The Complete Idiot's Reference Card

2000 NASCAR Winston Cup Series Schedule
(tentative, subject to change)

Date	Track
February 13	Daytona International Speedway (Bud Shootout)*
February 20	Daytona International Speedway
February 27	North Carolina Speedway
March 5	Las Vegas Motor Speedway
March 12	Atlanta Motor Speedway
March 19	Darlington Raceway
March 26	Bristol Motor Speedway
April 2	Texas Motor Speedway
April 9	Martinsville Speedway
April 16	Talladega Superspeedway
April 30	California Speedway
May 6	Richmond International Raceway
May 20	Lowe's Motor Speedway (The Winston)*
May 28	Lowe's Motor Speedway
June 4	Dover Downs International Speedway
June 11	Michigan Speedway
June 18	Pocono Raceway
June 25	Sears Point Raceway
July 1	Daytona International Speedway
July 9	New Hampshire International Speedway
July 23	Pocono Raceway
August 5	Indianapolis Motor Speedway
August 13	Watkins Glen International
August 20	Michigan Speedway
August 26	Bristol Motor Speedway
September 3	Darlington Raceway
September 9	Richmond International Raceway
September 17	New Hampshire International Speedway
September 24	Dover Downs International Speedway
October 1	Martinsville Speedway
October 8	Lowe's Motor Speedway
October 15	Talladega S
October 22	North Car
November 5	Phoenix In
November 12	Homestead
November 19	Atlanta Mo

* Nonpoints events

D1379415

alpha books

tear here

NASCAR Busch Series Schedule

Date	Track
February 19	Daytona International Speedway
February 26	North Carolina Speedway
March 4	Las Vegas Motor Speedway
March 11	Atlanta Motor Speedway
March 18	Darlington Raceway
March 25	Bristol Motor Speedway
April 1	Texas Motor Speedway
April 8	Nashville Speedway
April 15	Talladega Superspeedway
April 29	California Speedway
May 5	Richmond International Raceway
May 13	New Hampshire International Speedway
May 27	Lowe's Motor Speedway
June 3	Dover Downs International Speedway
June 10	South Boston Speedway
June 17	Myrtle Beach Speedway
June 25	Watkins Glen International
July 2	Milwaukee Mile
July 16	Nazareth Speedway
July 22	Pikes Peak International Raceway
July 29	Gateway International Raceway
August 4	Indianapolis Raceway Park
August 19	Michigan Speedway
August 25	Bristol Motor Speedway
September 2	Darlington Raceway
September 8	Richmond International Raceway
September 23	Dover Downs International Speedway
October 7	Lowe's Motor Speedway
October 21	North Carolina Speedway
October 29	Memphis Motorsports Park
November 4	Phoenix International Raceway
November 11	Homestead-Miami Speedway

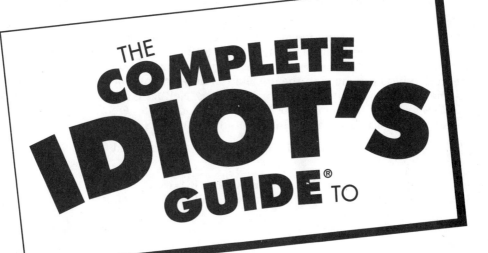

THE COMPLETE IDIOT'S GUIDE® TO

Stock Car Racing

by John Cerbone and Peter Monte

**alpha
books**

Macmillan USA, Inc.
201 West 103rd Street
Indianapolis, IN 46290

A Pearson Education Company

International Standard Book Number: 0-02-863181-1
Library of Congress Catalog Card Number: Available upon request.

02 01 00   8 7 6 5 4 3 2 1

Interpretation of the printing code: The rightmost number of the first series of numbers is the year of the book's printing; the rightmost number of the second series of numbers is the number of the book's printing. For example, a printing code of 00-1 shows that the first printing occurred in 2000.

Printed in the United States of America

Publisher
Marie Butler-Knight

Product Manager
Phil Kitchel

Managing Editor
Cari Luna

Acquisitions Editor
Amy Zavatto

Development Editor
Nancy D. Warner

Production Editor
Christy Wagner

Copy Editor
Heather Stith

Illustrator
Jody P. Schaeffer

Cover Designers
Mike Freeland
Kevin Spear

Book Designers
Scott Cook and Amy Adams of DesignLab

Indexer
Amy Lawrence

Layout/Proofreading
Angela Calvert
Mary Hunt

Contents at a Glance

Appendixes

Contents

Foreword

I wish this book was around when I was starting out. Back in 1990, when I began racing go-karts, there wasn't a book or guide to help me along. I had to work really hard to speed my learning curve.

Stock car racing is now my chosen career and I drive the no. 27 Castrol GTX Chevrolet Monte Carlo in the NASCAR Busch Series. NASCAR racing has enhanced my life and given me the chance to fulfill my childhood dreams and do what so many wish for and only a few achieve—compete against the greatest drivers in the world.

The best thing about NASCAR is you don't have to be a driver to be a part of the action. Many make careers building cars, fabricating, designing and engineering, engine building, and still more in management, public relations, and promotions. And there's always plenty of room for more well-informed fans.

There's something for everyone in NASCAR, and this book will help get you started by giving you the knowledge that professional racers have. No matter what part of NASCAR stock car racing you dream of pursuing, you will be participating in the world's fastest-growing spectator sport. I hope you enjoy this book and find it as informative and fascinating as I have. So sit down, strap in, and hang on, we're going racing!

—Casey Atwood

Casey Atwood drives the no. 27 Brewco Motorsports Castrol GTX Monte Carlo in NASCAR's Busch Grand National Series, and in 1999 was the youngest driver ever to achieve pole position and a race win.

Introduction

We have been in love with the automobile for years. The styling of the cars catches our eyes, the low rumble of the raw power in the motor makes our heart rate increase, and the idea that we can climb into this mass of steel and power and release the beast that lingers within it is exhilarating.

We all have a certain sense of adventure in us. Some of us have more than others. It is the desire to fill this need that motivates us to do things we would not normally do. This desire for adventure can be fulfilled in many ways. For some it is the need to explore new lands, while for others it is the need to push themselves to their limits.

Stockcar racing fills several needs. The first is to prove to yourself that you can climb into that car and can conquer the fear of the speed. Let's face it, it takes a lot of nerve to drive a car at over 150 miles per hour. The other need stockcar racing fulfills is the need for competition. It provides us with the forum to go out and compete against others and ourselves and prove that we are the best at what we do. Everyone wants to be the best or be Number 1, but there can only be one champion.

It is the satisfaction that comes from victory that makes the long hours and hard work all worth it. It is the feeling of accomplishment, the satisfaction of obtaining our goals that makes it all worthwhile. It does not matter if your are a racecar driver or a businessperson or a parent. It is the feeling we get from reaching our goals that continues to drive us.

How to Use This Book

Part 1, "Before You Burn Rubber," starts out by describing what it takes to become a racecar driver. It talks about the type of person and the basic skills needed. It also talks about how a racecar driver can get or refine these skills to become an even better driver. We also spend time talking about the tools and equipment needed to race. Most people do not realize how much equipment is needed both at the race shop and at the racetrack.

In Chapter 3, "The Silent Team Member," we discuss the importance of a sponsor to the race team. With the cost of racing increasing every year, the only way race teams can continue to compete is by finding and keeping sponsors.

Part 2, "Equipment Needed to Race," goes into detail about the types of equipment race teams use day in and day out. We give you an insider's look at the development and construction of the NASCAR racecar. We also detail what each member of a pit crew is responsible for. Finally, you will get a firsthand look at what is involved in transporting a NASCAR Winston Cup team to and from the racetrack.

In **Part 3, "Preparing for a Race,"** we take you through the process of setting up a NASCAR racecar for a race, give you an understanding of how shocks and springs affect the racecar, and explain the importance of a good set of tires. We then take you through the process of testing a racecar and running a practice session.

Before you can race 500 miles, you need to be able to turn a good qualifying time.

Part 4, "Showing Your Stuff," tells you about qualifying for a race, including how to set up the racecar for maximum speed during the qualifying run, and how racecar drivers prepare themselves for a qualifying run. Qualifications are your first chance to show your stuff on the racetrack, so make sure you do your best. After all, you can never make a first impression again.

Part 5, "Gentlemen, Start Your Engines," talks about racing strategies. Drafting, bumping, passing, and being patient are important factors in racing success. Pit crew performance is also an important factor. After reading this section, you will appreciate the hard work, dedication, and good luck required to reach victory lane.

Extras

Besides the insightful information on the sport of stock car racing, you will also see racing definitions, hints, and fun facts.

Inside Track

These are tips and suggestions on certain aspects in racing. All of these tips are based on experiences from competing in NASCAR races.

Yellow Flag

These warnings alert you to things to watch out for. Some of these we have learned about the hard way. There's no sense in letting you make the same mistakes.

Track Terms

These are terms and definitions of things you will hear around the garage area at a NASCAR event. Use these terms to impress your friends on how knowledgeable you are on the sport of stock car racing.

Under the Hood

This trivia will probably get you nothing special in life, but it will increase your overall knowledge of the sport of stock car racing.

Acknowledgments

We would like to thank the many people who provided time, information, and resources to this project. Without their help, this book would not be possible. Thanks to the editors at *The Complete Idiot's Guide* series for making an idea a reality, especially Amy Zavatto and Nancy Warner, whose hard work and saintly patience made our words and ideas into a wonderful book. Thanks also to Dave Baker for his technical editing.

Thanks to Vince Valeriano and Penske shocks for their information. Thanks to NASCAR and the entire France family for making stock car racing what it is today. Thanks to Race Basics for providing some of the tools and parts pictured in this book. Thanks to Howard Hodge for his great professional photographs. Thanks also to Tom Gallo for his professional photography efforts. Thanks to Penny Degree and the SPEEDWAY SCENE for their insights into media coverage. Thanks to the team, especially John "BUDA" Budakowski, Chris "The Handle" Vanzile, John "Little J" Arcardi, Richard Brandstetter, Damon "Static Man" Boccadoro, Anthony Abbondola, and Robert Vigliotti. Thanks to Ralph Mucci and Todd from Ultraflex fiberglass products. Thanks to Tracy Gordon for keeping the rain off our heads at the track. Thank you to John Drugach for his insights into sponsorship and marketing. And thanks to Bob Ingles and all the guys at J&B Performance.

Dedication

From Peter:

This book is dedicated to the people in my life who have put up with all of the weekends I have missed, dinners I was late for, and that pile of dirty, greasy clothes by the washing machine. Had it not been for their understanding and forgiveness, I would not be able to live the dream of being a member of a NASCAR racing team. To my loving and understanding wife, Lisa, and to my two sons, Nicholas and Anthony, who one day may decide to follow in their dad's footsteps and enter the world of auto racing, I dedicate this book to you. Nothing in the world means more to me than you. I love you all.

From John:

This book is dedicated to all the people who make racing possible for me. They selfishly give up their weekends and nights. They work hard, never complain (well, almost never), and lose sleep, all for the love of racing. It's said that you need to sacrifice in order to gain in this world; if that's so, then these people have at the very least gained my love, friendship, and loyalty. To my mother, father, sister, and brother, who have all at one time or another, probably more times than I can remember, given up something they wanted or needed, so that I may have more to race with. From the hundreds of dinners brought to the shop, to the 50-mile Friday night drives to bring me a part so I can race the next day, my family has been supportive in more than one way, have stood by me in the bad times, and rejoiced in the good. I can never repay you for all you have done. Finally, I dedicate this book to the woman I love and cherish. You have been there for me always. You showed me love, happiness, and friendship. With you, I experience true life and love, and I watch the sun rise and set on you. And through you, I have gained the strength and will to pursue my dreams. Donna, I have, do, and will always love and adore you.

Special Thanks to the Technical Reviewer

The Complete Idiot's Guide to Stock Car Racing was reviewed by an expert who double-checked the accuracy of what you'll learn here to help us ensure that this book gives you everything you need to know about stock car racing. Special thanks are extended to David Baker.

David Baker owns an auto repair and wrecker facility called J&L Service Center in St. Albans, Vermont. He has been a NASCAR technical inspector since 1988. David became Technical Director for the NASCAR Busch North Series in 1997. He and his wife Sharon have three sons: Mat, Pat, and Seth.

Trademarks

All terms mentioned in this book that are known to be or are suspected of being trademarks or service marks have been appropriately capitalized. Alpha Books and Macmillan USA, Inc. cannot attest to the accuracy of this information. Use of a term in this book should not be regarded as affecting the validity of any trademark or service mark.

Part 1

Before You Burn Rubber

So you think you want to be a stock car driver. Before you climb behind the wheel of a 700-horsepower racecar, let's make sure you know what you are about to get yourself into.

Being a racecar driver requires a lot of skill and nerves of steel. If you get nervous when driving at a high rate of speed or when someone gets too close to you on the highway, chances are you aren't cut out to be a racecar driver. When you finish reading these chapters, you will have a better idea about what it takes to be a racecar driver.

Chapter 1

So You Want to Be a Stock Car Driver?

In This Chapter

➤ Why people race cars

➤ How to become a stock car driver in three easy steps

➤ What it takes to be a stock car driver

Stock car racing is a sport that is fun, fast, and exciting. It is also a serious business that requires a large financial investment and long hours of hard work. When things are going well, racing can make participants (and fans) feel as high as a kite, but when things are not going so well, you may wonder why anyone would want to be involved in such a sport. Fully understanding the why, how, and what of racing will increase your appreciation of the work and dedication necessary to be successful in it. In this chapter, we are going to talk about why people want to drive stock cars, how to get into racing in three easy steps (yeah, right), and what it takes to be a racecar driver.

As If You Didn't Already Know Why

Why do people want to climb into a racecar and drive in a circle as fast as they can? The answer is simple. For years, people have been in love with the automobile. The styling of cars catches their eyes, the low rumble of the raw power in the motor makes their heart rates increase, and the idea that they can climb into this mass of steel and power and release the beast that lingers within is exhilarating.

Feeding the Desire

We all have a certain need for adventure. Some of us have a deeper need for it than others. The desire to fill this need motivates us to do things we would not normally do. This desire for adventure can be fulfilled in many ways: some people explore new lands; others, such as stock car racers, push themselves to their limits. It takes a lot of nerve to drive a car at over 150 miles per hour; most people are not comfortable at those speeds. Most stock car drivers start out by needing to prove to themselves that they can climb into that racecar and conquer the fear of the speed.

Most stock car drivers are also driven to compete. Racing provides a forum to compete against others and yourself and prove that you are the best at what you do. Everyone wants to be the best, but only one driver can win the race. The satisfaction that comes from victory makes the long hours and hard work all worth it. Whether you are a racecar driver, a businessperson, or a parent, the feeling of accomplishment you get when you reach your goals is what drives you.

The Need for Speed

Stock car drivers are—we hate to say it because we hate this term, but it is descriptive—thrill junkies. We get a thrill from the speed of the cars and from the challenges the tracks and other competitors present. If you think driving at 150 miles per hour is thrilling, just try doing it with 30 or 40 other racecars on the track at the same time. Not only do you have to worry about keeping your racecar under control, but you also have to worry about the other racecars around you that are *rubbing* up against you in order to pass you.

Track Terms

Rubbing is term used to describe when two racecars get too close to one another and touch slightly.

A few years ago, a movie about stock car racing was released named *Days of Thunder*. In one scene, a new racecar driver, who had just made the field for his first race, was excited and anxious. A few laps into the race, the driver of the racecar behind him wanted to pass him and decided to let him know it by hitting him in the back bumper. The hit was not hard enough to cause him to lose control of the racecar, but it was hard enough to make the racecar wiggle and make the young, inexperienced driver a little nervous. Shocked that he was just hit, the young driver radioed to his crew chief that the car behind him just hit him in the rear. The experienced crew chief radioed back to his driver and said, "No, he didn't hit you; he rubbed you. And son, rubbing is racing." That statement is so true.

Most people think that the only time racecars touch each other is in an accident, but the truth is that more rubbing goes on during a race than most fans realize. Rubbing to pass is an accepted method of communication between racecar drivers. Can you imagine what it would be like if, while you were driving down the highway at 65 miles per hour, the driver of the car behind you let you know he or she wanted to pass you by rubbing up against your car's back bumper? You would probably find yourself spinning off the road. So just because you are comfortable at driving 65 miles per hour or 75 miles per hour does not mean that you are ready to drive a racecar.

Follow Your Way to Success

There are three easy steps to racing: Start the engine, go fast, and accept the trophy. Of course, behind these basic steps are a lot of complex details, but if you keep to the basics at first, you will better understand the more complicated things later on.

KISS (Keep It Simple, Stupid)

An important part of stock car racing is trying to figure out how you can go as fast as possible or at least faster than all of the other cars on the track. Numerous items can affect how well a racecar can perform, including, but not limited to the engine, tires, shocks, springs, the track, and even the weather. Because of all of these variables, the racecar driver and, more importantly, the crew chief need to be constantly evaluating how well the racecar is performing.

It is not uncommon for drivers and crew chiefs to overadjust a racecar in an attempt to make it faster. It takes a lot of experience before someone can be an expert in making adjustments. Drivers and crew chiefs can very easily get caught up in a problem, and not see the answer because it is too basic. Remember to keep things simple. Stepping back from a problem allows you to see things more clearly.

Although there are a lot of variables involved in determining what makes racecars go fast, there are just as many, if not more, rules that limit what can be done to a racecar. If you have an idea on how to make your racecar faster, but are not sure if it is legal or allowed under the rules, check your series rule book or with a series official before using the adjustment in a race.

Inside Track

Do not try to solve multiple problems in one shot. Make one change and see how it affects the racecar. Then try something else and see how that change affects the car.

Yellow Flag

Do not wait until a race to find out if an idea you have to make the racecar faster is legal under the rules of the series you are in. In most racing series, if something is determined to be illegal on your racecar after a race, you may lose any or all prize money or series points for that race.

More Than Stepping on the Pedals

Going faster is a lot harder than it sounds. There is a lot more involved than just stepping on the gas pedal. Many factors affect a race, and one of these factors is driving style. All drivers have their own style of driving. Sure, they all step on the gas, brake when needed, and turn the steering wheel, but how each driver does these basics can affect the performance of the car.

Track Terms

The **term lap** times refers to the amount of time required to complete one lap around a race track.

For example, a driver who uses only one foot to control both the gas pedal and the brake pedal will not be as fast as a driver who uses both feet (one foot for the gas pedal and one foot for the brake pedal) to drive. The reason is that it takes less time to press on the brake pedal if you do not have to move your foot off of the gas pedal to do it. I know what you are thinking: Moving your foot from the gas pedal to the brake pedal and back again doesn't take that much time. You're right: it only takes a small amount of time, but over the course of a race, all of those small amounts add up. By the end of the race, the driver who only uses one foot could be turning in substantially longer *lap times*.

Knowing Whether to Follow the Track Line

Another item that affects how fast a racecar will go is the line the driver takes around the racetrack. Every racetrack has at least one line that is the fastest way to get around the track. Some tracks, such as the superspeedways of Daytona International or the California Speedway in Southern California, have two lines around the track, which are equally fast. However, the fastest line for the track may not be the fastest way around the track for a particular racecar or a particular driver. The problem or challenge is trying to find that line or the line that works best for both the driver's style and the racecar.

If the driver is not comfortable following the fastest line around the track, he or she probably will not be keeping his or her foot on the gas pedal for as long as he or she should. Drivers will never say that they eased off the gas, but you will know it is happening when you start to see slower lap times. Even if a driver finds the fastest line on the track and is comfortable driving that line, that driver still may not be going as fast as other drivers, because the racecar may not be comfortable with that line. Yes, it is possible for an inanimate racecar to be comfortable or uncomfortable on a racetrack.

Being comfortable or uncomfortable in a particular line on the racetrack is determined by the driver by the feeling he or she is getting from the racecar. If a racecar does not travel smoothly around the racetrack, it is trying to tell the driver that it does not like that line or there is an adjustment needed on the racecar.

Racecar drivers and crew chiefs have a sort of bond between them; each can tell when one of the others is not comfortable with a certain scenario. Do not ask us to explain it; we know we sound crazy when we talk about this bond, but believe us, it exists. This bond is one key to being successful. Crew chiefs and racecar drivers both are able to tell how well a racecar is performing in a particular line on the racetrack. While both are evaluating the same racecar, each uses a different set of inputs to come up with his answer. The driver has direct input from the racecar as it goes around the racetrack, while the crew chief uses a stopwatch to determine lap times.

Inside Track

Racecar drivers will never tell you when or if they lifted their foot off of the gas pedal because they were scared of the speed.

If the fastest line around a racetrack is not the fastest line for you, the driver, what do you do? In order to find the fastest line around a racetrack, you need to get onto the track and try different lines. Try entering into the turns on the high side of the track. Run a few laps like this and write down the lap times. Then try entering the turns on the low side of the track; write down your times and see how they compare to the previous times. Keep trying out different lines until you find which line around the racetrack works best for you. Remember that not all drivers drive the same way, not all racecars react the same way, and not all tracks have the same line. You will need to try all the different lines in order to find out which one works best you and your racecar.

Inside Track

Drivers keep a log of all of the lap times they turn at a particular track. This way, the next time they race at that track, they will know what worked and what did not.

The Third and Final Step

Accepting the trophy is the last step in the three steps of racing. Victory lane is the place the winner of the race goes to celebrate and receive the trophy and prize money for the race, and nothing is more exhilarating than the feeling of being in victory lane. In Chapter 26, "The Sweet Smell of Victory Lane," we will talk more about victory lane and the thrill it gives.

What Does It Take?

With the increase in popularity in the sport of stock car racing, the question of whether stock car drivers are athletes is often asked. One opinion is that racecar drivers are not athletes because they do not run like a track and field athlete, throw a football like a quarterback, or slam-dunk like a basketball player. All they do is sit in a racecar and turn the steering wheel. How can that be considered an athletic sport?

The other side of the argument is that racecar drivers are athletes because of the level of skill involved in maneuvering a 3,000-pound vehicle around a racetrack. Racecar drivers also need to be physically fit in order to endure the heat in the racecar and the G-forces created from the racecar's speed. Although racing has not traditionally been considered an athletic sport, it is a demanding sport that requires its participants to have both stamina and skill.

Getting the Skills

So where do hopeful racecar drivers go to obtain such skills? Racing schools throughout the country teach hopeful drivers how to handle a racecar. They teach how to find the best line around the racetrack, how to maneuver the racecar in certain situations, and what to do if you lose control of the racecar. These schools combine the theories they teach in the classroom with real driving experience behind the wheel of a racecar to give hopeful drivers a real understanding of the lessons being taught. Refer to Appendix A, "Track Directory," for a list of some of the more popular racing schools located around the country.

Most racing schools offer different levels of classes. Basic, one-day courses allow someone who is interested in racing to get a feel of what it is like to drive a racecar. The more advanced courses are several days long and teach people how to drive a racecar. These courses are only for people who want to become racecar drivers or for anyone who does not mind spending several thousand dollars on something that they will probably never use again.

Inside Track

For a listing of racing schools, check the Internet or in the back of racing magazines such as *AutoWeek*. You will find advertisements for many different types of racing schools.

Several of the more successful racecar drivers started racing at a very early age. Instead of going to a racing school to learn how to drive a racecar, many of today's drivers built their basic racing skills by starting in smaller, slower racecars and then moving up to bigger, faster racecars. As they progressed through each class, they learned more and more about how to drive a racecar. After building on their basic driving skills through real-life experience, these drivers then went to racing schools to help refine their skills. Refining one's skills in a racing school makes the transition to a higher level of racing much easier.

Nerves of Steel

What type of person becomes a racecar driver? One of the more important aspects needed to be a racecar driver is nerve. It takes a lot of nerve to climb into a racecar and drive at speeds in excess of 150 miles per hour. Because most people never see speeds of this level in everyday driving, it is hard to imagine what they feel like. Obviously, things happen a lot faster at these speeds, and the driver's reactions need to be just as fast. If something goes wrong on the track, there is usually not enough time to think about what is happening. Racecar drivers must rely on their skills, their reactions, and their intuition to keep them out of trouble on the racetrack.

Mr. Cool

Driving a racecar can be one of the most stressful things a person can do for a living. If a racecar driver cannot keep a cool head in stressful situations, he or she will not be able to think clearly and will not make the proper decisions.

Everyone on a racing team is doing his or her best to make the racecar as fast as possible. When working so hard, people can easily become agitated by the actions of someone else. The key to being a member of a successful race team is to remain calm, level-headed, and clear-thinking and not to let the actions of others distract you from your focus. This is not to say that others on the racetrack are out to get you, but everyone else is also trying his or her best to win the race.

It is very easy to lose your cool in a race. Sometimes things happen, and although you can do your best to avoid these things, you may not be able to avoid them every time. If you can keep your focus and stay aware of what is going on around you, your chances of succeeding are greatly increased.

For example, if another driver is doing something you know is foolish on the racetrack, like rubbing up against you for no reason. Instead of getting mad and distracted, which can cost you the race, relax and let them go by. Getting revenge on someone for something stupid is not worth loosing a race over. Be aware of what is going on around you, but stay focused on your race strategy.

The Great Communicator

Besides being a skilled driver and someone who can keep a cool head in stressful situations, a racecar driver needs to be a good communicator. Earlier we talked about the need for the racecar driver and crew chief to constantly evaluate how the racecar is performing. This process of evaluation involves input from both the driver and the crew chief. The way these two communicate with one another is critical to the success of the team.

Although crew chiefs make the decisions on what to do to the racecar to make it faster, they rely on the information racecar drivers give them. The

Inside Track

A driver's ability to remain calm under pressure is key to his or her success on the racetrack. Getting angry or upset because of something that happened on the racetrack just distracts a driver from the race.

racecar driver is the one person who knows exactly how the racecar is reacting while on the track. The driver can feel if the car is too lose or too tight or if the car is accelerating properly or decelerating properly. The driver is the best indicator of how the car is performing. If the racecar driver is unable to communicate or communicate clearly what is happening with the racecar, the crew chief will not be able to make the necessary changes to the racecar.

The Least You Need to Know

➤ Stock car racing is a serious business that demands a large investment in time, money, and labor from all involved.

➤ Not everyone can be a racecar driver. Racing requires skill and nerves of steel.

➤ When you try to fix a problem, keep things simple.

➤ Keep a thorough log of your performance at each track; this information will help you the next time you race there.

➤ Driving schools are an excellent place to go to learn how to drive a racecar.

➤ A racecar driver must be able to maintain a cool head in stressful situations.

➤ Communication between the driver and the crew chief is critical to the success of the team.

Chapter 2

This Doesn't Look Like My Car

> **In This Chapter**
>
> ➤ The difference between your car and a NASCAR racecar
>
> ➤ What the bells and whistles do
>
> ➤ How the car protects the driver

The cars we drive everyday on the streets of our hometowns are mass-produced by the automobile manufacturers such as General Motors and Ford. Sure, the model you purchase may have certain available options, but the cars are just cookie-cutter models mass-produced on assembly lines with a few minor options added to them.

On the other hand, racecars are custom-built cars. Sure, some racecar parts are standard, but for the most part, everything else on the racecars is custom-made. Almost every racecar in the NASCAR series is a custom-built racecar.

Mass-Produced or Custom-Built?

Stock car racing is an interesting name for this sport. When the sport started over 50 years ago, the name was appropriate. Folks would take the cars they bought at the local dealership and race them on the tracks. The term *stock* meant that the car was original (or stock) from the dealership.

These days, there is not much that is stock about a stock racecar. You can go to your local dealership and order a Ford Taurus, Chevrolet Monte Carlo, or Pontiac Grand Prix, which are the types of cars you will see at races such as the Daytona 500, but the car you will pick up from the dealership will be very different from the car you see at the racetrack. The car you purchase from your local dealership is designed to seat passengers comfortably, get good gas mileage, and have room for several bags of groceries in the trunk. The racecars you see competing in the races on television are built for speed, have only one seat, and have no room to carry groceries.

Under the Hood

Before you get into the car the next time you need to go run an errand, take a minute to open the hood of your car. Chances are that what you will see is a mix of different types of hoses and electrical wires running all over the place. We like to think of it as a bowl of spaghetti. It is a pretty complex system, but all we need to know is that it works. We put the key in the ignition, turn the key, and if it starts, we are happy. Okay, close the hood.

A typical car's engine.

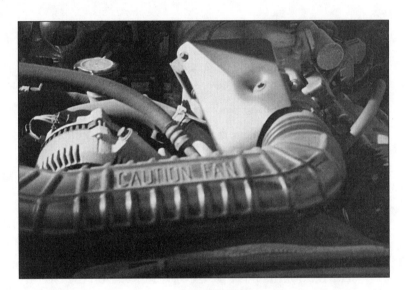

A racecar's engine looks nothing like the engine in your car, as you can see in the following figure. Instead of a bowl of spaghetti, a racecar engine just has some stray noodles, a few hoses and a few electrical wires. If you are a *shadetree mechanic,* you can probably identify all or most of the major components of a racecar motor. Racecar motors don't have exhaust emissions to worry about, and they don't carry an on-board computer. As a result, working on a racecar motor is much easier than working on a regular car's motor.

Racecar motors are simple motors built for speed and power. When we say power, we mean a lot of power. A new Chevrolet Monte Carlo from a dealership can have as much as 200 horsepower. In contrast, the engine in Dale Earnhardt's Monte Carlo racecar has over 700 horsepower.

A stock racecar's engine.

Where's the Door Handle?

This may sound like a silly question, but how do you get into your car? You lift the handle, and the door opens, right? Racecar drivers get in a different way. They climb in through the window. Why? Because there are no doors on a racecar. For that matter, there are no driver- or passenger-side windows, either. We like to think of this setup as built-in air conditioning.

Sit in your car. The seat is probably nice and comfy and made of cloth or even leather, if you could afford the extra money. Instead of sliding onto fine Corinthian leather, the racecar driver climbs into an aluminum seat covered with inch-thick foam padding. The seat is designed to be as light as possible while still providing as much protection as possible for the driver. In addition, the driver's seat has a head restraint built into the right side of the seat. This restraint prevents the driver's head from being tossed around in the event of an accident. Today, some teams are even installing a head restraint on the left side of the seat as well.

Track Terms

Shadetree mechanic is a term used for nonprofessional mechanics who work on cars in their own garages or backyards.

How Do I Put This Thing On?

Now that you're sitting in your car, it's time to buckle up for safety. A standard seat belt goes across your lap and across your chest. It is what is called a three-point seat belt. The points refer to the number of places the belt is connected to the car: one point on either side of your lap and one point over your shoulder. The purpose of your seat belt is to help prevent you from being injured in a car accident. Most cars today travel at speeds of 55 miles per hour to 75 miles per hour, depending on which state you live in and the road you are traveling on. Racecars travel at speeds anywhere from 100 miles per hour on some of the smaller racetracks to almost 200 miles per hour on some of the superspeedways, such as the Daytona International Speedway. Therefore, the racecar driver's seat belt has to be a little more complex than your seat belt in order to protect the driver.

A racecar driver's seat belt or harness has five points at which it connects to the car: one over each shoulder, one on either side of the driver's hips, and one between the driver's legs. All five points come together and connect to one another at the driver's chest. This style of seatbelt keeps the driver firmly secured in the driver's seat. The driver cannot slide down out of the seat because of the belt between his or her legs. The driver cannot be thrown forward toward the windshield because of the belts over his or her shoulders. The driver is fully strapped into the seat, almost to the point where he or she becomes part of the seat.

A typical racing harness used in stock car racing.

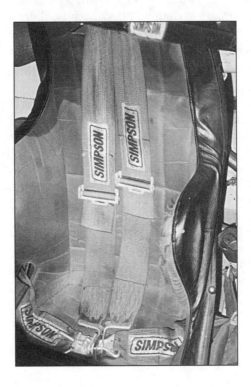

By the Dashboard Light

Now that you are strapped into your car, take a look at the dashboard. Your Chevrolet Monte Carlo has all of the basics to monitor the car's engine:

➤ The **speedometer** is a gauge that measures how fast a car is traveling in miles per hour.

➤ The **tachometer** is a gauge that counts the number of revolutions per minute (RPM) the engine is making.

➤ The **temperature gauge** measures the internal temperature of the engine.

➤ The **fuel gauge** measures the amount of fuel in the car by percentage.

These gauges are usually on the more sporty cars or available in an option package:

➤ The **oil pressure gauge** measures the pressure of the oil moving through your engine in terms of pounds per square inch (PSI).

➤ The **volt gauge** measures the amount of electrical energy in your car in term of volts.

A typical dashboard from an everyday car.

Watch the RPM Gauge

The first thing you probably notice when looking at the gauges in a racecar's dashboard (see the following figure) is that there is no speedometer. So how is the driver supposed to know how fast he or she is going? Believe it or not, the driver does not need to know exactly how fast he or she is going; racecar drivers simply drive their racecars as fast as they can. All a driver needs to watch is the tachometer in order to keep track of the number of RPMs that the engine is turning. If the RPMs get too high, the engine could blow up.

A typical dashboard from a stock racecar.

The number of RPMs a racecar engine will turn depends on a number of items. The first factor is the engine itself. A six-cylinder engine will turn at a higher RPM than an eight-cylinder engine at the same speed. The reason for this difference is that each cylinder in a six-cylinder engine will need to work faster than each cylinder in an eight-cylinder engine to maintain the same speed. Think of it this way: Two people can push a car easier than one person can. The same is true for the cylinders in an engine. The more help each cylinder has, the easier it is on each cylinder.

The Drive Train: Choo, Choo

Another item that affects engine RPM is the size of the gear in the *rear end* of the car. The rear end of the car contains a gear, which is attached to a drive shaft, which is attached to a transmission, which is attached to the engine. All of these components in the car work together to move the car forward. On most racecars, the gear in the rear end of the car can be changed. The smaller the gear in the rear end of the car is, the higher the engine RPM will be. A larger gear will require less engine RPM to maintain the same speed.

To give you an idea about the numbers that we are talking about here, consider that the engine of a new Chevrolet Monte Carlo purchased from the local dealership will probably produce about 2,100 RPMs at 55 miles per hour on the highway. Dale Earnhardt's Chevrolet Monte Carlo will turn about 8,700 RPMs at 185 miles per hour. That is more than four times the number of RPMs that the regular car is producing. That many RPMs creates a lot of stress for any engine;

Track Terms

The **rear end** of the car refers to the axle in the back of the car that the tires are mounted to.

16

too much stress will cause the engine to break. The bottom line is that the driver needs to watch the number of RPMs the engine is producing.

Oil Gauges: The Life Blood

The next most important gauges on the dashboard for a racecar driver are the oil gauges. Oil for an engine is like the blood in our bodies. We could not live without blood, and an engine cannot live without oil. The oil in an engine keeps all of the moving parts lubricated.

If the oil in a racecar engine gets too hot, the oil cannot protect the parts of the engine, and they will burn up and not work. The engine parts will burn up and not work if the engine loses oil, too. You may have heard people saying that their engine seized. What they are referring to is what happens when the parts of the engine become so hot that the metal starts to melt and the parts stick to each other. When this happens, it is not a good feeling.

Here is a brief story about engine oil and the heartbreak it can cause: On one hot summer weekend, I was racing at the New Hampshire International Speedway in Loudon, New Hampshire. It was Winston Cup weekend, which meant that all of the big names were going to be in town and everyone wanted to show their stuff on the track in the hopes of catching the eye of a Winston Cup team owner. Everyone who has ever driven in a stock car race, me included, hopes and dreams of one day making it to the big leagues as a NASCAR Winston Cup driver.

My team had set up the racecar perfectly for the race (John was the driver and Peter was part of the pit crew). The team double-checked everything to make sure nothing was missed. The engine was perfect, the tires were perfect, and the car handled like it was traveling down the track on a set of railroad tracks instead of tires. The team was set to go, and I was excited about my team's chances of winning.

I (John) started the race in the middle of the field and began moving up quickly. I passed the car in front of me coming off of the first turn. Then I moved to the outside of the track down the back straightaway to get a better angle to enter turn three. The car drove to the bottom of the track going into turn three just like I told it to. The car hugged the track; it turned when I wanted it to and gripped the track like it was covered in glue. I was moving up fast.

By lap 10, I had passed several cars and was running in fourth place. The crew chief radioed to ask how the car felt. It was perfect, and I said, "I'm going to the front." These are the words that a team loves to hear. Several of the other teams had noticed how well my team was getting around the track and decided to follow behind me in my line rather than fight for a position.

The day was perfect: It was a Saturday afternoon, the sun was shining, I was racing, and best of all, I was on my way to the front of the pack. The sun was so bright that at times when I was going down the back straightaway, it was hard to see the gauges on the dashboard because of the glare from the sun on the windshield. During lap 12,

I was going down the back straightaway, and the sun glare popped up again. So I took the opportunity to check my position in my mirror. I was getting ready to dive to the bottom of the track to enter turn three. Over the radio, my spotter said I was clear on the inside, so down the track I went. The sun glare cleared just as I entered the turn, and then I saw it. That big red light on the steering column was glaring at me with the intensity of a flare. It was the oil pressure light. I had lost oil pressure in the motor. My engine's life blood was gone, and the cardiac machine was reading flat line. Usually, as soon as that light goes on I see it and can shut down the motor to prevent engine damage. But the sun's glare on the windshield had blinded me and had prevented me from seeing the light when it came on.

At 8,200 RPM and no oil pressure, it only takes a few seconds for a $30,000 race engine to become a pile of junk. As soon as I saw the oil pressure light, I reached up and hit the kill switch to the motor and shut it down. I pulled the car onto the apron of the track and coasted in down pit road. My crew chief radioed me and said, "What's wrong?" I radioed back and said, "No oil pressure." He knew exactly what that meant. Our day was done. We went from being on our way to winning the race to finishing almost last. What had happened was that the belt on the oil pump broke and came off. This meant that for some period of time before I shut down the motor it was running without its lifeblood, oil, being pumped through its veins and arteries.

The moral of this story is to keep an eye on the oil in your car. It is more important that you think.

Just the Basics

The other thing you will notice about the dashboard in a stock racecar is that it is made of steel with no frills on it. It contains only the bare necessities to race. The rest of the interior of the racecar is pretty bare as well. There is only one seat for the driver; the rest of space is filled with metal tubes.

A typical stock racecar roll cage.

The Cage: You Gotta Get In

The metal tubes in the interior of the car protect the driver in the event of an accident with another car or an unplanned meeting with the outside wall. These steel tubes are called the *roll cage*. Just by their name you can figure out why they were put in the racecars. In the early days of racing, the roll cage was added to the racecar to protect the driver if the racecar rolled over on its roof in a crash. The roll cages of today surround the driver and protect him or her from all types of crashes, not just rollovers. However, even with this protection, injuries still occur.

Manufacturers are always looking for new ways to increase driver safety. For example, many drivers were being injured in side-impact crashes. A side-impact crash is when the racecar is hit in the door area by another car or object. To better protect the drivers from these types of crashes, extra steel tubing was added to the roll cage in the door area. The additional steel tubing provided a strong roll cage around the driver, which increased the chances of a driver walking away from a crash.

If you look at the interior of a standard Chevrolet Monte Carlo, you will not see the same steel tubing that you see in a racecar. But don't think that there are no similarities. The automobile manufacturers use stock car racing as the testing ground for things to put into their production cars. Over the past few years, for example, automobile manufacturers have been adding more steel in the doors of their production cars to better protect the driver in a side-impact crash. This is just one example of how stock car racing affects the cars we drive everyday on the road.

Inside Track

Many of the automobile manufacturers are using the things race teams learn on the track in the cars you and I can purchase at our local dealerships.

Under the Hood

All NASCAR racecars are required to have a fire extinguisher system installed in the racecar.

This practice of using stock car racing as a testing ground does not stop at the auto-mobile manufacturers; the tire companies are also doing it. Goodyear uses the ideas and information developed at the racetrack and incorporates them into its manufac-turing process for developing a better tire for regular consumers. A recent example is the new Goodyear Run Flat tire. The idea to create a tire that could be driven on for 50 miles with zero air pressure was developed based on the Winston Cup Series tires. If a tire on a Winston Cup stock car goes flat or loses air pressure, the driver can still drive the car to safety before the tire becomes completely flat or destroys the car.

The Trunk: No Room for Groceries Here

Let's climb out of the car and take a look at the trunks of the street car and the race-car. The Chevrolet Monte Carlo you purchased at the dealer has a roomy carpeted trunk with a spare tire. The trunk of the racecar is not very roomy or even carpeted, and it doesn't have a spare tire. After all, racecar drivers don't need spare tires; they have pit crews instead. The pit crews take care of changing the tires, jacking up the car, and filling it up with fuel.

Track Terms

Roll cage is the center of the racecar chassis that protects the driver in the event of a crash. **Frame rails** are the two rails on either side of the racecar that the roll cage attaches to.

The steel tubes of the roll cage go all the way into the racecar's trunk. The reason for this is that distributing the force over a larger area allows for better protection to the driver. The round steel *roll cage* connects to rec-tangular steel rails in the trunk. On both the driver side and passenger side, these same rectangular rails run the entire length of the car. These two rails are called *frame rails*.

It Will Save Your Hide

The steel roll cage and the frame rails make up the skeleton, or the chassis, of the racecar. Without the chassis to connect all of the parts to, there is no race-car. All of the components used in the racecar are welded to, bolted to, or sitting on the chassis of the racecar.

The outer metal of the racecar, which covers the chassis, is the skin of the racecar. If you were to take the outer metal layer off of the racecar to reveal the chassis, you would not see very much difference from one racecar chassis to another. The reason for this similarity is to ensure that all drivers are equally protected from a crash.

The Skin

Let's talk about that outer layer of metal, which covers the chassis and makes the racecar look more like the cars at the local dealership. This metal outer layer, known as the body, has several basic parts. From front to back, the following are the only body parts on the racecar that are produced from the manufacturer:

➤ Nose

➤ Hood

➤ Front windshield

➤ Roof

➤ Rear windshield

➤ Trunk

➤ Rear bumper

All of these parts, with the exception of the front and rear windshields, are the same parts used by the automobile manufacturer in producing the car you can buy from the dealership. The hood that is on Dale Earnhardt's Chevrolet Monte Carlo is the same as the one on your Chevrolet Monte Carlo.

You may be wondering about the sides of the car. Where do those parts come from? The sides of the racecar are nothing more than flat pieces of steel bent to look like the sides of the car. The reason that the sides of the car are nothing more than ordinary steel is because if the teams had to buy new doors from the manufacturers every time they traded paint with one another, there would be a lot of very rich car door salesmen in Detroit. Seriously, at the speeds these cars travel and in such close proximity to one another, the sides of the cars usually end a race with more than a few dents. It is cheaper to use a fabricated door or fender than a real door or fender from the manufacturer.

So as you can see, other than some resemblance in the body style, there is not much stock about racecars. But they are exciting to watch and a lot of fun to drive.

The Least You Need to Know

➤ Always wear your seat belt.

➤ Check your engine oil on a regular basis.

➤ A motor can have too much horsepower.

➤ Not much is stock about racecars.

21

Chapter 3

The Silent Team Member

In This Chapter

➤ Everyone needs a little help

➤ Finding the right sponsor

➤ Advertising on the car, yourself, and everywhere

➤ The benefits of self-promotion

Most people think stock car racing is a sport. It is a sport, but it is also a business. Like any other business, racing requires the hard work of several people. Most race fans only see about eight or nine people per team at the track: the driver, the crew chief, and the pit crew. What most fans do not see is all of the people behind the scenes preparing the racecar and race team for the race on Sunday. For example, a crew works on the racecar both in the race shop and at the track, someone manages all of the work that needs to be done on the racecar, and someone manages the business aspects of the race team. All of these people need to be paid, and that cost is added to the significant costs of maintaining a racecar. If you added all of the costs involved in competing in one season of NASCAR's elite Winston Cup Series, the total would be in the millions of dollars. This chapter explains how race teams raise the money to compete.

Help, I Need a Sponsor

If you just hit the super lottery or inherited a large family fortune, financing a race team is not a problem, but most race teams look to other businesses for financial help in the form of sponsorships. The idea is that in exchange for the much-needed financial help, the race team will plaster the sponsoring company name all over the racecars, trailer, equipment, and team uniforms, making the race team a living, breathing, and, when it comes to the racecar, a very fast-moving advertisement for the company.

Big Bucks for Big Exposure

Let's step back for a moment and put things into perspective. One option for a company looking to advertise their products to millions of people is to advertise on television. In order to advertise on television, a company needs to produce a commercial. That alone can cost a small fortune. Once a company has a commercial, it has to buy air time from the networks to show its commercial. This can cost another small fortune. Most commercials are only 15 seconds long, so the company can easily end up paying hundreds of thousands of dollars for 15 seconds' worth of exposure. The exceptions to this are the ever-popular commercials during the Superbowl, which are usually 30 seconds in length, but those time slots have astronomical costs.

Another option for a company is to sponsor or advertise with a stock car racing team and receive exposure for almost a 12-month period and in front of millions of people for less than what a single commercial would cost. Sponsoring a race team offers great exposure for the company and allows the race team to compete in more races. Without this kind of help, race teams would not be able to compete.

What a Race Team Has to Offer

What does a stock car race team have to offer? A NASCAR Winston Cup season includes over 30 races. The season goes from early February to late November, and every race is shown on national television. An average stock car race is about three hours in length. That means that the racecars are on national television for an average of three hours every race weekend. That works out to be at least 90 hours of national television exposure for almost an entire year. That is a lot of exposure and that is just the television coverage.

A NASCAR Winston Cup race, depending on the track, can draw over 100,000 race fans to the track. Every year, race fans purchase toys, T-shirts, and other merchandise. People who do not even go to the races will go out and buy a little Dale Earnhardt or Jeff Gordon racecar for their kids to play with. Combine these figures with the television rating and the stock car racing team has a lot to offer a potential sponsor.

NASCAR tops the charts in 18 of 20 categories rating sports sponsorship, according to a survey published by *Street & Smith's Sports Business Journal*. In the survey, which was sent to more than 1,200 corporate sports sponsors, major sports leagues and associations were ranked in various categories, including: do a good job marketing their sport; are client-centered and service oriented; deliver good business building programs; are innovative and aggressive marketers; provide good service after sale; and have a sport with a strong future. In the category of marketing their sport, NASCAR was first with a 96.6 grade from all sponsors, followed by football's NFL (86.4), PGA (76.6), WNBA (54.5), MLB (54.5), Olympics (45.3), and NHL (45.0). When asked to rank sport with a strong future, NASCAR again was tops with a 95.5 grading, followed by the NFL (86.5), PGA (82.6), Olympics (66.1), and Minor League Baseball (65.7). In a separate sponsorship survey, the *Sports Business Journal* found that NASCAR ranked highest of any other major sport when fans were asked to name any sponsor associated with it. Of those surveyed, 81.6 percent said they could correctly name a NASCAR sponsor, beating out PGA (72.2), NFL (70.3), and NBA (64.8). (Taken from the December 1999 issue of *NASCAR Magazine* with the permission of Paul Schaefer, Senior Editor.)

Good Luck Trying to Find One

One of the major challenges racing teams face is trying to find sponsors. As we know from personal experience, going door to door and asking companies to sponsor a race team is not easy. Usually, the company slams the door in your face, but sometimes you do get the opportunity to talk to someone. The key is finding the right person at the company to talk with. This task alone can be a challenge. If you do not find the right person to talk with, you can be wasting that person's time as well as yours. The other challenge is finding a company that thinks advertising in racing is a good mechanism for reaching its customers. If a company's customers are not likely to be watching or attending a stock car race, that company is not likely to want to advertise with your team. So the first challenge is to find a company whose customers are likely to be watching or attending a stock car race.

Everyone Is a Potential Sponsor

In the past, one type of business that sponsored stock car racing was automotive companies. Oil companies were, and still are, big sponsors in the sport. The themes of their advertisements were, "If our oil can protect this car's engine, it can protect your engine, too." Beer companies and tobacco companies were also big sponsors. Today, the types of businesses sponsoring stock car racing are very diverse. Some of the "newcomers" to the sport are candy companies, banks, laundry detergent makers, paint companies, cereal companies, and fast-food chains. Stock car races have become major sporting events, and businesses are realizing this.

Inside Track

Do not limit your thinking to any one specific type of business. With the growing popularity of the sport, every type of business is a potential sponsor. However, you will probably have more luck with a business whose products are targeted to the general public. Business to business sponsors do work (having companies that can interact with other NASCAR sponsors even if they do not have public-oriented products).

Do Your Homework

After you have selected some specific business to go after, do your homework on them. Find out as much information as possible on the company and its products and services. When the time comes for you to meet with people from that company, the more you know about the business, the better your chances for securing the sponsorship will be.

One of the easiest and best places to go to look for information on a business is the Internet. Most companies today have a Web site that contains some information on their businesses. Some of the types of information you can find on the Internet include addresses, phone numbers, type of business, and the products or services the businesses offer. Some companies even list the names of a few senior people in the companies. No matter what the company, you will know more about it after visiting its Web site.

Inside Track

Even though you are not an employee of the company sponsoring you, you are representing that company to the public, so be sure to present yourself in a professional manner. Remember that your actions both on and off the track are a reflection on your sponsors.

Inside Track

When calling a business to ask about a sponsorship, ask for the head of the advertising department.

How to Reach Out and Touch Someone

After you learn about the company, you need to find a way to contact the appropriate person to start talking about the opportunities you can offer the company. There are a few ways of doing this. The first is to pick up the phone and call the company. The problem with this approach is that you will probably have a hard time finding the right person to talk to.

If you are unable to reach someone by telephone, another way to get your foot in the door is to mail a letter briefly explaining your proposal to several key employees of the company. You want your letter directed to the marketing or advertising department, so try to find out the names of the heads of these departments. Although it may be easier to mail a letter then place a call, mailing a letter alone is the least effective way of getting noticed. Think about all of the junk mail that you receive every day and what you do with it. Chances are the same thing is happening to your sponsorship letter.

Whether you choose the phone route or the mail route, always follow up your efforts. If you mailed a letter, call the person to say you are following up on the letter you sent to see if he or she has any questions. If you telephoned someone at the company, follow it up with a letter thanking the person for taking your call and saying you look forward to speaking with him or her further. The goal is to schedule a face-to-face meeting where you can discuss a sponsorship. Companies will not come to you; you will need to go to them. After all, they are the ones writing the check.

Talking the Talk

You made the call, followed it up with a thank-you letter, and scheduled a face-to-face meeting. When you go to the meeting, the first thing to do is look professional. Do not go to a business meeting with oil on your hands to show how good a mechanic you are. Companies are looking for someone who will present a positive image to the public. Think of all of the spokespeople you know or see for companies. The one thing in common about all spokespeople is that they have charisma and charm. So turn it on. You want to show the company that you can be a great spokesperson. If the company sponsors you, you will have to talk about how good its products are, how dedicated a company it is, and how you can't imagine how you survived without its product for so long. Show the company that you can promote it without coming across as being pushy.

The biggest thing you have to offer is the exposure you bring to the company. Race teams have many ways in which they can promote their sponsors. Sure, you can display logos on the sides of the racecar or the hood of the racecar, but you need to offer sponsors something really eye-catching. These days, many race teams are building what is called a *show car*.

Many teams are taking the show car concept a step further and building interactive show cars. Instead of just being an older or retired racecar, show cars are sometimes equipped with racing video games to give people the feeling of what it is like to drive a racecar. This is just one example of offering something that will catch someone's attention. Be creative in this area. The more you can offer the sponsor, the better your chances are of closing the deal.

Inside Track

When you are close to finalizing your sponsorship, ask the company what activities or things you or your team can do to help promote its business. Demonstrating that you are someone who takes a genuine interest in the company, not just someone who wants a check, will make a lasting impression on your potential sponsors.

Track Terms

A **show car** is a racecar that is used by the sponsor at trade shows, business meetings, or store openings to draw the public's attention.

Ads in Motion

Now that you have a sponsor, you need to make sure you promote it. Of course, you will put the name of the sponsor on the car, but where should it go? What happens when you have multiple sponsors? Read on to find out how to increase exposure for your sponsors both inside and outside of the racetrack.

Places for the Sponsor

When you are trying to secure a sponsor for your race team, what you are really doing is selling advertising space. The racecar is your advertising space, and there are at least eight major places on a racecar where you can promote your sponsor:

➤ The hood

➤ The upper quarter panel

➤ The lower quarter panel in front of the tire

➤ The lower quarter panel behind the tire

➤ The B post (between the two side windows)

➤ The C post (between the side window and rear windshield)

➤ The trunk lid

➤ The light panel on the rear bumper

In many cases, race teams with multiple sponsors will divide up the racecar for each sponsor. One sponsor might have the entire hood of the car, another sponsor may have the sides of the car, and still a third sponsor could have the entire trunk. By dividing up the space on the racecar, you may be able to secure smaller sponsors, instead of trying to find one for the entire car.

Inside Track

Try obtaining several smaller sponsors instead of searching for only one big sponsor. You may have better luck at getting more businesses to give you a small check for a small place on the racecar.

Trailer Time

While traveling to and from the races, you haul your racecar and all of your equipment in a big trailer. Think of that trailer with all your equipment in it as a rolling billboard. By displaying your sponsor's name on the trailer while you travel to races, you are reaching more than just the folks that attend the races. When figuring out how and where to place your sponsor's name on the trailer, work with your sponsor. It may want to take the opportunity to design something special or use the space to announce a new product. Either way, the sponsor will be happy to see that you are working with it to help promote its business.

More Exposure Means a Happier Sponsor

The more places you can put your sponsor's name, the better exposure it will receive. The more exposure you give your sponsor, the better your chances are at keeping that sponsor for next year. Besides advertising or promoting your sponsor on the racecar or trailer, you can also promote your sponsor on the driver and crew uniforms.

Some of the most exciting action in stock car racing happens during the *pit stops*. Because the racecar must get back on the track as quickly as possible, the pit crew works to change four tires and fill the car with gas in 17 seconds. The excitement surrounding this activity creates another opportunity to promote your sponsor. Because everyone likes to watch the pit crew work on the racecar, the crew uniforms also carry the sponsor's name. Having the sponsor's name on the crew uniforms significantly increases the exposure for the sponsor.

In the early days of racing, crew uniforms were nothing more than a pair a blue jeans and a T-shirt. As sponsors signed up with race teams, their names were put on the back of the T-shirts in a rather crude fashion. But today, like everything else, crew uniforms have evolved.

Crew uniforms today are designed with safety in mind. With all of the potential hazards on *pit road* from flammable liquids to pressurized air bottles and speeding racecars, the need for protection for the pit crew has grown. Today's crew uniforms are made of a fire-retardant material, similar to the material in the drivers' racing suits. The idea is that in case of a fire on pit road, the pit crew should be given the greatest chance possible of escaping unhurt. In addition to being made of fire-retardant materials, crew uniforms have padding sewn into the knee and elbow areas as well. This padding helps protect the pit crew from minor injuries.

Track Terms

A **pit stop** is when the racecar pulls off of the racetrack for service or repair. Some of the more common items performed during a pit stop include changing tires and filling the racecar up with gas.

Track Terms

Pit road is the road usually located on the infield along the front straightaway. On this road teams are assigned a stall, or spot where they may perform routine or emergency maintenance during the race.

Everybody Loves Style

In addition to safety, the style of the pit crew uniforms is also important to the sponsors. Everyone likes to watch the action on pit road, and the sponsor wants to make sure that its team looks good both on and off the track. The number of style options for crew uniforms has increased over the years. In the early days of racing, only a few style and color options were available. But today, race teams and sponsors have the option to design their own crew uniforms. Color options appear to be unlimited, and the style options are limited only by the need for function and safety. To put it simply, the fashion industry has a whole market to get into. It's only a matter of time before Armani starts designing crew uniforms. What is this sport coming to?

Walking the Walk

Even with all of the items we have talked about so far, there are still some things a sponsor could want from a race team. Earlier in this chapter, we talked about the sponsor using the racecar at trade shows or at grand opening events to attract the attention of the public. This is an example of a typical off-track event. Off-track events draw attention to the sponsor and increase the exposure for the driver and team to the general public, so they benefit both parties.

One of the more common activities that a race team is asked to perform for a sponsor is driver appearances. During driver appearances, the driver of the racecar attends a business function to sign autographs and shake hands with the public. The average person does not often have the opportunity to get a close look at a racecar or shake the hand of a racecar driver. If a person receives an autograph from a racecar driver, the next time he or she goes to or sees a stock car race, he or she will say, "Hey, I know that guy. He gave me an autograph once." This type of interaction with the general public helps to build fans for the driver, sponsor, and the sport itself.

Shameless Self-Promotion

Fans are very dedicated and loyal to their teams. The more people you can get watching you and your team, the better off you will be. If possible, try to organize a fan club. Any fans that a racecar driver has automatically become the fans and supports of that driver's sponsor. This fan base can be a very powerful negotiating item when you are trying to find a sponsor.

Don't underestimate the power of meeting fans face to face. Fans like to get close to the team and the tracks. When negotiating with your sponsor, talk about the activities you may want to do that involve your fans. One example would be to have a raffle for one lucky fan to become an honorary pit crew member at a race. An activity like this brings increased exposure to the sponsor and allows the fans to get closer to the team.

Another example would be to have your sponsor host a pre-race party at the track. The sponsor could invite the driver's fan club as well as several of its customers. You could set up the racecar in an area in which the attendees could sit in it. Another idea would be to have the pit crew put on a pit stop demonstration for the attendees. In the time it takes a pit crew to change four tires and fill the car with 22 gallons of gas, most people are just getting out of their car at the local gas station. When most people see how fast the pit crew can service a racecar, they are amazed.

These are all types of ideas that a race team can do to help promote its sponsor, show-case its skills, and draw fans to the sport itself. The more you do for your sponsor, the happier your sponsor will be, and a happy sponsor is a good thing. Happy sponsors return year after year and allow you to keep doing what you love to do.

What It All Means

The sponsor does not work late hours in the race shop to prepare the racecar for the coming weekend or go to the track and change tires or fill the racecar with gas during a race. These types of activities require a different kind of assistance. But even if you had all of that help, you still would not be able to race without the assistance of the silent crew member, the sponsor. Racing sponsors allow race teams to build the race-cars, get to the tracks, and compete in the races. Without a sponsor, most race teams could not race.

If there is one thing you should remember about the importance of sponsors, it is this: It is much easier to keep a sponsor than it is to find a new one. Every year, more newly formed race teams are looking for sponsorship. Take care of your sponsors and keep them happy. Treat them more than just as companies that give you a check every year. Treat them as partners and keep them involved. If you do not, some other race team will.

The Least You Need to Know

➤ Do not limit your thinking to only automotive companies for sponsorship.

➤ Find out as much as possible about potential sponsors.

➤ Turn on the charm when meeting with sponsors to show that you would make a good "company person."

➤ Be professional when dealing with your sponsor.

➤ The more you do for your sponsors, the more they will do for you.

➤ Do not underestimate the importance of a sponsor.

➤ To keep your sponsors, treat them like partners.

31

Chapter 4

The Arena

> ## In This Chapter
>
> ➤ Determining whether track size matters
>
> ➤ Banking with your car, not your cash
>
> ➤ The ins and outs of flat tracks
>
> ➤ The pros and cons of road courses and right turns

Does size matter? Yes! Drivers who spend most of their careers on one track that is a quarter of a mile to a third of a mile will tell you that if you can drive in a bull ring you can drive anywhere. That's so untrue! The size of the track determines the terminal speed of the racecars. Higher speeds change the equipment a car needs to have to be competitive. Higher speeds also require that the drivers have the skills necessary to negotiate the higher speeds and handle the g-forces that they will encounter.

This chapter deals with the size of different tracks in stock car racing. The track shapes and configurations change the way the drivers and crews prepare for a race, and a team's success is determined by how much effort and knowledge it has about different tracks. You will learn how to drive on banked tracks, flat tracks, and road courses; you will also learn the equipment needed to race on these tracks.

Let's Make Tracks

NASCAR tracks range from ¼ mile to more than 2½ miles. Their shapes also vary: Some are ovals, some are D-shaped ovals, and some more round than others. Triovals are a driver favorite because they add another turn in one of the straightaways.

Under the Hood

The 1960s and 1970s were the major growing periods for racetracks around the country; more than half of the tracks used today in NASCAR were built during these times. The 1990s proved to be another growth period; seven major super speedways were built for use in NASCAR competition during this time.

Short Tracks

Short tracks are the mainstay of the racing world. Nearly every racing series in the world is run on tracks that measure a half of a mile or less. These tracks come in different shapes and sizes ranging from a quarter mile to half or five eighths of a mile. Some short tracks are banked higher than others, and some are more round than oval. Others are D-shaped or trioval.

Success at these tracks doesn't guarantee success at the higher levels of NASCAR, but it does give you a great head start. Racing on short tracks requires great concentration and the nerve to withstand constant contact with other cars. Close racing and a lot of light contact is not uncommon in short-track races. The car is going to be roughed up a bit on a short track, no matter how skilled you are as a driver. On short tracks, handling is more important than horsepower. Without a car that handles properly, you can kiss winning good-bye.

Aerodynamics isn't as much of an issue as it is on longer tracks because of the slower speeds; more attention should be paid to the suspension rather than the body shape. However, you can't run a box-shaped car or have the fenders hanging off the body with the hood flying up. Air does play a role on short tracks. Hold your hand out the window traveling at 50 miles per hour. Notice how the air forces your hand around. This air is also blowing on your car, but the *drag* on the car is not as drastic as it is on bigger speedways.

Track Terms

Drag is the effect air has on the car as it travels through the air. Air doesn't really move as compared to the car, the car travels through it and moves it either out of the way or directs it around the car (drag).

Superspeedways

Every young racer dreams of running 200 miles per hour down the back straightaway of the premier superspeedway, Daytona International Speedway, and drafting with the best Winston Cup racers NASCAR has to offer. The incredible speeds and close racing on the superspeedway requires all the skills of the short track and the nerve of a fighter pilot. One wrong move will result in a high-speed traffic accident, which probably will be disastrous for more than one racer.

The first televised 500-mile NASCAR race was broadcast live from Daytona in February 1979. This race was to be a test for the networks and cable television companies, and it delivered more than what could have ever been expected. The northeast was covered with snow, and the outlook was for more snow. With a captive audience watching, the race delivered excitement and one of the most spectacular endings ever for any Daytona 500 race. A last lap crash between Donnie Allison and Cale Yarborough caused a fight between the two. Donnie's brother Bobby then jumped in the mix. The three tangled on the track outside of their cars on national television. The race ended with Richard Petty taking the checkers, but the talk was all about the awesome racing and the wild fight at the end. This race kicked off a frenzy of cable television companies bidding for more of these exciting races.

Inside Track

Before trying your hand at the superspeedways, you should amass years of short-track experience. Those valuable laps of experience in handling a racecar and avoiding incident will help you avoid the rapid accidents that happen on the high-speed speedways.

Under the Hood

During NASCAR's first 30 years, television coverage of NASCAR races was limited to highlights on ABC Sports or a mention on local newscasts. The first televised race needed to be a big one, and what was to become one of the world's most famous superspeedways, Daytona International Speedway, was chosen to host this event. In 1979, CBS showed the Daytona 500 live to the world for the first time, and the world reacted like no one could have expected. With one of the most exciting races ever held at Daytona, NASCAR and its drivers were introduced to the entire world as the real people they were. After this broadcast, interest in NASCAR increased, and drivers became heroes in what would become the fastest-growing sport in America.

The Daytona 500 was also the start of Bill Elliot winning the Winston Million in 1985. Winston developed this program to give a million dollars to any driver who wins three of the big races. Weeks after winning the Daytona 500, Elliot came from an unprecedented five laps down to win at Talledega. With two of the big races won, he had only to win in Charlotte to win the million, but he could manage only a nineteenth-place finish. The next race took place at one of the most brutal super-speedways in the country: Darlington International Speedway. This track, dubbed "too tough to tame," became a frenzy of excitement and anticipation. Could Bill Elliot win the coveted Winston Million? Only true superspeedways could bring this kind of excitement to television. Elliot did win the million, and with it, he garnered more attention than he bargained for. Television brought hero status to this NASCAR driver, and it all happened at a superspeedway.

Banking (Do I Get Free Checking with That?)

The term *banking* is usually associated with big institutions that pay you about 2 percent per year to keep your money. In the world of NASCAR, banking is the wall of asphalt that stock car drivers love to climb. It is the angle of the track off zero degrees, measuring from a low of about 8 or 12 degrees to as much as 33 to 36 degrees.

Banking allows drivers to go faster by holding them onto the track by taking away the *slip angle* associated with flat tracks. By angling the track at various degrees, banking provides traction to racecars. Gravity plays the biggest role here. High-banked tracks aid traction by using what would be side load and changing it to down force because of the angle at which it is applied. As a result, cars not only go into the turns faster, but they also travel through the turns and out of the turns faster, resulting in rapid action and quick lap times.

Banking means to incline laterally, and the amount of this lateral incline determines how much faster a car will travel. Dover, Delaware, has one of the fastest 1-mile tracks in the country, Dover Downs Speedway. Another one of the north's crown jewels is New Hampshire International Speedway in Loudon, New Hampshire. Although each of these speedways is 1 mile in length, Dover allows for a much faster lap time and greater speeds because it has double the amount of banking that Loudon has. (Loudon has 12 degrees of banking, and Dover has 26 degrees of banking.) The difference in banking between these two tracks means that the average qualifying lap at Loudon is around 29 seconds at an average speed of 130 miles per hour. A qualifying lap at Dover averages about 23 seconds at about 153 miles per hour. That's a

Track Terms

The **slip angle** is the difference between the wheel and tire as the steering wheel is turned. You can turn your steering wheel, as you watch the wheel turn, the side wall flexes and the tire's contact patch stays momentarily and then turns after the wheel. This situation causes the driver to turn the steering wheel more at higher side load turns. Radial tires removed some slip angle, but certainly not all.

difference of about 23 miles per hour and 6 seconds in the same distance because of the increase in lateral traction.

Banking uses the same principle runners use as they sprint around a track. They lean over and allow some of the forces that would normally be a side load to become down force and help their running shoes grip the ground and adhere to the surface of the track. With banking, cars have more traction, and speeds increase because of it.

Flat Tracks

Flat tracks are defined as low-banking tracks, usually with under 15 degrees of banking. Without banking, drivers sometimes try to get on the inside of other drivers and use them as banking to *lean on* to gain more traction and remove the other drivers' usable side bite. Side bite is a term used by racers to define how good or bad the traction is in the corner. Side bite is the traction achieved by a tire while being stressed and asked to turn.

The following are examples of flat tracks:

➤ Loudon, New Hampshire: New Hampshire International Speedway

➤ Phoenix, Arizona: Phoenix International Raceway

➤ Martinsville, Virginia: Martinsville Speedway

➤ Stafford, Connecticut: Stafford Motor Speedway

All of these tracks have similar characteristics.

Inside Track

When driving on a flat track, be as smooth as you can and use the forces of inertia to propel the car around the track. Hustling the car around the track will not work as well as the smooth approach. Let the car and suspension match the track surface and try not to upset this delicate balance.

Track Terms

Lean on is when the car on the inside, or lower on the track, will actually put his car right up against another car traveling on the outside of them, it takes the load off the inside car's tires.

Why Are They So Tough to Get Around?

Flat tracks pose a problem not found on high-banked tracks: reduction of traction. With the flat corners, crew chiefs must work extensively with soft shocks and springs to help tires adhere to the track. Without the banking, flat tracks make the car feel as though it might tip over. The left side wheels seem to want to lift off the ground and tumble like a bad stock.

Inside Track

Running the car into the corner on a flat track a little softer than usual will save the right front tire. Front tires wear down fast on flat tracks, and care is required to make them last.

Inside Track

Driving on flat tracks comes close to driving on a rain-slicked road. Smooth easy transitions from corner to straightaways are needed, and light braking is a must for entry into the corner.

Flat tracks also pose some problems unseen by most racing fans, such as right-side tire wear, especially the right front tire. Although this tire is always the most worn on ovals, it especially takes a beating in a flat-track situation. The next tire that gets a beating is the left rear tire. This happens due to the sliding of the car while it's turning and the spinning of the left rear tire while the right rear tire is being planted. Flat tracks often require more stagger. *Stagger* is the difference between the circumference of the right side and left side tires. A larger right side tire allows the car to turn more freely while keeping the wheels turning at the same speed. We cover stagger further in Chapter 12, "A Good Set of Rubbers."

A Left-Foot Track

Flat tracks often require a good left foot. The left foot works the brake in a stock car, and braking becomes more important as the race wears on. With the low or no banking, flat tracks are driver-oriented tracks, and the smoother the driver is, the faster the car goes. You don't have the banking to lean on or catch you if you overdrive a corner.

Throttling the car on a flat track becomes a situation in itself. When getting back into the throttle at Dover (a banked track), you may just squeeze it right to the floor. But at tracks like Loudon (a flat track), you need to squeeze the throttle softly, feathering it softly and maybe never reaching full throttle until almost all the way through the corner and onto the straightaway.

You Mean I Have to Make a Right Turn?

NASCAR drivers encounter a multitude of different track configurations; one oddity is the road course. Road courses bring to NASCAR racing several different things that ovals do not. The first and main difference is that drivers need to make right turns on road courses. Unless a right turn is necessary in the pits, the only other time a driver needs to make a right turn on oval tracks is to catch the car from coming around on him or her or to crash into someone coming off the corner. Other than that, making a right turn would immediately introduce a driver to the outside retaining wall.

Comparing Apples to Ovals

Aside from the right turns, road courses are very similar to ovals. But they do pose different problems. One of the major differences is that shifting is needed to get around a road course. Drivers have to shift as many as 20 or more times each lap around a road course; they never shift after getting up to speed on an oval.

The second difference is the shape of the track. Unlike ovals, the turns on road courses are not all the same. Some are hard rights, some are soft lefts, and still others are 90- or 180-degree turns that require a reduction of speed from 160 miles per hour to about 50 miles per hour. The lengths of straightaways on the track are also different. Some straightaways require a short acceleration and one shift; others require three shifts and a 1,500-foot run. Drivers need to be prepared for the constant change in track design.

Inside Track

A road course can be run in two different ways. You can try to make smooth, easy transitions into the corners, or you can slip and slide your way around the corners. Both of these types of drivers have won on road courses.

Under the Hood

In the 1970s and early 1980s, drivers would just coast through a road course race and use it as a throwaway race. They wouldn't prepare very well, and most didn't aspire to excel at road racing. By the late 1980s and early 1990s, more and more drivers were looking for instruction from road course specialists to accelerate their road course programs. They saw the need for running this race like it mattered, and it did. With the points races tightening more and more each year, teams saw the opportunity to use road courses as a springboard to jump past competitors.

This shifter from Hurst Racing Products provides a good base for road racing. We built the shifter linkage with straight rods made of tubular, thin-walled steel and aluminum; it's sturdy, without flex, and light-weight.

Another difference in road courses is the way you need to drive them. On an oval, you run the car into the corner, brake, set up for the middle, and jump on the throttle to exit the corner. On a road course, you run into the corner, brake hard, downshift, set up a kind of apex into the corner, finish all your downshifting by the entry to the corner, and accelerate off the corner harder than the entry. The exit from the corner is where you will try to gain all your advantage. You run down whatever length straightaway confronts you, shifting only enough to reach the next corner, and then you start the process all over again. There is so much more to do on a road course than there is on the common oval. Drivers must be prepared to shift upwards of a few hundred times during a road course event and brake quite a bit.

Road Course Equipment

Road courses require many of the same parts and equipment as short tracks. As with other tracks, heat is a major factor and is the enemy of your drive line parts as well as the driver. Oil coolers are mandatory on rear gears and transmissions. Not running a cooler would be like sentencing both these parts to death.

Road courses also require the use of the "clutchless" transmission. This transmission allows drivers to shift without the aid of a clutch. Once the driver lets out the clutch to get the car moving, the clutch is no longer needed. The clutch should be used for downshifts, but it's not completely necessary. The addition of this type of transmission has brought newfound reliability, and missed shifts are now kept to a minimum. It also has decreased lap times by allowing quicker shifts and more speed. As a result, road courses have become more fun.

Some examples of clutchless transmissions are:

➤ Jerico Transmissions

➤ Tex Racing T101

➤ G-Force transmissions

On road courses, braking is more frequent and is harder than on ovals, so the most efficient braking systems needs to be used. NASCAR also allows the use of a third brake-cooling hose and has increased the size of the cooling ducts allowed in the front of the car. Cooling the rear brakes also becomes an issue. Both front and rear brakes are tested to the limits on road courses, and durable heat-resistant units are recommended.

Rear sway bars in NASCAR were introduced at road courses. These bars allow more rear suspension control and provide a more confident feel for the driver. When using a rear sway bar, remember to soften the rear springs because the sway bar will add the "wheel rate" of the spring. We will talk about this issue further in Chapter 16, "Foot to the Floor."

The tracks used for NASCAR racing all have personalities of their own. No two are alike, and no two can be driven the same. To race successfully, teams need to adapt to the size and shape of each track by adjusting the car and driving style.

The Least You Need to Know

➤ Size does matter in racing. Different track sizes require different driving styles and equipment.

➤ Superspeedways, such as the Daytona International Speedway, are the big guns of NASCAR.

➤ Banking holds a car onto the track, making the car go faster.

➤ Flat tracks require a lot of finesse to negotiate.

➤ Road courses require drivers to turn both left and right.

Part 2

Equipment Needed to Race

You've made it this far, and you still want to be a racecar driver. Before you can turn a few laps on the racetrack, you need some pieces of equipment in order to get started.

In this part, you'll read about the equipment and the costs associated with being a successful racecar driver. You need a lot of stuff in order to be a competitive racecar driver. Don't say we didn't warn you.

Chapter 5

The Stock Car Itself

In This Chapter

➤ Understanding front end styles and suspensions

➤ Working with rear end suspensions

➤ Getting car, driver, and track feedback

➤ Following the rules of performance

➤ Using body styling for different results

This chapter talks about the racecar itself, including the different types of front ends and suspensions. You will learn how changes to the rear end suspension affect the ways the racecar, the driver, and the racetrack relate with one another. This chapter concludes with a discussion on the evolution of the body styling.

What Is It Made Of?

Each stock car is made up of hundreds of feet of round and square steel tubing. The tubing is bent, shaped, and fitted to the body style. The rules regulating the construction of the car also determine the car's skeleton. A NASCAR-style stock car is made up of a 3 × 4 × .120 wall-based frame, rails, and cross members. The roll cage is seamless round tubing, which is 1¾ diameter and a minimum of .090 wall thickness.

An example of a frame with a roll cage.

The chassis is the base for all suspension and body mounts. There are many small variations in the chassis that make the difference between a good and a great car. The following sections cover the different types of chassis and suspension styles used in NASCAR.

Front-End Suspension: A-Arm

The most widely used suspension is the conventional A-arm style suspension. Today's A-arm suspension is modeled after the early Chevrolet Malibus and Chevelles and utilizes A-frame upper and lower control arms. This suspension is dependable, rugged, and stiff in structure, which makes it a good base for racing. The drawback to this style is its weight; it is quite a heavy package.

A-arm suspensions come in many different styles, including the following two:

Track Terms

Darty is the feeling of the car being aggressive or reactive.

➤ **Standard snout.** The name of this style refers to the roll centers of the control arms, with the roll centers being the intersection of the control arms. The standard snout has a high roll center, and the car rotates closely to the center of gravity. This high roll center makes the car roll evenly and smoothly. The low snout car has a low roll center, which makes the car roll over more with the same center of gravity. It almost flops over on the tires, making the car a bit *darty*, or aggressive.

➤ **Strut.** Modeled after the early Ford Torinos of the '70s, this style is somewhat lighter and more adjustable than other styles, but it is a bit touchy for the driver. It is used mainly as a low snout or low roll center style suspension. This front-end style uses a straight, somewhat lighter lower control arm with a strut support.

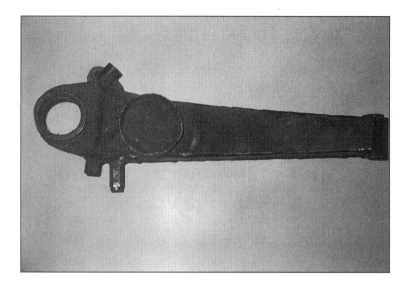

A strut style control arm.

Rear Suspension: Truck Arm

Rear suspensions have been narrowed down to just one style, the truck arm suspension. NASCAR allows only this style in order to make the cars easier to police during the technical inspection and to keep costs down. In the past, too many styles were being used, which made it difficult to enforce the rules. Truck arms shaped like I-beams apply the power softer to the rear suspension, whereas tubular truck arms are more unforgiving.

A rear housing centering device called a track bar or a *panhard bar* (which is covered in more depth in Chapter 11, "Rocking and Rolling") helps control rear end side-to-side motion. It's also the adjustment to rear roll centers; moving the mounting points of the bar either raises or lowers the roll centers.

Track Terms

The **panhard bar**, or track bar, controls the rear roll centers. Raising the bar can help loosen up the rear of the car. Lowering the bar tightens up the car by making it roll over more on the rear tires and planting the tires harder to the track.

47

The track bar is a good tuning device. For example, if you have a car that pushes entering the corner, you can help fix that by raising the bar evenly. If you have a car that is loose entering the corner, lowering the bar will lower the roll center, making the car roll more and lean on the rear tires. If you have a car that drives in good, gets off the corner well, but doesn't turn right in the middle, you can lower one side of the bar and help it turn only in the middle.

Car and Driver Feedback

Drivers, like cars, have characteristics of their own. Two drivers can each have different feelings about the same car. Getting the correct style of chassis is important to obtaining the best feedback from your driver. One driver may like the easy roll of a high roll center car; another may not feel it turns to his ability. If a driver has no confidence in the car, he will not ever reach his potential.

Yellow Flag

Be careful of what the driver tells you. Some know what they're talking about; some don't. More than a few times you may not get the whole truth.

The feel of the front end has become paramount with drivers. Many drivers are now chassis specialists or chassis tuners. Some of the best drivers in the world win as much as they do because they know about chassis tuning and know exactly what they want to feel.

Driver feedback is one of the most important tools used to tune the car. The driver needs to relay information about what the car is doing and what it needs to do. Only then can a team adjust a car to achieve its full potential. Many drivers are able to race well, but they are unable to help the team adjust the car to the conditions or a particular track. This lack of communication makes for a very difficult day for the crew. Drivers who can help the crew progress quickly through practice, and their cars become fast more quickly.

A driver's personality and ability determines what he or she can do with the car, and the car must be matched to those traits. For example, aggressive drivers need a car that can withstand the abuse of hard driving. Smooth drivers need a car geared around careful driving and calculated moves. Out-of-control drivers who drive over their heads may be the worst type of drivers for crews to handle because their driving style changes all the time, making for a very difficult setup.

Car and Track Feedback

Matching the car to the specific track and to the driver is all interconnected and necessary to the success of the team. Although crews mainly like to have a lower roll center for flatter tracks and a higher roll center for very high-banked tracks, this guideline doesn't work for all drivers. Some drivers just don't like the feel of the low snout car, making it difficult for them to negotiate the turns properly.

Ideally, you need a car that can drive into a corner and turn itself to the middle with the driver controlling the speed and direction of the entry. The driver must then have total control of the car during the exit and accelerate to the limits of the car.

Under the Hood

Superspeedway cars use a window in the right side door on tracks of 1½ mile or longer. This window helps lessen the chance of air picking up the car during a spin.

The Shape of Performance

The body of the car plays a crucial role in its performance. The shape of the car moving through the air has a direct effect on the performance of the chassis. The down force is the pressure of the air pushing on the car as it travels. The air doesn't travel across the car, rather the car punches a hole through the air, forcing the air away from the car and causing pressure on the car.

To get an idea of what air does to the car, think back to when you were a kid and you would hold your hand out the window while being driven down the street. Your hand would be pulled up and down by the position in which you held it. (That would keep you occupied for hours wouldn't it?) And that was only at 30 to 50 miles per hour. Imagine what that air can do at 200 miles per hour or more!

Changing the shape of the car causes the down force to be applied to different parts of the car and helps the chassis. The following changes have different effects:

➤ Flatter, wider front fenders direct more down force to the front of the car, making the front end stick better. Widening the front width of the lower fenders does the same thing.

➤ Flattening the sides of the car, which means bubbling out the front and rear fenders, makes the car glide through the air and pulls air into the car, causing down force.

➤ Raising the angle of the rear spoiler helps traction in the rear of the car.

On a flat track at high speeds, a car can benefit greatly from the use of the air around it. Large front and rear fenders create the pressure needed to hold the car to the track under the great side loads of this kind of track condition.

Change It All!

Aerodynamics has been one the greatest influences on the handling of a car in the past few years. A small spoiler change, front or rear, can make a big difference in speed, especially at the larger tracks. One strip of tape can determine whether a team qualifies or not. You may notice that team members adding or removing tape on the front of the car during a pit stop. Removing tape means the car was too loose for the driver; the car wanted to spin around. Adding tape means the driver couldn't turn as well as he wanted; adding tape allows more pressure to be applied to the front end, which helps the tires stick to the track and aids in turning the car.

No part of the car is safe from change in order to gain an advantage in down force. Even the bolts and screws used on the outside of the car are rounded and made smaller. The edges of every window are made smooth and level with the next edge. The edges of the front of the car are made smooth and round to cut through the air cleanly. The rear of the car gets sharp or slightly waved edges. This design cuts through the air, but grabs onto it as well, utilizing every bit of pressure available.

Oh Yeah, There Are Rules

Ideally, if the rules allowed, crews would build cars as low to the ground as possible and make the front and rear fenders flat, with a slight *rake* to the rear. The rear spoiler would be large, and front spoiler would be low, as close to the ground as possible. But this is NASCAR, and they regulate the rules closely.

Some safety rules have made the current stock cars safer. The addition of roof flaps has saved more than a few cars from flipping over during high-speed spins. As the car spins, the flaps, one on each side of the roof, open and disturb the air. Not allowing the air to travel over the roof keeps the car from going into the air like the wing of a plane.

Track Terms

The **rake** is the angle and rate of angle of an object.

Evolution of the Body Style

The evolution of the body style shows where we may be heading in the future. The first stock cars were cars right off the showroom floor. Drivers raced what they brought, without making any changes. The original cars were not at all aerodynamic, at least by today's standards. They were large and high and had very few down force characteristics. They didn't even have racing tires. They needed to fit the people of that time. Imagine Fatty Arbuckle or Lou Costello trying to stuff themselves into a new Saturn or Geo!

Each year, the cars got a little smaller. They also became flatter, shorter, and lighter. The first cars capable of obtaining high speeds with comfortable driving conditions didn't arrive until the 1970s. These cars also started to develop more usable chassis and body styles. Some, such as the Dodge Daytona, made aerodynamic advancements such as a V-shaped front nose and a huge wing mounted off the trunk of the car. This wing was soon disallowed for use in competition because of its aerodynamic advantage and odd look.

In the 1980s, racers saw the need for a more aerodynamic car that could attain high rates of speed with safety and stay stable with many other cars around them. The first of these cars were the Ford Thunderbird, Chevrolet Lumina and Monte Carlo, and Oldsmobile Cutlass Supreme. These cars had all the basic requirements of today's modern day racecars. These cars were all specifically made by the manufacturer to cut the wind and create down force.

Track Terms

A **wind tunnel** is a controlled environment of forced air travel to test the flow of air over objects. These were first developed to test plane shapes and wing designs, but are easily adapted for use testing racecars.

The more these cars were raced, the more changes were made to enhance the aerodynamic package of the bodies. Teams found a new tool to make the cars go faster: The *wind tunnel* allowed teams to work to improve the car without having to go to the track.

Today's racecars are made from stock roof, hood, trunk lid, and fiberglass or carbon fiber nose and tailpieces. The remainder of the car is fabricated by car builders or the teams themselves. The body panels start from flat sheets of steel. These sheets are cut, formed, rolled, shaped, and welded together to form the cars you see on the track. To shape the panels and form compound curves, car builders use a sheet metal tool called an *English wheel*. Made over 100 years ago, the English wheel presses its two heavy wheels together with the steel sheet between them. The sheet is rolled back and forth until the desired shape is obtained.

An English wheel is a tool used to form body panels.

Forming the Perfect Body

Templates are used to keep cars within the NASCAR rules; each car has many templates. NASCAR officials take templates to the track, so not having your car fit these templates will ensure that your team has plenty of work to do before practice.

Teams work within the guidelines, but they sure do try to stretch every rule. Basic body rules include roof location as well as roof and rear quarter panel heights. After these measurements are established, the remainder of the body can be mounted. The hood and trunk lids are usually next, followed by the nose and tailpieces. After these pieces are located and mounted, the next step is fabricating the sides of the car and front and rear fenders. Most of the speed gains come from changes to these last areas; paying close attention to detail here can pay large dividends at the track.

Inside Track

Round, streamlined bodies work better on superspeedways; cars shaped more for heavy down force work better almost everywhere else.

Track Terms

Templates are precisely made tools made to fit the outside shape of an object in order to keep close tolerances.

Drafting is a term used for the practice of two or more cars running closely together. In doing this, each car can go faster because the air is divided between the two of them.

Popular Styles

Each body style used in stock car racing has its own benefits and drawbacks. The current Monte Carlo may just be the most universal car now available to racers. Used in short track or speedway form, it offers great down force and straightaway speed. The car has produced more wins than any other car currently being used. A new Monte Carlo is currently in the works and testing is being done as of this writing. However, until the beginning of 1999, the older Ford Thunderbird still made for a faster and better speedway car.

Although it's a new car for Ford, the Taurus has come along very quickly in a short time. It has shown itself to be a front-runner in the high down force tracks. Its large facial area and sharp high rear deck and bumper are basic needs for aerodynamic domination. The small, round-style roof and lay-back windows make the Taurus a very aerodynamic vehicle. But don't underestimate its ability to run the superspeedways. It *drafts* well and can be shaped to run to the front.

The other GM product, the Pontiac Grand Prix, has also shown its winning capability on both short track and speedways. With the long front hood and nose, lay-back front window, and formed rear deck, the car can easily be shaped for heavy down force or *low drag* speedway form.

What's Next?

This chapter shows that many factors are involved in the creation of a NASCAR racecar. In this chapter, we have only talked briefly about a few things. To go into every area of the racecar and cover all of the details, we would need a series of books more like an encyclopedia.

If you want to learn more about the racecar chassis and the effects of aerodynamics on the body styling of vehicles, check the Internet, browse your local library, or watch shows such as *NASCAR Garage*. The wealth of information out there is improving everyday. The only problem is finding it.

Track Terms

Low drag is a term used for how much air pulls on a car, causing down force or restriction through the air.

The Least You Need to Know

➤ The most widely used suspension is the conventional A-arm style suspension, which is modeled after the early Chevrolet Malibus and Chevelles.

➤ Choosing the correct suspension for your driver's style and getting the correct style of chassis is important to obtaining the best feedback from your driver.

➤ Driver feedback will be the most important tool on practice day.

➤ A driver's personality and ability determines what he or she can do with the car, and the car must be matched to those traits.

➤ The shape of the car will determine where it can be used successfully because the shape of the car moving through the air has a direct effect on the performance of the chassis.

Chapter 6

Getting Around

In This Chapter

➤ Getting your equipment to the track

➤ Getting your team to the track

➤ Getting around the track without using the racecar

Stock car racing involves a lot of equipment and a lot of people. Getting all of the equipment and the necessary crew members to and from the racetrack can be a major process. After all, the crew can't just pile into the racecar and drive to the track. Trying to coordinate transportation is more of a challenge than it may first appear to be. In this chapter, we talk about how race teams accomplish this task.

Getting to the Track

A race team can transport all of its equipment and its racecar to the track in several different ways. The deciding factor on which method to use depends on how much money the team has to spend on transportation. The NASCAR Winston Cup teams go in style, primarily due to the fact that their races are all over the country. The middle-of-the-road teams or teams who race regionally will not travel quite as well as the Winston Cup teams, but they do get the job done and make it to every race. Local weekend racers who may race only at one track all season long do not have to worry as much about how to get to the racetrack. They are able to go bargain-basement style.

Under the Hood

The amount that some NASCAR Winston Cup teams spend on transporting the equipment and the crew to the races is equal to or greater than the total amount teams in other series have to race with.

Going in Style

In addition to knowing how to race, the NASCAR Winston Cup teams know how to travel. These teams use the best of everything, including transportation.

Winston Cup teams will use several vehicles to transport everything to and from the racetrack. They have 18-wheel tractor-trailers for the racecars, equipment, and all of the spare parts. Then they usually have passenger vans for transporting the crews back and forth to the racetrack. The big teams, such as Dale Earnhardt and Jeff Gordon, have a tour bus brought to the racetrack as well. The tour bus is primarily for the families of the driver and car owner. It gives the families a place to stay at the racetrack that is not too close to the tractor-trailer, where they might get in the way of the crew working on the racecar. These buses also give a place for drivers to rest between driving sessions and a safe haven from the crowds of people seeking autographs or who just want to be near.

The race teams get to the racetrack in style as well. They are flown into a nearby airport by a private plane and then picked up and taken to the racetrack. By flying to the racetrack instead of having to drive, the teams have more time to spend at the shop working or at home with their families. With the season lasting from February to November, traveling that much can take a toll on anybody. Flying the team in and out makes the travel a little easier on everybody.

Traveling in this kind of style, although very comfortable, requires a lot of money. That is why only the very well-financed teams, like the Winston Cup teams, can afford to travel this way.

Inside Track

Many of the NASCAR Winston Cup teams travel to and from the racetracks by airplane. It is the quickest way these teams can get from racetrack to racetrack.

Middle of the Road

The teams that don't have a big travel budget still make it to the racetrack, but not in the same style as the Winston Cup guys. These teams use a smaller trailer that carries only one racecar and can be towed with a large pickup truck. These fully enclosed trailers vary in size from 50 feet to 20 feet long. They are usually just big enough to carry the equipment and few critical spare parts. Instead of having a crew lounge, these trailers have a platform on the roof for watching the race.

The team, which does not have the luxury of flying to and from the racetrack, travels in the pickup truck pulling the trailer, or the crew members drive their own cars to the racetrack. Only a few of the team members are paid a salary; the other team members volunteer their time to work on the racecars. They stay in an average hotel and share rooms in order to keep the hotel bills to a minimum. The team owner pays most of the expenses for the crew, but it is anything but a luxury trip. The majority of the money for the team is spent on the racecar.

Bargain Basement

The local weekend racer, who probably cannot afford either a tractor-trailer or an enclosed trailer, uses something a little more economical called an open trailer. As you may have guessed, an open trailer has no walls or roof to it. It is just a flat-bed trailer that the racecar sits on and that can be pulled by a regular pickup. There is no room for any spare equipment on it. It is just big enough for the racecar. All of the tools and spare equipment have to be loaded in the back of the pickup truck and brought to the track that way.

The crew drives themselves to the racetrack, and all of them are volunteers or are family members of the driver. Because the races are usually at a racetrack that is close to home, traveling to the track is not a big problem. The primary thing is to get to the racetrack and not worry about comfort or style. The races are only one day or night, so there is no need for any hotel rooms or additional vehicles to get to and from the racetrack. The people who use this type of trailer are usually just starting out in racing or race in a series that does

Inside Track

A fully enclosed trailer, although not as comfortable as a custom-built tractor-trailer, allows regional race teams to transport everything they need to and from the racetrack.

Inside Track

An open trailer is a good inexpensive trailer for a weekend racer who has to travel only a limited distance to the racetrack. The downside to an open trailer is that there is no place to put any equipment on it other than the racecar itself.

not require teams to bring a lot of equipment to the racetrack. There is no big sponsor, no big crew, and no big race hauler for the racecar or the equipment. These teams get to the racetrack any way they can just for the love of the sport.

The Equipment Hauler

No matter how teams get to the racetrack, whether it is first-class, business class, or economy, the important thing is that they get there. Let's talk a little more about the different types of equipment trailers race teams use to get to and from the racetrack.

Gold Is Best

The NASCAR Winston Cup teams, which are pretty well financed, have a custom-built tractor-trailer that can carry two racecars, all of the equipment and tools needed for the race, and usually enough spare parts to completely rebuild a racecar right at the racetrack. The tractor-trailer itself is used primarily to transport the racecars and the equipment to and from the racetrack. It is not used to transport the team.

A typical lounge area in a Winston Cup tractor-trailer has a couch, a table and chairs, a television, a VCR, and a refrigerator. The lounge area is where the driver and crew members stay when they are not working on the racecar at the track. It usually does not have a sleeping area because the team stays at a local hotel. The lounge area is just a comfortable place to hang out or to have a meeting while at the track.

Under the Hood

A custom–built NASCAR Winston Cup race trailer can cost up to $250,000.

Depending on the distance to the racetrack, one or two truck drivers will take the tractor-trailer for the trip to the racetrack. Because the majority of the races are located on the East Coast, where most of the race shops are, only one driver is needed to take the tractor-trailer to the racetrack. For long trips, like the races in Las Vegas or California, two truck drivers take the trip. As one driver sleeps, the other driver continues driving to the racetrack. Having two drivers means that the equipment can arrive at the track in the least amount of time.

These large tractor-trailers, or 18 wheelers as they are more commonly known, can be up to 53 feet long. The rear door is a lift that extends from the back of the trailer and is used to roll the racecars in and out of the top portion of the trailer. The lower half of the trailer is built to the specifications of the race team with storage cabinets, countertops, closets for uniforms, and anything else a race team could need or want. The front half of the trailer is the lounge area, which can seat up to 10 people comfortably. If you can afford the $250,000 price tag that most of these trailers also carry, it is worth it.

The only down side to this type of trailer is that not just anyone with a driver's license can drive it. In order to drive one of these big rigs, a person must have what is called a CDL, a commercial driver's license. Because these trailers are so big, the person driving them must be trained. Before you run out and buy one for your race team, make sure that you know someone who has a CDL and is willing to drive your stuff to the racetrack every weekend.

Silver Is Better

The middle-of-the-road race trailer is the most common trailer that race teams use. You will see this type of trailer at your local racetrack. This type of trailer is enclosed and can carry one racecar and all of the equipment you will need at the racetrack.

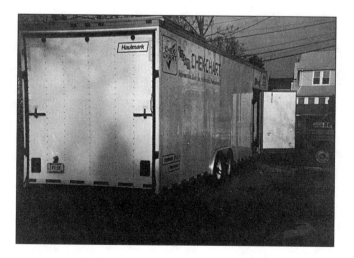

This is a typical one-car race trailer.

Enclosed trailers come in a variety of sizes from 20 feet long to as big as 45 feet long. Teams can order the interior to include a series of storage cabinets and a closet for team uniforms or any other clothing the teams may want to bring to the track. These trailers are small enough to be towed by a large pickup truck or a Suburban-style truck, and drivers do not need a CDL to tow the trailer. The important thing is to get a truck designed for towing such a large trailer.

The most common style of pickup used for pulling a race trailer is what is called a dualie pickup truck. A dualie pickup truck has four wheels in the back, which allows for greater stability when towing such a large trailer. Because the trailer is much longer, taller, and heavier than the dualie pickup truck, the extra wheels in the back make for a better ride and can distribute the extra weight over a wider distance. For example, if you have driven over a bridge on a windy day, you know what it feels like when the wind hits the side of your car and the car wobbles from side to side. When the wind hits the side of a 30-foot-long trailer, the feeling is a lot worse. A dualie pickup lessens that feeling. The feeling is still uncomfortable, but not as bad.

Inside Track

An enclosed race trailer, depending on size and configuration, can cost up to $75,000. Added to that price is the cost of something to tow it with, which can be up to $40,000.

In addition to the extra wheels in the back, most dualie pickup trucks have four doors, instead of just the two doors that most pickup trucks have. Pickup trucks with four doors instead of just two are called crew cabs. The cab of the truck is big enough to hold a crew of four people comfortably and a crew of six people who don't mind getting to know each other very well.

This is a crew-cab dualie pickup truck.

Each of the major truck manufacturers makes a crew-cab dualie pickup built for towing. Just as sport-utility vehicles have become popular over the last few years, crew-cab pickup trucks are the thing now. It is not just the highway crews or construction crews that are buying these trucks anymore. These trucks are becoming so popular with the general public that the truck companies are even making them in a smaller size for the everyday family. Of course, the increase in popularity of these vehicles has also caused an increase in their price tags, so be prepared when you go to buy your crew-cab dualie from the local dealership. A typical crew-cab dualie that can tow a 30-foot-long race trailer can cost up to $40,000.

Bronze Is Good

The open race trailer can carry one racecar and no equipment. It is an inexpensive way to get a race-car to and from the racetrack. These trailers can cost from $3,000 to as much as $10,000. When you compare this cost to the cost of an enclosed trailer at $15,000 to $30,000 and the cost of a custom-built 18-wheel Winston Cup-style trailer at $250,000, you know why we call this a bargain-basement deal.

The goal is to get to the racetrack so you can race. If you do not need the king-size Winston Cup trailer, why spend the money? Most new race teams do not have that kind of money anyway. Even the larger enclosed trailers are sometimes out of a team's financial reach. There is nothing wrong with an open trailer. It is easy to tow and easy to see around and is inexpensive. If you do not need to bring a lot of equipment to the racetrack, it is a perfect option for you.

If you choose an open trailer, make sure that you buy a very good car cover. Because your trailer does not have walls or a roof for that matter, it will be exposed to the wind, rain, stones, road dirt, and other outside elements while you are going to the racetrack. All of these can do some nasty damage to the body and the paint job on your racecar. Spend a few of those bucks you saved on the cost of the trailer on a good car cover. It will protect your racecar from the nasty elements while you travel to the racetrack. It will also create a bit of mystery for the folks who see you traveling down the road. They will be thinking, "I wonder what's under there?"

Yellow Flag

Towing a 30-foot race trailer is no small responsibility. Most people are not accustomed to pulling something this tall, heavy, and long. Remember that there is a lot of time and money sitting in that trailer while you are on the way to the racetrack. Be careful as you drive, and re-member that you need a lot of room to stop that thing, so don't tailgate anyone.

Yellow Flag

Open trailers are an inexpensive alternative to enclosed race trail-ers. However, they have some downsides. They don't have room for equipment and spare parts and provide limited security for the racecar.

This is a typical open-style race trailer.

The Team Hauler

Now that you know how you are getting the racecar and the equipment to the racetrack, you need to decide how you are going to get the team to the racetrack. As with the equipment hauler, there are three basic styles of getting a race team to the racetrack. Once again, it comes down to how much money the team has and is willing to spend on transportation. A team can go in style, take the middle-of-the-road approach, or figure out a more economical way.

Top of the Line

Almost all of the NASCAR Winston Cup teams transport their teams the same way to a race. You might think that because these guys are racers and love cars that they would drive to the racetrack, but driving to the races would be impractical because many of the Winston Cup races are scattered about the country. Catching a ride on the race trailer is no picnic either.

The race team travels to the racetracks by airplane. The team owner, driver, and crew fly to an airport close to the racetrack and then hop into a waiting vehicle that takes them to the racetrack. Many of these teams even own their own airplane. Some of the racecar drivers own their own planes and even fly themselves to and from the racetrack. Imagine owning your own plane to commute back and forth to work in!

The crew arrives at the racetrack usually on a Wednesday or a Thursday before the race, just as the race trailer shows up. They spend the next several days working on the racecar in preparation for Sunday's race. Then right after the race, after everything is loaded back onto the race trailer, the team members jump into a van and head back to the airport, where the plane is waiting for them for the quick flight back home. By Sunday night, they are all back home with their families.

Middle of the Line

As you can probably guess, most race teams cannot afford to fly their crews to and from the racetrack, never mind own their own airplane. So how do they get to and from the racetrack? They drive.

Some teams coordinate a meeting time at the race shop or some other central location where everyone who is going to the race carpools together to the racetrack. This way, each member of the crew is not driving to the racetrack by himself. The other benefit of meeting and driving together is that it confirms who is going to the racetrack and when they will be there. Because the racetracks are usually not too far from the location of the race shop, the team members either ride in the crew-cab dualie that is towing the trailer or just follow in their own cars.

We find that the ride to and from the racetrack with the crew in the truck is usually one of the better parts of the race. It allows us to discuss strategies, the setup of the racecar, and any other last-minute thing that might need to be discussed. Once we get to the racetrack, we have to be all business. Having a few hours in the truck on the way to the racetrack gives everyone some time to review the game plan before getting to the game.

Traveling to the race is also a good time in itself. The crew pokes fun at one another about some dumb thing they did at the last race. Everyone is in a good mood and excited about the fact that they are going racing.

Yellow Flag

Most of the regional series teams transport their crews to and from the races in the hauler that tows the race trailer or in a minivan.

Inside Track

The trip to the racetrack in the hauler is an excellent opportunity for a team to go over its plans and strategy for the race before getting to the racetrack. It is kind of like a traveling meeting.

End of the Line

For those who cannot afford to fly their race team to the track or haul everyone to the racetrack in crew-cab pickup truck, the other alternative is just to have everyone meet at the racetrack. This alternative is usually not a problem because the weekend racer does not have to travel far in order to get to the racetrack. Most, if not all, of the races are held at a local racetrack, which makes it much easier for the team to get there. There is no need for lots of money to transport the team nor is there a need to coordinate meeting places and times. Everyone knows that he or she must be at the racetrack at a certain time.

When We Get There, How Do We Get Around?

Once a race team has made it to the racetrack, there is usually little need for traveling around. After all, it's not like the teams are on vacation and need to go sightseeing. After a team arrives at the racetrack, the only need for transportation is to move the crew back and forth from the hotel to the racetrack.

Depending on how far the racetrack is from the race shop, teams may have one of the crew members drive a passenger van to the racetrack. The passenger van is used to get the team members back and forth from the hotel where they are staying. For racetracks that are too far from the shop to drive the passenger van, teams will just rent one from a local car rental place.

A Winston Cup race team brings at least 10 crew members to every race. That is a lot of people to have to shuffle back and forth to the racetrack. Remember, these people are at the racetrack from Thursday to Sunday. That's four days of shuffling back and forth to the track. Using a large passenger van, either their own or a rented one, is the most convenient way to move these people around. With a van, the team does not have to worry about how many cars it needs to get everyone back to the hotel, who is going to drive, and how much gas and tolls for the extra cars will cost.

The common way of transporting the crew back and forth from the racetrack is to use the crew-cab pickup truck. After the team hauls the race trailer to the racetrack and parks it in the pit area, the trailer is going to stay there until it is time to head home. (Hopefully, that time is after the race, but those teams that do not qualify for the race usually leave the racetrack early to get a jump on the traffic.) Teams disconnect the crew-cab pickup truck from the trailer and use it for transporting the team back and forth from the racetrack. Because the trailer is big enough to carry most of the team to the track, it is also big enough to carry them back and forth to the hotel.

In cases where there are more crew members than can fit into the crew cab, some crew members may have to catch a ride with another team staying at the same hotel or drive themselves back to the hotel if they brought their own cars. At this intermediate level of racing, teams help each other. All the teams are watching the expenses very closely and trying to do the best they can. Helping out another team when it is in a bind is good thing to do. Sooner or later, you will be part of that team needing assistance, and it is good to have a favor owed to you. So the next time another team comes over and asks for a favor, just do it.

For the weekend racer, track travel is not a problem because these local races are only held on one day. There is no need to show up at the track several days

Yellow Flag

After you disconnect your truck from the race trailer, do not expect to try and move the trailer before the race is over. The race trailers are usually parked so close to one another that it would be almost impossible to pull out your trailer early.

in advance of the race for things such as inspection, practice, and qualifying. All of the pre-race activities take place on the same day or night as the race itself.

The only need there may be for transportation after a team arrives at the racetrack would be if the team left something necessary back at the race shop. If this happens, there are plenty of vehicles that someone could take to go back to the race shop. Remember, most of the time, the crews on these teams all meet at the racetrack, so there are plenty of vehicles there if needed.

The Least You Need to Know

➤ Tractor-trailers are great because they can carry everything a team needs at the racetrack; however, only truck drivers with a commercial driver's license are allowed to drive these big rigs.

➤ A crew-cab dualie pickup truck is a great vehicle to tow an intermediate-size race trailer and also doubles as a crew hauler.

➤ Although you do not need a special driver's license to tow a 30-foot-long enclosed trailer, you should not underestimate how the added weight and size will affect your driving.

➤ A passenger van is a great way to get your crew back and forth from the race-track, although there are usually numerous vehicles to use.

Chapter 7

Racing Stuff

In This Chapter

➤ Pit cart, the rolling house of tools

➤ The importance of fuel cans

➤ All of the necessary tools and equipment

➤ Ways to listen in on the competition

Every racer and crew member needs an assortment of tools and equipment. This assortment can rival that of the best mechanics and make them envious of the quality and incredible variety of tools that racers have and need to compete. This chapter discusses all the tools needed to race one car for one day. You will be amazed at the amount of equipment needed. We will talk about basic hand tools, support equipment, and pit stop tools. You will soon read about the cool equipment you see on television. By the end of the chapter, you will know how to identify and use this equipment on practice, qualifying, and race day.

The Pit Cart

The main toolbox, which is called the *pit cart*, is full of almost everything needed to perform repairs and basic maintenance on the racecar. Most pit carts are very big, taking several crew members to move them. Some even have chairs mounted on top of them for spotters, crew chiefs, and scorers.

Yellow Flag

Always use eye and ear protection when using tools. Drills, air tools, and machines run at high speeds and can cause severe injury if used improperly or if they malfunction. You only get one set of eyes and ears, and you will need them for life.

The pit cart has drawers full of hand tools, wrenches, sockets, screwdrivers, hammers (because "rubbing is racing"), pliers, and so on. Each drawer is labeled and filled to capacity with neatly assorted tools. Also on the pit cart are compartments and storage areas containing the air hoses, electrical cords, small generators, jack stands, compressed air bottles, and extra parts for the car.

The pit cart must be completely accessible. In the heat of battle, crew members can't spend time fumbling around looking for that special tool. Have you ever looked for that screwdriver to tighten something as simple as a door hinge, and you can't find it? Imagine what drivers say to crew members as they look for a tool that they should have had handy. All crew members need to be familiar with every aspect of the cart because they need to be able to retrieve any tool at any time to make speedy repairs and get the car back on the track.

Pit carts come in a variety of shapes and sizes. They carry what the crew deems necessary to make quick repairs. When the crew members build a cart, they must already know what they're going to put in it and make room for stuff they never knew they even used. Once the crew members are on pit road, they are there until the end of the race; they can't take a taxi to Home Depot. A good idea is to assign a crew member the responsibility of checking to see if all the equipment and tools are in place and in proper working order before leaving the shop.

Building your pit cart should be as important as building your car. Quality and performance are paramount. Make sure your pit cart is arranged so that all crew members are comfortable using it.

The Quick Fill Can

The quick fill can is used to fuel cars quickly during the pit stop. This lightweight aluminum can is manufactured to NASCAR specifications: it can be a minimum of .064 inches thick, 33 inches in total height, and 11½ inches wide. In addition, it must incorporate a 1-inch vent tube and have a 2¼-inch fill tube.

The top of the can incorporates a filling device called a *dry break*. The car houses the female side of the device. When the dry break is inserted into the car, the shouldered female dry break opens the locking device, allowing the gas to flow quickly into the car—11 gallons can be put into the car in less than 7 seconds.

This fill can is made to meet NASCAR rules requirements.

Make sure you connect both dry brakes the first time; missing the hole in the car can get you a face full of fuel and a hefty dent in the quarter panel.

The gas flowing into the fuel cell forces air out. The fuel cell in the car also has a vent tube with a check valve. This valve must be opened by another crew member with a *catch can*. This small aluminum can has a tube or rod protruding out the front of it called the catch tube. This tube is inserted into the vent tube/check valve in the car and allows the forced air to exit the cell. It also catches any overflow of fuel.

Track Terms

A **dry break** is an air tight mechanical device installed on the end of the quick fill can to facilitate fast fuel delivery to the fuel cell. A second part is installed in the side of the quarter panel which receives the fill can end and allows fuel to flow smoothly.

Dry breaks come in a couple of different sizes.

Catch cans can be fabricated in different shapes; this piece is nicely manufactured.

Track Terms

A **catch can** is a can with a tube top that's inserted into the vent hose end on the car opening the vent hole to allow fuel to flow into the cell. It catches fuel as it overflows from a topped off cell.

The Tire Cart

The next tool is a tire cart, which is basic in design and very useful. These carts carry 8 to 12 tires and many times the quick fill can and nitrogen bottle (for pressuring the tires). The tire cart allows one person to move all those items at the same time. Not all carts are the same. Some teams opt for the smaller four-tire cart, designed similarly to a handcart. These carts are easier to store and more maneuverable.

This tire cart enables one crew member to transport eight tires.

The Jack and Jack Stand

Jacks and jack stands are some of the most used tools in the pits. Every time a car comes in from hot laps, it's jacked up and put up on jack stands for inspection.

The following are just a few of the many types of jacks:

➤ **Basic hydraulic steel design.** Rigid and tough in design, these jacks are worthy, long-lasting tools with very little failure. Although they are tough and trustworthy, they are also very heavy; some weigh as much as 70 pounds or more. This weight makes them quite the obstacle in a hurried situation, such as the pit, but they remain the top choice for the garage area.

Quality steel jacks are durable but heavy.

➤ **All-aluminum design.** These jacks in most cases are half the weight of their steel counterparts and require less handle pumping to lift the car into the air.

A lightweight and highly maneuverable aluminum jack makes for quick tire changes.

➤ **Single pump jack.** The quickest of the jacks, this type requires only one pump to lift the car after contact, but it also needs a strong operator.

➤ **Three pump model.** This jack's lightweight and strong design lifts the car quickly for fast pit stops.

Every jack needs to be kept in top condition, whether it is a garage or pit road jack. If a jack fails, the car falls, and then trouble begins. If the tires are off when the jack fails, the car will fall to the ground, potentially damaging brake or suspension components. Never use your race jack to lift the truck or trailer, doing so will shorten the life of your jack and may cause it to fail during a pit stop.

Jack stands need to be rugged in design and the correct height for the car they're being used on. Stands come in various weight capacities and heights. Choose your stand wisely, because you may be under the car it is holding up. Remember, safety first! If you jack up a car and plan to be under it, you need jack stands. Always buy quality stands.

Use only quality jack stands to support your racecar.

Generators

Generators are portable electric power plants. Run by gas or diesel, they run independent of any other power source. Each race team may have as many as three or more generators in their trailers. The first generator would power the main trailer and truck. This power is needed for power drills or battery chargers. Generators also provide power for lights and fans in the trailers and even air conditioners for the driver and crew lounge (should you be lucky enough to have that). Smaller generators are used for heating the oil in the racecar, charging the batteries on pit road, or doing small repairs during a race.

Generators come in various sizes.

You need to be sure you have the proper size of generator for the purpose for which it's intended. A small trailer may require a 5,000-watt generator. A tractor-trailer with a lounge area may need 10,000 or 15,000 watts. The generator for pit road should be about 1,500 to 1,800 watts, and qualifying generators can be 750 or as small as 500 watts.

Compressed Air, Nitrogen Bottles, and Air Guns

Air bottles are very basic but important items. They contain all the air needed for race weekend. This compressed air is used for pressuring tires and powering air guns to remove and replace tires. Using air from a compressor instead of air bottles can damage air guns and put unwanted moisture in your tires, causing uneven tire growth and increasing operating pressures. Using nitrogen in air bottles ensures that you are using pure, dry air.

Yellow Flag

Be careful to properly regulate the nitrogen bottle. The bottle initially comes with about 2,200 pounds of compressed air. If this air is not controlled, it could result in an immediate bursting, which could prove catastrophic if hoses or tools were overpowered with air.

73

Yellow Flag

Never pick up an air gun–removed lug nut without hand protection! Lug nuts can be as hot as 240 degrees after being removed from a racecar.

The air guns used in NASCAR racing are high-performance versions of the normal air guns used in corner garages everywhere. They run at a higher rate of speed and produce more power, which is needed to remove those tough, hot lug nuts (lugs) on racecars. These guns are lighter for quicker tire changes and ease on the operator. Today's powerful air guns run at such high speeds that they need constant maintenance to ensure their proper operation.

To remove lugs with such great speed, special sockets are used with the air gun so that the gun never slows down. The crew member needs only to firmly apply the gun to each of the lugs to send them flying.

Air guns like these are widely used throughout the NASCAR series.

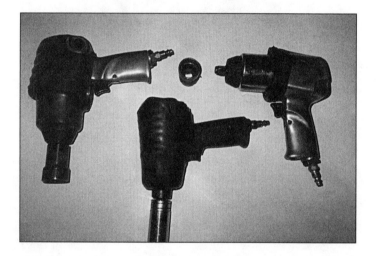

Duct Tape

The last tool we cover in this chapter is duct tape. The duct tape used in NASCAR is the same used to seal the air ducts in any building, but racers got a little fancy and made the tape in many colors to match the cars.

While watching racing on television, you may not notice all the tape on the car. Tape is applied to the grills of the car to prevent air from entering the radiator or brake duct area. This allows more air to travel around the car rather than through it to make it a more aerodynamic package. But covering the grills also may cause excessive temperatures. A crew member can easily take off some tape or apply some to correct a problem.

Duct tape is surprisingly sturdy and is frequently used. Most commonly, it is used during a crash situation. Crew members will hold fenders together, keep hoods down, and close holes in the car with it. In these situations, duct tape is a temporary fix to enable a car to finish a race or keep from having the car make an extended pit stop.

Duct tape is the racer's friend; from quick repairs to major crashes, this tape never lets you down.

Communications

In racing, teams use two-way radios to communicate. These radios are invaluable tools. Every serious team has at least two and may have up to 20 or more depending on how many crew members need to be in constant communication. Radios are used between driver and crew chief, crew chief and crew, spotter and driver, and spotter and crew. The use of the radio became common in the 1970s; now radios are essential to success.

Typical radio and headset used in racing.

Radios need to be used properly; only important conversation should be spoken on the air. Useless jabber will only irritate and distract the driver. (It sure irritates us when we're driving.)

Spotting

Radios are a key piece of equipment for spotters. A *spotter* is a crew member who feeds the driver constant information about the race, nearby cars, and pit information. A spotter finds a good point of sight high enough to see the entire track and then uses the radios to relay positions about cars racing with his team's driver. If another car is directly behind and constantly looking to get by his driver, the spotter can relay this information and his driver can counteract any move made by the opposing driver.

Yellow Flag

Never just accept everything you hear on a radio or scanner. Many teams feed incorrect information to confuse other teams.

Another great use for the radio is notifying a driver of an incident or crash in front of him and directing the driver to a clear track area, so he may get through the accident trouble-free.

Scanners

Another form of radio is a scanner. A *scanner* is a multichanneled, revolving radio capable of listening to many channels at one time. A team might be tempted to use a scanner to monitor other competitors and their conversation about race strategy, but teams have been known to give out false information to create diversions. Being honest racers, we, of course, would never do that.

Scanners such as this one are used by racers and fans alike.

Scanners are also used to monitor NASCAR. NASCAR constantly feeds information to the race teams. This information includes such details as whether pit road is open or closed, which car needs to report to pit road to answer a black flag, and what track positions drivers are running in.

There are many uses for and many different types of radios. These tools are not only useful, but they are also necessary for all teams to have.

Take Care of Your Tools

This chapter has covered some of the tools and equipment needed to compete on the stock car circuit. Many of these tools are specialty pieces that need special handling and care. Proper use of these tools awards your team a chance to run well and finish the race, and those are the two most important requirements needed to win! Take care of your tools, and they will take care of you. No team can win without having all the tools we have talked about and a few more. No matter what their size or finances, all racing teams need the same basic pieces of equipment. The difference between winning and losing is how a team uses its equipment.

Inside Track

Fans use scanners to listen to their favorite drivers and crew chiefs. All scanners have a priority channel. If you set that channel with your favorite team and find the correct frequency for your favorite driver, you will never miss anything. To obtain the frequencies available, you can contact radio suppliers, Web sites of your favorite drivers or use your scanner on automatic, or use binoculars to watch crew chiefs speak and match them to the voices on the scanner. The last method may take a while, but you may find a secret nonposted channel and really hear some great driver to crew conversations.

The Least You Need to Know

➤ Check your list of equipment before leaving the shop.

➤ Arrange tools in a pit cart in an order that all crew members find quick and easy to use.

➤ Always make sure the car is secure on jack stands before getting under the car.

➤ Use all your tools for their intended purposes. Using a tool improperly almost always causes injury.

➤ Buy quality equipment; inferior tools will cost you more than just the difference in price.

➤ If at all possible, have more than one channel in the radio sets to keep scanning of other teams to a minimum.

Chapter 8

The Posse

In This Chapter

➤ The team owner: all the bills and no glory

➤ The driver: no bills and all the glory

➤ The team manager: Mr. Coordinator

➤ The pit crew: all the work and very little glory

The title of this chapter may sound a little odd for a book about stock car racing, but it does give you the idea we are trying to get across. A race team consists of many individuals who all have a specific job function and play a vital part in the overall success of the team, just as each member of a posse is vital to the overall success of the posse. The purpose of a posse is to find a criminal and bring him or her to justice. Each member of the posse is critical to the hunt, and each person in the posse must pull together as a team to find the criminal.

This same philosophy is true for a NASCAR racing team. Team members have specific job functions they are responsible for accomplishing to the best of their ability. If every person on the race team does his or her part to the best of his or her ability, the chances of success are greatly increased.

In this chapter, we talk about the members of a race team, what their job functions are, and how critical those functions are to the overall success of the team. Some of the positions on a race team will be familiar to you, and some will be unfamiliar. The thing to remember is that regardless of whether the position is high profile, racing success cannot be achieved unless everyone pulls together as a team.

And You Thought Your Car Was Expensive

The owner of a NASCAR race team is the person who owns the racecar, the equipment, the race shop, and probably the racecar hauler. The team owner is responsible for paying most, if not all, of the bills and expenses incurred by the race team. Because the owner is the one paying the bills, he or she is the overall boss of the team; what he or she says goes.

The most obvious owner expense is the racecar itself. A complete rolling racecar chassis costs anywhere from $5,000 for a two- or three-year-old used one to $20,000 for a brand-new one. This cost is just the chassis; most racecars are not sold with a *drivetrain*, which is a necessary part of the racecar. A drivetrain can cost an owner anywhere from $30,000 to $75,000.

You Have to Tow It

One complete racecar costs anywhere from $35,000 to $95,000, but that's just the beginning of a team owner's expenses. The racing team has to be able to get the racecar to and from the racetrack. That means the owner needs to buy or lease a pickup truck and a trailer or a tractor-trailer.

Most race teams use the pickup truck and trailer option. It is less expensive than a tractor-trailer, and you don't need a special license to tow a trailer with a pickup truck. Most smaller teams use this option because they do not have a lot of equipment to bring back and forth to the racetrack. Racecar trailers can vary in size from a simple one-car open trailer to a 40-foot-long, two-car enclosed trailer. Obviously, the larger and heavier trailers require larger and stronger trucks to pull them. A new pickup truck big enough to pull a one-car enclosed trailer costs anywhere from $30,000 to $45,000. A 30-foot-long, enclosed, one-car trailer can cost anywhere from $15,000 to $20,000. A low estimate for a new pickup truck and trailer is about $45,000, bringing the total owner's cost with the racecar (using the lowest estimates) to $80,000.

Track Terms

The engine, transmission, and rear end of a racecar are referred to as the **drivetrain** of the vehicle.

In case you're curious about the tractor-trailer option, a two-car race tractor-trailer complete with custom cabinets and a small living area in front can cost anywhere from $250,000 to $500,000. Only the very well-funded race teams are able to buy or even lease one of these puppies. They are, however, an unbeatable way to get to and from the racetrack.

How Much for That Screwdriver?

Another major expense is the tools and equipment to work on the racecar. The cost of all of the wrenches, screwdrivers, drills, and so on adds up very fast. Tools and equipment can end up costing anywhere from $50,000 to $100,000. The owner can easily spend $130,000 on the racecar, trailer, and tools before his team turns a single lap on the racetrack.

Part of the expense of racing is purchasing backup equipment. Usually teams buy another complete racecar. At the least, they buy two or three spare engines in case one is broken and several transmissions and rear end units. Because the engine and transmission take the greatest abuse during a race, most teams bring a spare of each to every race. The NASCAR Winston Cup Series teams bring a complete backup racecar and enough spare parts to build a third one if they had to.

You Want to Get Paid, Too?

Every race team needs a crew to work on the racecar. Most of the crew members on smaller race teams are volunteers. They work on the racecars at the race shop and at the racetrack for the love of the sport. In this situation, the team owner has one less expense to worry about. However, most NASCAR Winston Cup team members are paid employees of the race team, so the team owner has salaries to pay, which is not a small expense by any means.

Under the Hood

Most crew members on small race teams volunteer their time to work on the racecar for the love of the sport.

Everything we have talked about so far is what could be classified as a fixed expense. A team has to have these items in order to go racing. We talked about the costs in terms of if an owner were to purchase the items outright; financing options are available to lower the initial costs to starting a team. But the owner is going to have enough expenses later on once his or her team starts racing, why add to it with a big loan payment for a trailer? Anyway, the owner will be spending every last penny on bodywork and duct tape.

Variable Expenses

When a team starts racing, the variable expenses kick in. Variable expenses are things such as the entry form fee, track fee, tires, oil, food, hotel bills, gas for the trailer, and gas for the racecar. Each time a team goes to the racetrack, it spends money. The only question is how much.

The team owner has the privilege of being responsible for paying all of the race team's bills. (Isn't he the lucky one?) The other side of the coin is that any money the race team wins goes to the team owner.

The Driver

The racecar driver is the most recognized member of the race team. He or she is the one who gets the most attention and also carries the greatest personal risk of being hurt. Although all team members risk some personal injury, the driver is more likely to be seriously hurt from a crash than say a tire changer is from dropping a tire on his or her foot.

Natural Athlete

Not everyone has what it takes to become a racecar driver. First of all, the person has to love to drive. Driving a racecar is a physically demanding job. It takes stamina, strength, skill, and strong nerves. As we talked about in Chapter 1, "So You Want to Be a Stock Car Driver?" racecar drivers usually possess a certain amount of natural driving skill. That skill is then refined through attendance at a professional racecar driving school and *seat time* in a racecar.

Track Terms

Seat time is the term used to refer to the amount of driving experience that a racecar driver has. The more seat time a driver gets, the more comfortable, and usually the quicker the car gets.

The job of the racecar driver is to win as many races as possible. What some people may not realize is that a racecar driver also has the responsibility for working with the pit crew and the crew chief on fine-tuning the racecar. The best person to know how a racecar is performing is the driver of that racecar. The driver must constantly communicate with the pit crew and crew chief about the racecar's performance. After the pit crew has made a change to the racecar, the driver must then communicate with the pit crew about how that change has affected the racecar. Working with the pit crew and crew chief to tune the racecar for maximum performance is a critical function the driver must perform in order to be successful.

Under the Hood

A racecar driver is as much of an athlete as a football or baseball player. Drivers endure tremendous heat and mental and physical stress. They need to think constantly and perform their jobs within extreme conditions. There aren't any timeouts or time between pitches. With very few caution laps in a four-hour race, drivers must condition themselves to have plenty of stamina.

Mr. Big Mouth

Another responsibility of the driver is to be the spokesperson for the team and for the sponsors of the racecar. Earlier in this chapter, we talked about the expenses involved in stock car racing. Many of these expenses are paid for through sponsorship money paid by large corporations. These corporate sponsors are expecting to receive positive and professional exposure from the driver of the race team. If the driver cannot positively and professionally represent the corporate sponsor, chances are that sponsor will look to another team and or driver.

Part of representing a sponsor may include activities off the track as well as on the track. If the sponsor of a race team wants the driver and the racecar to attend a corporate function, the driver must satisfy this obligation.

Stock car drivers not only have to be skilled drivers, but they also need to possess a certain amount of charm, be well spoken, and conduct themselves both on and off the race track in a professional manner. Most corporate sponsors would not want an ill spoken, rude, and unprofessional racecar driver representing them.

The Pit Crew

Pit crews consist of several members who all have different jobs or functions to perform for the race team. Some race teams have pit crew members who specialize in one area. For example, one crew member may work just on preparing the shocks of the racecar. A race team may try several combinations of shocks during a practice or test session. A shock specialist will have the sole responsibility to ensure that all the shocks are assembled and configured properly for the racecar to give the driver the best handling performance possible. Most of the NASCAR Winston Cup teams have specialized pit crew members.

83

Under the Hood

Most racecar shocks can be disassembled and reconfigured to work differently for each track. This is because different track configurations require many different shock pressures. This is discussed in detail in Chapters 11 and 13.

Other race teams way not have the luxury of having specialized pit crew members. Most of the smaller teams' pit crews are volunteers. When teams have a small number of pit crew members, they cannot afford to have one person dedicated to one specialized area. Each pit crew member needs to be more of a generalist who can work on many areas of the racecar. Having this type of pit crew means that any one crew member can perform almost any function or job on the racecar. The down side to this type of crew is that a person may not be an expert on the job he or she is currently asked to perform. This leaves the door open for errors, which can have some serious effects at over 150 miles per hour.

Whether the crew consists of specialists or generalists, every crew has basic jobs that need to be performed. The following sections explain these pit crew jobs in detail.

The Crew Chief

Every team needs a coach. In stock car racing, the coach of the team is the crew chief. The crew chief calls the shots for the team and has the overall responsibility to ensure that everything has been taken care of, every job has been completed, and the racecar is ready to go.

Under the Hood

The crew chief can be fined for the inappropriate actions of his or her crew members.

The crew chief makes the decisions on how to set up the racecar before the race, decides what to change on the racecar to make it faster, and has overall responsibility for the actions of everyone on the team, including the racecar driver. If something goes wrong with the racecar, the racecar violates rules, or a crew member's actions are deemed to be inappropriate, the crew chief is held responsible.

Although the driver receives the most attention of anyone on the race team, the crew chief receives a lot of attention as well. Crew chiefs are multifaceted people. They need to be top automotive technicians, decision makers, people managers, and spokespeople. Often during a race crew chiefs have to make critical decisions about a pit stop or keep their drivers in a positive upbeat mood, regardless of what is happening on the track. While this is going on, the crew chiefs need to keep track of their competitors and changing conditions on the track and even answer a question or two from a television reporter covering the race. The position of crew chief carries a great amount of responsibility and duty with it. Not everyone can work under the pressures a crew chief must face.

The Spotter

One of the keys to winning a stock car race is a driver's ability to stay out of trouble and to avoid crashes as they happen. Although the driver has total control over the racecar, he or she has only limited visibility to see what is happening ahead of him or her. Having limited visibility means that the drivers have limited time to react and avoid any crashes. To improve or increase the drivers' visibility and their reaction time, each race team now has someone stand above the racetrack with a radio to tell the driver when there is a crash. This person is called the *spotter*.

The spotter is in direct radio communication with the driver, crew chief, and pit crew. The spotter has the responsibility to keep the driver informed of what is happening on the track. The spotter lets the driver know when a crash occurs on the track as well as where the crash is. As the driver approaches the crash, the spotter must direct him or her safely past the crash.

Under the Hood

The spotter for a race team has the responsibility for directing the racecar around crashes and other obstacles on the racetrack.

In addition to informing the driver of crashes on the track, the spotter lets the driver know when another racecar is nearby. The driver is concentrating on driving the racecar around the track and has limited visibility of when a car is coming up beside him or her.

In order to ensure the driver and spotter clearly communicate with one another, the spotter uses certain terms to identify where another racecar is in relation to the driver's racecar. When drivers hear their spotters say "Outside," they know that another racecar is on the right side of their racecars. The right side of the racecar is also referred to as the high side of the racetrack. When spotters say "Inside," the drivers know that another racecar is trying to pass them on the inside of the racetrack, which is the left side of the racecar. Just as the right side of the racecar is referred to the high side of the racetrack, the left side of the racecar is referred to as the low side of the racetrack.

Spotters also tell drivers when the other racecars are no longer on the side of their racecars by using the following terms:

Inside Track

Passing a racecar on the high side of the racetrack is a greater risk than passing a racecar on the low side of the racetrack. This is because most tracks have greater traction on the low or inside lane. Even if this isn't the case, and a particular track has greater traction on the high or outside lane, having a car on the edge of control on the inside of you puts you in direct danger of being slid into, or being pushed even further up the track. Almost always the inside car has the advantage.

➤ "Clear" means no other racecar is on either side.

➤ "Clear low" means that the racecar on the left side is no longer there and it is safe for the driver to move down the track.

➤ "Clear high" means that the racecar that was on the high side, or right side, is no longer there and it is safe for the driver to move up the racetrack.

The key to being a successful spotter for a NASCAR racing team is to speak clearly over the radio. Talk with the driver and crew chief to set the standard for how you will communicate with one another. When you do need to radio the driver, be clear, accurate, and brief with your message. You do not want to talk a lot or about unnecessary things over the radio. Most radios are one-way communication devices. This means that while you are talking over the radio, no one else can talk until you stop talking. Racing radios are not like telephones, where two people can talk at the same time.

The Scorer

The scorer for a race team has a simple but very important job: This person keeps track of the number of laps his or her team completes during the race. This very important position can have a major impact on the success of the race team because the number of completed laps determines the amount of championship points a race team receives. After each race, the scorer provides a copy of the score sheet to the NASCAR officials, who use the sheet to verify the number of laps completed and to determine the number of championship points awarded.

The Tire Changer

At some point during most NASCAR races, the racecar needs to come to pit road for service. The most common services provided on pit road are changing the tires and refueling.

To change the tires during a pit stop in the least amount of time, several crew members are required. Two of these crew members are called tire changers. The job of a tire changer is to change tires as quickly as possible. One tire changer is responsible for changing both of the front tires, and the other tire changer has the responsibility for changing both of the rear tires.

If you look in the trunk of your car, you will see a wrench that is used to remove the lug nuts that hold the tire on the car. A tire changer for a race team uses an air gun with a special lug nut socket on the end. (Chapter 7, "Racing Stuff," has a picture of an air gun.) The air gun allows tire changers to remove the lug nuts much quicker than if they were to use the wrench that is in your car's trunk.

When the racecar comes down pit road for service, the tire changers prepare to service the racecar. When the racecar reaches the pit stall, the tire changers immediately go over the pit road wall and head to the right side of the racecar. There are two reasons why the right side tires are changed before the left side tires. The first reason is that because the racecar goes around the racetrack in a counterclockwise direction, the right side tires wear out faster than the left side tires. The other reason is that the right side of the racecar is the farthest away from the pit equipment. It takes more time to get there initially, but overall the pit crew has to do less running around the racecar if the right side is serviced first.

After the right side of the racecar is serviced, the tire changers come around the racecar and service the left side tires. By servicing the racecar in this order, the tire changers have to pass the racecar only twice: once to service the right side and once to return to the left side. If they serviced the left side of the racecar first and then serviced the right, the driver would have to wait until the pit crew returned to the left side of the car before leaving the pit stall. In most cases, the driver can exit the pit stall immediately after the racecar is lowered from the jack. Most times the tire changers are still on their knees as the racecar leaves. These few seconds can mean the difference between first and third on the racetrack.

The Tire Carrier

As we have been saying, the goal of a good pit stop is to get the racecar back on the track as quickly as possible. Another way race teams accomplish this is to have people dedicated to carry the new tires for the tire changers. The tire changers can get to the racecar faster if they do not also have to carry the new tires. Just like the tire changers, there are two tire carriers for each team: one to carry the tires for the front of the racecar and one to carry the tires for the rear of the racecar.

While the tire changer is removing the lug nuts from the wheel, the tire carrier carries the new tire for the changer. By the time the tire carrier gets to the tire changer, the lug nuts have been removed, and the old tire is already off of the racecar. The tire carrier then can put the new tire directly on the racecar, and the tire changer can immediately begin to tighten the lug nuts.

In addition to carrying the new tires for the tire changers, the tire carriers also have the responsibility for carrying the old tires back over the pit road wall. During most NASCAR races, you see only the front tire carrier immediately carrying the old tire back over the pit road wall. The reason for this is that the driver needs to have an unobstructed path back onto pit road. If the old front tire were left on the ground, it would be in the way of the racecar. The old rear tire is usually not in the way of the racecar and can be carried over the pit wall after the racecar has returned to the racetrack. Also if a tire would get away from crew members and cross pit road, a penalty would be assessed to the team by bringing their car back onto pit road for a stop and go penalty.

Inside Track

Tire changers should always service the right side of the racecar first because the right side tires wear out faster than the left side tires and the right side of the racecar is the farthest away from the pit equipment. Servicing the left side last puts crew members in a safer position for the car to pull away during quick exits, since the car will turn right to exit from their pit stalls.

Besides carrying the new and old tires for the tire changers, both tire carriers also have another responsibility. As the tires on a racecar wear, they leave little pieces of rubber on the racetrack. These little pieces of rubber can get stuck in the grill of the racecar. As more pieces of rubber get stuck in the grill, the amount of cool air to the engine is reduced. Limiting the amount of cool air to the engine causes it to run hotter than normal and can damage the engine. The front tire changer is responsible for cleaning the front grill.

The back of the racecar doesn't have a grill, so the rear tire carrier has a different additional responsibility from the front tire carrier. The rear tire carrier is responsible for making any adjustments to the racecar chassis. On the sides of the racecar just above the rear tires is the point where chassis adjustments can be made to the racecar. To adjust the chassis, the tire carrier uses a long bar with a ratchet attached to it. As you can see from their job descriptions, tire carriers need to be strong, quick, and agile in order to perform these duties in less than 17 seconds.

The Jack Man

So far we have talked about changing tires, cleaning the front grill, and making chassis adjustments. It would be very difficult to change the tires on a racecar if you did not have someone to jack up the racecar. Race teams have one person whose sole job is to jack up the racecar during a pit stop—the jack man.

The job of the jack man is both simple and very important. In addition to lifting the racecar for the tire changers, the jack man also communicates with the driver. The jack man ensures that everyone who is servicing the racecar during a pit stop has completed his or her job before the racecar is let down. By lowering the racecar, the jack man is communicating to the driver that the pit stop is complete and that it is okay to return to the racetrack. If the jack man lowers or drops the racecar before a service is completed, the driver will have to come back to pit road in order to complete the service. Doing this can and usually does cost the team valuable track positions.

Under the Hood

The jack man is responsible for telling the driver when it is okay to return to the race-track. This is because he is usually the only crew member standing and able to see all other crew members. He will hold the car in the air until all work has been performed and crew is clear. As he drops the car the driver will leave instantly, so the jack man will dictate when the driver can go.

You may be wondering how the jack man knows when everyone servicing the racecar has completed his or her respective tasks. That is the easy part. Instead of using radios, pit crew members put their arms in the air to signal that they have completed their task. When everyone has his or her arm in the air, the jack man drops the racecar and pulls the jack out from under the racecar. This action tells the driver to head back to the racetrack.

The jack man also needs to be strong, quick, and agile. The racecar cannot have its tires changed until the jack man lifts the racecar into the air. You may see the tire changers starting to remove the lug nuts before the jack man lifts the racecar, but they obviously cannot remove the tires until the tires are in the air.

The jack man uses a special jack to lift the racecar. It is not something that you would see in your car's trunk, but it may look like something you would see at your local service station. It is a lightweight jack, usually made from aluminum, that can lift the racecar high enough in the air with only one or two pumps of the handle. (Refer to Chapter 7 for a picture of an aluminum jack.)

The Gas Man

Having enough gas or fuel in the racecar to complete a race is very important. In the NASCAR Winston Cup Series, the races are too long for a racecar to finish the race without stopping for fuel. Therefore, pit crews have two people who are responsible for fueling the racecar during a pit stop: the gas man and the catch can man.

The gas man is the person who puts the fuel into the racecar, ensuring that every drop of gas gets into the racecar during a pit stop. When you go to the local gas station to put gas into your car, you pull up to the gas pump and use a nozzle to put the gas into the car. In stock car racing, fueling is done a little differently. Instead of a gas pump, the gas man uses two 11-gallon gas cans to fuel the racecar. The gas tanks in a NASCAR stock car can hold 22 gallons of gas, but each gas can is only allowed to hold 11 gallons. The 11-gallon per can is a rule. Since the car can be filled with 22 as stated, NASCAR allows teams to do it in two stages. It's about the same time it takes to replace four tires. One 22-gallon can would be around 150 pounds, a bit heavy to carry over pit wall and be safe considering it's extremely flammable.

At the local gas station, an electric pump puts the gas into your car. Because there are no electric pumps on pit road, the gas man uses gravity to get the fuel into the racecar. The gas man picks up the gas can, turns it upside down, and puts it on his shoulder. When he turns it upside down, the gas does not immediately come pouring out; a pressure valve on the end of the gas can prevents the gas from coming out. (Refer back to Chapter 7 for a picture of a gas can.)

Under the Hood

A full gas can weighs as much as 75 pounds. This is because gas weighs just over 6 pounds per gallon, and the can weighs about 10 pounds with the dry break installed.

When the driver pulls down pit road and into the pit stall, the gas man immediately begins to fuel the racecar. Most pit stops average 17 seconds, which is not a lot of time for a gas man to put 22 gallons of gas into the racecar. (The next time you go to fill up your car see how long it takes you. We bet that it will take more than 17 seconds!) An opening on the side of the racecar allows the gas man to quick fill the racecar. This quick fill opening opens the pressure valve on the gas can and allows the gas to flow into the gas tank. It takes about 8 seconds for the gas to empty into the tank. After the first gas can is empty, the gas man gets another can of gas and continues to fill the racecar until it is full.

If the gas man does not put the gas can properly into the quick fill opening on the racecar, the gas will not flow into the tank. It will, however, flow out of the can and onto anything in its way, as we found out in the summer of 1997. We had our first race at the Dover Downs International Speedway. It was a very hot summer weekend and changing your mind made you sweat. We qualified for the race, and we were excited about racing at what is referred to as the Monster Mile. During the race, we needed to pit for fuel and decided to come in during a late race caution flag. As John pulled into the pit stall, I immediately jumped over the wall with the gas can on my shoulder and headed for the side of the racecar. John and I had decided that all we needed was a "splash and go." I did not have to worry about filling the racecar because all it needed was a few gallons of gas to have enough fuel to finish the race.

What I did not know is that when John pulled into the pit stall, he overshot the stall, and the nose of the racecar was over the line. The NASCAR rules state that you cannot service your racecar unless it is in your pit stall. Just as I went up to the racecar to fuel it, John put the racecar in reverse and backed up the racecar. This move caused me to miss the quick fill opening, and what seemed like all 11 gallons of gas went over the back of the racecar, over the rear windshield, and all over me. It was so bad that I was spitting gas out of my mouth like water. After the initial hit, I realized that I was not putting the gas into the racecar, but rather all over it. I readjusted and put the remaining fuel in the racecar, which turned out to be only a few gallons, and off John went.

After I climbed back over the pit road wall, the safety crew members, who are on pit road for every race, looked at me and said with a grin, "Did you get *any* gas into the car?" At the time, standing there covered from my head to my waist in fuel in 90-degree weather, I did not see the humor in their comments. At least now I can laugh about it.

Yellow Flag

Be sure your gas man uses eye protection and fire retardant clothing to protect himself from any potential mishaps. Many gassers now wear a protective fire suit, and extra layer of fire retardant over wear, and a race helmet with a full shield.

The Catch Can Man

NASCAR rules state that a crew member must hold a catch can in the gas overflow tube while the racecar is being fueled up. The gas overflow tube allows air to escape from the gas tank as the gas goes into it. The purpose of the catch can is to catch any excess fuel that may flow out of the overflow tube for the safety of the crew members, drivers, race officials, and everyone on pit road. If the excess gas were allowed to flow out of the overflow tube and onto pit road, it would present a dangerous hazard. Racing fuel is slippery, which can cause a crew member to fall when running around the car. Also, it is very flammable, and the heat from brakes or any spark could ignite the fuel and create a disastrous situation on pit road.

To make things as safe as possible, the rules state that if a racecar is fueled during a pit stop, the catch can must stay in the overflow tube until the racecar returns to the track. The catch can man has the responsibility for complying with this rule.

Yellow Flag

Racing fuel is very flammable and slippery and should be handled carefully. If you spill any fuel on the ground or on your skin, be sure to clean it up immediately. And treat your skin for chemical burns especially in the heat, where a rash could form.

Earlier we talked about the gas man using two gas cans to fill the racecar. The catch can man helps the gas man do this. As the first gas can empties, it becomes lighter and lighter. When only a few gallons are left, the can is light enough for the catch can man, who is standing behind the racecar, to hold it in the racecar while the gas man gets the second can.

You may be wondering how the catch can man, who is holding the catch can in the overflow tube, can also hold the gas can in the quick fill. The way he does this is to use his thigh to hold the catch can in place. This frees up his hands to hold the gas can in place, until the gas man returns with the second gas can. This position is a little tricky, but the catch can man only has to do it for a few seconds.

The Pit Road Sign

In the early days of racing, before race teams started using radios, the pit road sign was used to communicate with the drivers. Today, crews use it to let the driver know where his or her pit stall is located.

When a driver comes down pit road, the pit road sign, which is mounted on a long pole, is held out in front of the pit stall and waved up and down. This is to get the attention of the driver and to let him know how far down the pit stall is located. The pit road sign is held out by a crew member who also services the racecar. After the racecar pulls into the pit stall, the crew member puts down the pit road sign and goes over the pit wall to clean the windshield.

Earlier in the chapter we talked about the tires wearing away and leaving pieces of rubber on the racetrack and stuck in the grill; tire rubber also leaves marks on the windshield, making it difficult for the driver to see. In addition to rubber marks, dirt, oil, water, and other debris can accumulate on the windshield, reducing the driver's visibility. You might think cleaning the windshield is an unimportant task, but you might feel differently if you tried driving at 150 miles per hour with limited visibility from your windshield.

When the windshield is cleaned, it is not just wiped off. There is a definite method to cleaning the windshield. The crew member wipes the windshield from top to bottom instead of from side to side or in a circle. The reason for the top-to-bottom method is in case the windshield is scratched or the cleaning leaves a streak. The streak or scratch will not impair the driver's complete horizontal line of sight. It is easier to move your head to the right or left to look around a scratch than it is to look over or under one.

The NASCAR Winston Cup teams have improved the method of cleaning the windshield. Instead of wiping the windshield with a cleaner, they apply thin layers of plastic film over the windshield. As the windshield gets dirty, they just remove the dirty layer of plastic, and the driver instantly has a clean windshield.

Inside Track

When cleaning a windshield, use vertical strokes instead of horizontal strokes. Using this method prevents the possibility that a scratch or streak on the windshield will impair the driver's complete horizontal line of sight. The sun causes glare on the windshields, and the polycarbonate windshields are more susceptible to scratching, and thus more likely to impair vision. Using vertical and horizontal strokes will cause a maze of scratches for the driver to try to see through. Glare like this could be compared to the glare you get on the highways at sundown, when the sun is in a perfect position to cause glare.

The Team Manager

Each of the NASCAR Winston Cup teams has a team manager. The team manager handles the finances for the team, coordinates all of the logistical issues involved in getting the team and the equipment to and from the racetrack, and works with the team sponsors and the team itself. The team manager is the primary coordinator for all activities that affect the race team.

The team manager receives the least amount of public exposure on the team, but he or she has just as much responsibility as the car owner, crew chief, or driver. Although stock car racing is a sport, each team needs to be run and managed as a business. If the team is not managed well, both financially and operationally, the team will not succeed. Team managers need to be smart businesspeople and strong coordinators.

In this chapter, we have talked about many of the people involved in a race team. Do not think that these are the only people required for a race team. In addition to the crew members who go to the racetracks every week, many other team members remain back at the race shop to continue working on other racecars, building new engines, and assembling chassis. Running a NASCAR Winston Cup team requires a large number of resources, both financially and personally. Many team members sacrifice a large amount to be involved in this sport. If you ask them why they sacrifice, they will all tell you the same thing: They do it for the love of the sport.

The Least You Need to Know

➤ Team owners need thousands and thousands of dollars to pay for the racecar, the trailer, the tools and equipment, crew salaries, and other racing expenses.

➤ Drivers must be skilled athletes, good communicators, and charming spokespeople.

➤ Each pit crew member has a specific job that he or she must do well for the team to be successful.

➤ Successful teams have team managers with business smarts and strong organizational skills.

Chapter 9

Paying the Bills

In This Chapter

➤ Balancing the team, talent, and expenses

➤ Getting the race shop together

➤ Paying fees to get the car on the track

➤ Making money in racing

In Chapter 8, "The Posse," we talked about the team and what all the different jobs are. The team owner, who we fondly call the money man, is the person who is responsible for shelling out the money needed to race. In this chapter, we are going to talk a little bit more about the expenses involved in racing. We will also talk a little about the how the team owner can recoup some of these expenses from team sponsors, series sponsors, prize money, and merchandise sales.

A Balancing Act

It is very expensive to run any kind of race team. The only difference between running a weekend team at the local racetrack and running a professional NASCAR Winston Cup team is the amount of money required to be successful. Every year, race teams need to improve on their performance to stay competitive. Each year, the lap times are faster, the cars are more aerodynamic, and the engines are stronger. The way teams improve their performance is by investing a large amount of resources into the team. When we talk about resources, we mean more than just time and effort. It also takes money to stay competitive.

Now I'm not saying that all it takes is a well-financed team to be successful. A combination of talent and resources is what makes a team successful. Either one of these things by itself will not make you a successful team owner. A talented team without financial resources cannot win, nor can a well-financed team with minimal talent.

Getting Started

Starting a race team is the first big obstacle a potential car owner needs to overcome. The two basic ways to start a race team are building one or buying one. Both options have benefits and drawbacks.

To build a race team, a team owner needs several things before he or she can start racing. These things include a race shop, tools and equipment, workers, transportation, and money to pay the bills for the organization.

The Race Shop

The race shop is the home of the organization. It is the place where the majority of the work is done, where the team stores store all of its tools and equipment, where the transporter and support vehicles are kept, and basically where the organization is run.

Inside Track

The size of the race shop a race team needs is determined by the type of work the team will be doing. If a team plans on doing most of the work on the racecar itself, it will need a big shop with a lot of specialty tools. If a team plans on having someone else do the specialty work, then it will not need a very big shop.

Race shops vary in size; they are as small as 5,000 square feet or as large as 150,000 square feet. It all depends on what the race team can afford and how much work the team plans to do on the car. Building a racecar requires a lot of specialty equipment that takes up space in the race shop. If you buy a racecar from a racecar builder, like most weekend racers do, you will not need this specialty equipment and can get away with a smaller shop. A local weekend racer may only have a 5,000-square-foot shop, which is enough room for one racecar and some equipment. Most NASCAR Winston Cup teams prefer to do all the work on the car themselves, which requires more space.

Every NASCAR Winston Cup team also has multiple racecars. It is not uncommon for a Winston Cup team to have as many as 15 racecars. As you can imagine, you cannot park a NASCAR Winston Cup racecar on the street or in a driveway. All of these racecars need to be stored inside the race shop. Think about how much room just parking the cars would take.

As you might imagine, a Winston Cup race shop is very large. It also is divided into functional sections or areas. The following sections describe what is in each area of a race shop.

The Engine Area

One of the most important factors to having a successful race team is having a strong motor in the racecar. Without a strong motor, you might as well not even race. All of the work required to build and or maintain a race motor is performed in the very clean and well-organized engine area. After running 500 miles in a race, motors can take a good beating. To make sure that the engine is strong for every race, the race team performs regular maintenance on the motors.

The Chassis Area

The chassis area is where all of the work is performed on the chassis of the racecar. The *chassis* is the skeleton of the racecar. Each chassis is made up of three sections: the front clip, the roll cage, and the rear clip. Each section is made independently from the other sections and then welded together to make a complete chassis.

The reason for this type of construction is two fold. The first reason is safety. Each section is made to an exact specification that allows for the greatest amount of strength to be built into it. Welding the sections together also creates joints in the racecar that help to protect the driver in the event of a crash. These joints are what some car manufacturers call *crumple zones*. When the three sections are welded together, the complete chassis provides a great amount of strength and safety for the driver.

The other reason for this type of construction is maintenance. When a racecar is involved in a crash, usually the front clip or the rear clip sustains the most damage. When this happens, race teams are able to cut off the damaged section and replace it with a new one. This design allows for relatively quick repairs and saves the team a lot of money. It is much easier and cheaper to replace a front or rear clip than it is to replace an entire racecar. Replacing front and rear clips are just some of the types of repairs that are done in the chassis area.

Inside Track

Replacing a front clip or a rear clip of a chassis is easier than building an entirely new chassis.

The Fabrication Shop

In Chapter 2, "This Doesn't Look Like My Car," we talked about the differences between racecars and the cars on the street. We said that the sides of the racecar are nothing more than pieces of flat steel formed and shaped to look like the sides of an everyday car. In the fabrication shop, the team makes the racecar sides and many other parts of a racecar. In order to fabricate these pieces of steel, teams use a series of specialty tools to shape the steel into the needed pieces.

The Body Shop

The body shop is where the race team prepares the body of the racecar for painting. In order to have an aerodynamic racecar, the sides of the racecar need to be as smooth as possible. Although the fabrication shop has the primary responsibility for the body of the car, there are some areas on the body that require a certain amount of bodywork in order to create the sleek, aerodynamic body. These areas include any place where two pieces of steel are welded together. These seams need to be filled with body filler and smoothed out before the racecar can be painted. Although bodywork covers or fills in any imperfections in a racecar body, the goal is to use as little filler as possible. The reason for this is that body filler is heavy. The more filler you use, the heavier the racecar will be. The heavier the racecar is, the slower it goes. And slowness is not a good thing.

Inside Track

Using body filler to fix a dent in a racecar adds unnecessary weight to the racecar. Instead of using body filler to repair the damaged area, cut off the area and replace it with a new piece. This repair helps keep unnecessary weight off of the racecar.

The Paint Shop

The paint shop is where the parts of the racecar are primed, painted, and detailed. Teams use a series of high-pressure paint guns to apply the primer and paint to the racecar. Paint shops are usually environmentally controlled areas and are the cleanest part of the entire race shop. They need to be environmentally controlled and clean in order to create the best conditions for the paint to bond to the body of the racecar. If the air is too cold or too hot, the paint will not adhere to the body. The paint shops need to be kept clean in order to prevent any dirt from being blown around by the paint guns. If dirt particles from the air land on a freshly painted racecar, they will ruin the appearance of the paint.

The Parts Area

Some race teams have a separate area dedicated to storing spare parts, accessories, and consumables used by the other areas in the race shop. Walking across the shop to get something you need from the parts area is much easier than going to the local auto parts store, and the local auto parts store does not carry many of the specialty products the race team needs anyway. Some of the typical items in a parts area include cleaners, paints, small engine components, electrical components, and raw materials such as aluminum and steel.

The Office Area

In addition to each of the functional areas we just talked about, every race shop needs some sort of office area. The office area is used for holding meetings, scheduling appointments, and handling all of the business aspects involved in running a race team. It is basically the quiet area in the race shop. It is also the area where the team owner and crew chief spend most of their time while at the shop.

Although not every race shop will have a separate area dedicated to each of these functions, most Winston Cup teams do. These shops are big and need to be laid out in such a way that allows a racecar to move around the shop efficiently, similar to an assembly line. The racecar should start at one end of the shop and move to each area until it reaches the other end of the shop as a complete racecar ready to go to the racetrack. Shops of this size and layout are quite large and expensive to run and operate. Consider the electric bill for a shop of this size, and that bill is only one of the utility bills team owners have to pay.

A shop of this size and configuration is just one end of the spectrum. The other end is the local weekend racers who do as much as they can from the small garages behind the houses they live in. Although they may do many of the same basic things as Winston Cup teams, such as pulling an engine from the racecar, replacing a bent tube on the chassis, or painting a new color scheme on the racecar, they do it all in one small little garage. Their racecars may not look as good as Winston Cup racecars, but they will be ready for that Friday night race at the local racetrack.

Bottom line, you need a place, no matter how big or small, to work on the racecar. Having a race shop costs money, and you cannot run a race team without one. So figure out what you need to do in the shop, draw out a rough floor plan to help you determine its size, and then double it. No matter how much space you have, it is never enough. Then figure out how much space you can afford to have and cut it in half. There are always hidden expenses in the shop that you did not plan on, so cover yourself by expecting the unexpected bill.

Basic Tools

After you have your race shop mapped out for the type of work you will be performing, the next thing you need are the tools and equipment to do the work. In Chapter 7, "Racing Stuff," we talked about the tools and equipment commonly used at the racetrack. Although these same tools are used back in the race shop, there are additional tools you need for use in the race shop only. Some of these tools are specific to a certain type of work; others are more general tools that are used by each of the areas in the shop.

The Basic Toolbox

Whether you are part of a race team or just a backyard mechanic who is going to change his own oil, you need a good set of basic tools. A set of basic tools includes screwdrivers, open-end wrenches, hammers, pliers, and a set of socket wrenches. These tools are the basics for any service you will need to do. Because these tools are used so often, many race teams have multiple sets of these tools in the race shop.

You can purchase a basic set of tools from any good hardware or auto parts store. Because every area in the race shop uses these tools, make sure you buy a high-quality set. A basic set of tools can cost anywhere from a few hundred dollars to a few thousand dollars, depending on the brand of tool you purchase. The more expensive tools may also come with a lifetime guarantee. This guarantee means that if the tool breaks the company will replace it for free. This is a good option, because your tools will be taking quite a beating, and a free replacement is a good thing.

All Snap-On and Craftsman tools come with a lifetime guarantee and free replacement. Although Snap-On makes an excellent tool, you can buy them only from a local distributor; Snap-On tools are not sold in stores. Craftsman tools that are just as good as Snap-On are a little easier to find. They are sold in hardware stores, home improvement stores, and at all Sears stores around the country. For this reason, we recommend Craftsman tools, but if you know a local Snap-On distributor and can afford the few extra dollars, Snap-On tools are excellent.

Inside Track

When you buy a set of basic tools, spend more money to buy a quality set of tools, which may include a lifetime guarantee. You may be able to save a few bucks now on a cheaper set of tools, but it will cost you more in the long run to replace the tools when they break.

Drills and Grinders

In addition to the basic toolbox, you also need a series of drills and grinders in the shop. These tools are used in a variety of functions and help the team to build and prepare the racecar. Several types of drills and grinders are available from your local hardware store. At a minimum, you need a small handheld drill for drilling out small holes on the racecar. Because the entire racecar is made of steel and fiberglass, you need to drill holes in order to attach the pieces to one another. Handheld drills come in a variety of sizes and speeds. A three-eighths drill is a good universal drill and is fine for most of the work you will need to do. You should have at least two of these drills in your race shop.

In addition to the handheld drills, you also need a more heavy-duty drill. This type of drill is usually mounted on the workbench or comes with its own stand and is commonly referred to as a drill press. The reason for this name is that the drill is pressed down onto the surface being drilled with a lever. A drill press provides for a more precise type of drilling.

Drill presses can cost anywhere from $250 to $1,000, depending on the manufacturer. The same rationale applies here as with the basic set of tools. Paying a little more now for a good drill press will save you money in the long run. The worst thing is to have your only tool break while you are using it and not have a replacement. There was a company with the slogan, "You can pay me now, or you can pay me later." Spend the extra money now and save yourself the headache later.

Grinders are also important tools in the race shop. They are used to grind down rough edges and cut pieces of metal. Because the majority of a racecar is welded together, a lot of items require the use of a grinder.

Air Compressors

Air compressors are another invaluable tool at the race shop. Although the average person may think of an air compressor only for inflating tires, race teams use them for much more. Many of the tools a race team uses are run by an air compressor. Wrenches, chisels, socket wrenches, and hammers are just some of the types of tools that can be powered by an air compressor. These tools are often referred to as air tools. They allow a mechanic to work more efficiently and faster than using electric or hand-powered tools.

Air compressors come in a variety of size and shapes designed for specific uses. Race teams use small, portable air compressors at the racetrack, but in the race shop, they may use much larger and heavier air compressors. One air compressor can be used for an entire area in the shop or, if the shop is small enough, for the entire shop. Air compressors are great, versatile tools for the race team. A small portable air compressor can cost as little as $200; one that is large enough to run an entire shop costs a few thousand dollars.

Specialty Tools

A specialty tool is a tool that is used for a specific purpose. Most specialty tools are not used at the racetrack; they are used in the race shop during the building or repairing of the racecar. These tools are usually very expensive and should only be used by people who are trained to use them. The following sections describe some of these tools and explain what they are used for and some of the hazards to avoid while using them.

Welders

Remember that the three sections of the racecar chassis are made of steel to protect the driver from injury. Welding machines are used to assemble the sections of the chassis. Think of a welding machine as a tube of glue. You use the tube of glue to make two pieces stick together. A welding machine does the same thing with metallic objects. Welding machines use a thin wire as the glue to hold the objects together. The machine heats and melts the thin wire as it is being applied to the two pieces of metal.

Most race teams have at least two welding machines in the race shop. A portable welding machine costs about $500. We recommend buying a small, portable machine because it enables you to reach into the small areas of the chassis.

Although you need to be careful with any type of tool, you need to be extra careful when using a welding machine. This tool can melt metal, so you can imagine how hot this metal must become before it melts. When using a welder, you have to wear a protective face shield to protect your eyes and face. Never use a welder without proper face protection. The bright light from the melted steel can burn your eyes, causing permanent vision damage.

Never use a welding machine around flammable objects or fluids. Never weld on anything that is flammable or contains a flammable substance either. Sparks from a welding machine can ignite a fire. Always have a fire extinguisher or a water hose near by when using a welding machine.

If you have not been trained on how to use a welding machine, do not use one until you are. It is better to be safe and have someone who is trained do your welding for you. In the meantime, go out and get yourself trained on how to properly and safely use a welding machine. You will need it more than you think.

Yellow Flag

When using a welding machine, always use a proper face shield to protect your eyes, hair, and face from the extreme heat and bright light given off by the welding machine. Only trained professionals should use welding machines. They are very dangerous and can cause a fire or extreme injuries if used improperly.

English Wheel

The English wheel is a tool with two oval-shaped ends that squeezes a flat piece of steel into a curved shape. Race teams use this tool to make the front fenders and rear quarter panels of the racecar. These parts are critical to the racecar because the shape of the front fender and the shape of the rear quarter panels determine how well the air passes over the racecar. A poorly shaped racecar does not pass through the air as well and is slower than a racecar with a good shape.

Think of an English wheel as a kind of rolling pin. A baker uses the rolling pin to flatten out and shape the dough to the desired form just as a crew member uses an English wheel to shape steel into the desired shape. Although this process may sound fairly easy, it is harder than you think. It takes a lot of experience to be able to shape a flat piece of steel into an aerodynamic fender.

Engine Dynamometer

The engine is one of the more important items in the racecar. Without a good, strong engine, you will never be competitive on the racetrack. Although most of the smaller teams buy or lease a race engine from a professional engine builder, some teams build their own. Whether you build your own engine or buy, rent, or lease one from a professional engine builder, you need to know how powerful that engine is. One way to determine how much power an engine has is to use what is called an engine dynamometer, or an *engine dyno* for short, to measure the engine's power.

Engine dynos are very expensive and should only be used by trained professionals. Engine dynos measure horsepower by revving the engine to extremely high revolutions. The engine dyno measures the amount of horsepower and torque being generated while the engine is being revved. Improper use of an engine dyno can cause severe damage to the engine as well as to anyone around it. If an engine is over-revved, the internal parts can break and cause internal damage to the engine. A typical race engine can cost $40,000 to $60,000 to build, which would be a very expensive lesson for an inexperienced engine dyno operator.

Track Terms

An **engine dyno** measures how much horsepower and torque an engine can produce.

Yellow Flag

Over-revving an engine on an engine dyno can cause severe damage to the engine and to anyone standing nearby. When an engine is over-revved, it can explode and seriously hurt someone.

The Worker Bees

So far we have been talking about the race shop and the tools in it. What we have not talked about yet are the people that make up the race team. A race team needs people who understand the mechanics of a racecar and know how to build and repair one as well. Working on a race team also requires dedication, hard work, long hours, and a lot of sacrifice. Crew members spend many hours during the week at the race shop working on the racecars and even more hours at the racetrack preparing and fine-tuning the racecar for the race. It is not easy work by any means, and people who have both the skills and dedication are tough to find.

Most local racers have their friends as their pit crew. These local people volunteer their time for the love of the sport. They are usually not paid for their time and do it because they just love racing. They usually have regular full-time jobs that limit the amount of time they can spend at the race shop or the racetrack.

The NASCAR Winston Cup teams are a little different. These teams consist of people who also love the sport and have the dedication needed to succeed. However, working on a NASCAR race team is a full-time job. NASCAR crew members go to the race shop every day and work a full day to prepare the racecar for the coming race weekend. Having a full-time, dedicated crew makes the team better prepared for the coming race weekend, but it does require a lot of money because the crew members must be paid salaries.

Starting a Team

We said on the first page of this chapter that there are two ways to start a race team. The first way is to build your own organization from the ground up. From the preceding pages, you can see that building your own organization from the ground up is no small task and requires a large investment up front.

The other way, which we have not discussed, is to buy into an existing race team. Team owners are always looking for people who are willing to invest in the race team.

Inside Track

Buying an existing race team is easier than starting one from scratch. The only problem is that if someone wants to sell a race team it is probably not doing very well on the track. You could be buying someone else's headache. But if you are getting into racing, you should expect to have headaches.

This allows them the opportunity to recoup some of the expenses they have paid for getting the team started. If you want to buy into an established and successful race team, it will cost you a lot of money, and you may not even be a major partner in the team.

The best way to get started quickly is to buy into a team from someone who is looking to get out of the sport. You will not be paying top dollar for the equipment because it is used and the current owner is probably looking to get out as quickly as possible.

On the Road Again

After you have your race shop up and running, the next step is to get to the races and start having some serious fun. Unfortunately, there is no easy or cheap way to get to and from a racetrack. The moment a team leaves for the racetrack, the team owner starts spending money.

In the following sections, we are going to talk about the types of expenses involved in getting the race team to the racetrack. Now you may be thinking that the cost to get to a racetrack does not start until you start off down the road to the racetrack. This is not true. The cost of going to the racetrack starts as soon as you decide you want to go to the racetrack. The reason is that once you decide you are going to the racetrack there are things you will need to have with you when you get there. These things are the first expenses involved in going to the racetrack. Just a few examples of what we are talking about are fuel for the hauler, fuel for the racecar, and food and water for the race team. Each of these items are things you need to spend money on before you even head down the road. After you are off and on your way to the race-track, additional expenses, such as highway tolls and hotel bills for those long overnight trips, start piling up.

Hotel Bills

In the NASCAR Winston Cup Series, a typical race weekend occurs over several days. Teams start to show up at the track on the Wednesday before the race and do not leave until the race is over on Sunday. That's five days that race teams spend at the racetrack preparing for a race. That also means that the team owner is looking at five nights of hotel bills for putting the team up. Most teams bring at least 10 team members to every race, which adds up to a lot of rooms per night, just for the team.

Hotel bills can eat into the racing budget very fast. In order to try and keep this type of expense to a minimum, team members often double up in one room, or some may even stay in a camper or the hauler located at the racetrack. Many of the Winston Cup teams bring a luxury mobile home with them to the racetrack in addition to the racecar hauler. The drivers and their family members use these luxury mobile homes while at the racetrack. These luxury mobile homes are an alternative to staying in a hotel, but they are not inexpensive as you might imagine. Only the well-financed race teams, like the Winston Cup teams, use luxury mobile homes at the races.

Because most of the races that weekend racers participate in are at local tracks or on only one day, teams do not have to worry about a big hotel bill for the team. As a team progresses from the local regional series to the national series, budgeting for hotel stays becomes mandatory.

Road Bills

Another expense that may not come to mind when planning a race budget is the amount of money spent just trying to get to the racetrack. In Chapter 6, "Getting Around," we talked about the different ways teams get to and from a racetrack. First, the owner must pay for a way to haul the racecar and equipment. Some of the obvious expenses are gas money, highway tolls, food for the driver, and emergency repairs for the hauler. (Because most of the large 18-wheel haulers have a small sleeper compartment for the driver to sleep in, hotel bills are not usually necessary.)

Of these road expenses, the biggest one is gas money. Your truck may get 20 miles per gallon of gas, but when you are towing a trailer behind you, it is not unusual to get only 5 to 7 miles per gallon of gas. Getting this type of gas mileage for the race hauler drastically increases the amount of money you will need for gas for the hauler. With the price of a gallon of gas increasing every year, it can cost even the local weekend racer a few hundred dollars in gas alone to get to the racetrack, and that is even before he or she unloads the racecar.

Paying to Play

In addition to all of the expenses we have been talking about so far, the team owner must pay certain fees in order to compete in the race. Each team member has to pay a fee for the license to compete. There is also an entry fee to enter a racecar in the race, an inspection fee to have a racecar inspected at the racetrack, and a track fee. The team owner usually pays all of these fees.

License Fee

Every member of the race team who will be attending the race to work on the racecar is required to have a NASCAR license. Being a holder of a NASCAR license means that you agree to abide by the rules and regulations of NASCAR. In addition to agreeing to the rules and regulations, you are also agreeing to the NASCAR code of ethics and conduct. What this means is that you will conduct yourself in a professional manner that accurately represents the true professionalism of the sport.

In reality, what this license means is that you have agreed to follow rules and not do anything to embarrass your team or the sport and that you have written a check to NASCAR for several hundred dollars. Anyone over age 18, regardless of their automotive knowledge and racing experience, can obtain a NASCAR license.

Racecar Entry Fee

The racecar entry fee is the fee paid by the team owner to enter the racecar into the race. Not every NASCAR series requires entry fees to be paid in order to compete in the race. The entry fee for a NASCAR Winston Cup race can cost as much as $500; the NASCAR Busch Series races cost about $250, and any one of the regional touring series races costs about $150 dollars. There is no rationale behind the cost of the entry fee. It is just an expense you have to pay in order to compete in the race. Don't ask or worry about it—just write the check.

Inside Track

To enter a race, you need to fill out and send in an entry form to NASCAR in Daytona Beach, Florida. As soon as the entry form arrives, write the check and send it in. It could mean the difference between racing and staying home.

Inspection Fee

The inspection fee is a similar type of fee to the entry fee. It is supposed to cover the cost of inspecting the racecar before the race. However, NASCAR requires that all racecars be inspected before competing in the race, so we're not sure why a fee has to be attached to it. Again, just write the check and don't ask why.

Track Entry Fee for the Team

In addition to the fees paid directly to NASCAR, each track also wants to get a piece of the action. Even though every team member is required to have a NASCAR license, which already costs about $250, each team member must pay an additional track entry fee. This fee can vary from as little $20 to as much as $50. This one time fee for teams per event is paid directly to the racetrack and allows team members access to the pit areas where the racecars are worked on. Again, just write the check and don't argue about it. You will not get a decent answer, and your team will not be able to get in without paying the fee.

Getting Some Back

As you can see, there are a lot—and we do mean a lot—of expenses that the team owner is responsible for paying. Unless they are multimillionaires, team owners have to find help to pay for these bills and expenses.

Team Sponsors

The first way team owners offset their costs is by looking for corporate sponsorship. Team owners sell space on the racecar to a corporation to help pay for racing expenses. Because NASCAR has become the fastest-growing spectator sport in America, it is a prime mechanism for large corporations to advertise and promote their products. In addition, all NASCAR Winston Cup races are televised nationally, which means millions of people every weekend are sitting in front of their television sets for hours to watch the races.

A typical Winston Cup race lasts about three hours. If a large corporation sponsors a Winston Cup team, it has the opportunity to have its company name broadcasted on national television for over three hours. If that company would try to buy that much national television coverage, it would cost them a fortune. Not to mention, when was the last time you sat and watched a three-hour commercial? This type of exposure allows team owners to obtain millions of dollars in sponsorship money from large corporations. Sponsors are the main way team owners obtain the money needed to race.

Track Terms

Team sponsors are the primary way owners fund the race team. There are multiple types of sponsors: primary sponsors, secondary sponsors, and associate sponsors. The difference between them depends on how big their checks to the racing team are.

Series Sponsors

In addition to team sponsors, some companies sponsor a racing series instead of just one team. These series sponsors donate prize money to the series for the drivers who finish the race. In exchange, the series sponsor sticker is placed on the front of each racecar. All of the small stickers on the front of the racecar are series sponsors who donate prize money to the series. How well a team finishes in a race determines how much money it will be awarded from the series sponsors. The better a team finishes, the more money it gets. Some series sponsors also pay some money to any team who enters the race. It is not much money, but every little bit helps, and no team turns down a check.

Prize Money

The second biggest way team owners pay for the expenses of racing is with prize money won from a particular race. This is more like gambling than anything else. You have to spend a lot of money first, and then hope you win the race to get back some of the money you spent. This is a very dangerous way to fund your race team. So many things could happen during a race, all of which could affect how well you perform in the race. In most NASCAR races, the winner takes all the prize money, so it is very hard to fund a team with just prize money unless you are dominant in your series. With racing getting more competitive every weekend, it is difficult for anyone to be dominant in this sport. Think of the prize money as a bonus. Do not count on it to pay the bills, but be happy when you do get the check.

Merchandise Sales

The NASCAR Winston Cup fan is a very dedicated fan who cannot get enough stuff with his or her favorite driver on it. These fans are so loyal to their drivers that they will buy anything—and we do mean anything—with their driver's name on it. In addition to T-shirts, teams sell towels, flags, die-cast replica cars, lunchboxes, jackets, watches, hats, flashlights, and anything else you can think of. Put the word NASCAR on it or the picture of a driver, and it will sell like crazy.

Team owners are aware of this fan craze and are using it to help fund the race team. The more popular a driver is, the faster those products will sell. Team owners and drivers license the right to use their image and or likeness to any company who is looking to increase its sales. Put Dale Earnhardt on a box of Wheaties cereal, and it will fly off the shelf at your local grocery store. Have Jeff Gordon do a commercial saying that he uses Quaker State oil in his racecar and watch how

Inside Track

Merchandise sales are a great way to supplement any race team's budget. The more popular you are or the more races you win, the more stuff you will be able to sell.

fast people are going to their local Q-Lube for an oil change with Quaker State. Team owners and drivers are riding this new merchandise wave. It is so big that many teams bring a tractor-trailer full of merchandise to sell to every race. Dale Earnhardt brings several tractor-trailer trucks to every race. (Now that his son, Dale Jr., is moving into Winston Cup for the 2000 racing season, we think he is going to need a few more merchandise trailers.)

The Least You Need to Know

➤ Owning a race team is expensive, regardless of whether it is a local weekend team or a NASCAR Winston Cup team.

➤ Building a race team from scratch requires a lot of money upfront just to get started.

➤ Buying an existing race team gets you to the track faster, but you may be buying someone else's headache.

➤ Traveling to and from the racetrack can cost more than just a few bucks for gas and tolls; make sure you budget for this expense.

➤ Nothing is free, including stock car racing; you have to pay fees just to be able to race.

➤ Sponsors are the primary way that team owners fund their race teams. The more successful you are, the easier it is to get sponsors.

➤ Sales of racing merchandise are a great way for teams to supplement their racing budget—fans are dedicated and will buy anything racing related.

Part 3

Preparing for
a Race

Now that you have all of the stuff you need to race, you need to get ready for the race. This includes preparing the racecar, preparing your crew, and getting through the technical inspection at the racetrack. After you have read this part, you should have a better understanding about what is involved in getting ready for a NASCAR race.

Dialing It In

Warning! Do not read this chapter outdoors. Do not operate your car or heavy machinery while reading. Refrain from alcoholic or beverages containing no caffeine. While reading this chapter, place yourself in a comfortable upright position and have nothing cooking in the oven. This chapter contains technical information. Please proceed with caution.

This chapter deals with some of the technical aspects of the chassis, including some of the procedures and adjustments teams make to prepare for a race and some they make during practice to make the car comfortable to drive. Some of these procedures and adjustments are very involved, but we will try to explain them as simply as possible.

Ride Heights: How Low Can You Go?

A ride height is the relationship of the lower frame to the ground. Ride heights are measured and recorded throughout the set-up period, and these measurements are referred to many times during practice, qualifying, and before and after the race. As teams make adjustments to their cars, they make sure the ride heights haven't changed, unless that's something they intended to do.

Cornering and the Center of Gravity

Ride heights have a direct affect on the way the car corners. Making the car lower to the ground lowers the center of gravity, and a car with a lower center of gravity (COG) is easier to turn given that everything else is equal. In a normal, circle-track stock car situation, a higher COG causes the left side of the car to lift, or lose traction, in a turn.

To understand how the COG affects cornering, consider a fullback in a football game. When he gets the ball and runs through the line, he lowers his body to give himself a lower center of gravity. With this movement, he can change direction more effectively and quickly avert opposing would-be tacklers. When he gets into open ground, he rises up and tries to get speed. But if another tackler gets in his way, he will lower his body and dart one way and then the next. Lowering his body like that gives him a lower center of gravity and enables him to make fast direction changes and elude opponents.

Stock cars are traveling at a high rate of speed and need to change direction in a relatively short distance. The lower the car can get, the better the chance that the car will turn without lifting or *unloading* the left side of the car and losing speed. Unloading the left side of the car results in a great loss of traction and increased lap times.

Inside Track

Always set the car as low as the track, rules, and suspension allow. It will almost always be faster through the corner this way.

Track Terms

The **unloading** of the chassis is when weight transfers off of wheels previously with traction, making traction for the remainder of the wheels.

Ride Heights and Roll Centers

A ride height affects more than the car's center of gravity. It also affects the ground clearance and roll centers of the front and rear suspensions. A *roll center* is the relationship between the upper and lower control arms of a suspension. These arms connect the spindle, to which the wheels are bolted, and the chassis. Where these arms pivot makes a tremendous difference in the way the car handles entering the corner and the exiting the corner onto the straightaway. The position of the roll centers basically controls the way the car rolls over in the corner and the amount of traction the front and rear tires give to the chassis. Looking at the diagram of roll centers, you can see how the roll centers are determined. The further away from center of gravity the roll center is, the more aggressively the car will roll.

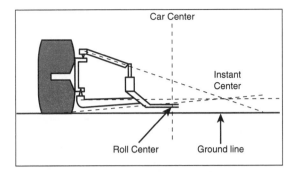

Car Center

Instant
Center

Roll Center

Ground line

*Roll centers control the
feel of the car and how it
rolls over in the corners.*

Engineers work for years to develop the correct roll centers for certain types of racecar chassis or the cars on the street. Racecars need more camber gain because of the high speeds in racing and the need for increased traction. We will talk about camber and what it does later in the chapter (see the following "Camber: A Top and Bottom Relationship" section).

Finding the correct roll center is also a matter of feel for the driver. A high roll center doesn't have the sensation of roll over that the low roll center does. A low roll center is used mainly for flat or tracks with little banking, but it is not limited to these tracks. Many drivers use this type of suspension on all tracks and feel that the side bite they get with this suspension style allows for greater adjustments. Other drivers say that high roll center cars roll over easily and smoothly, making them easier to control.

I have driven both styles. Although I like the feel of the high roll center cars, I have always been faster with low roll centers. Perhaps I get lulled to sleep by the comfortable, easy feel of the higher roll centers, and I "get after it" with the more aggressive-feeling low roll center.

Caster: An Upper and Lower Relationship

Caster is the relationship between the upper and lower ball joints. The inclination of the ball joints determines the degree of caster in a front suspension. Why would you need to know about caster as

Yellow Flag

Roll centers are developed from years of track experience and engineering science. Don't try to change a car's roll centers unless you have researched what could happen. Do the research before you make test runs on the track.

Track Terms

If a car **tracks straight,** you can let go of the steering wheel while driving and it will go straight and it won't pull to one side or the other.

115

a racer? Caster affects the feeling you have in the steering wheel. The more caster you have, the better you can feel what the car is doing.

If your car pulls to one side when you let go of the wheel while driving, your car has caster problems. That's why you bring it in to the repair shop for a wheel alignment. When the caster is good, the car *tracks straight* and doesn't wear tires irregularly.

Camber/caster settings are made with the same gauge. This one is a good example of an affordable, portable gauge.

Yellow Flag

Try not to use too little caster. It may make the car feel better, but this sensation is more of a feeling of security, not one of feeling what the car is doing. More caster gives you a better feel of the car and enables you to give more feedback to the crew, resulting in more positive changes in the suspension.

In stock car racing on an oval-shaped track, race teams do something called *caster split*. By putting more degrees of caster on the right side and less on the left side, the car has a head start turning into the corners, which results in less driver fatigue in long races. But too much stagger split makes the car turn into the corner too fast and takes away the feeling of the racecar. The typical caster split is two or three degrees. So if you have four degrees of caster on the right side of the car, you can have one or two degrees on the left. This is a good starting point for most cars. Using excessive amounts of caster forces the need for a strong power steering unit or a good set of forearms, because it adds to the necessary force needed to turn the car.

The first time we tried to run a mile track, we had three degrees of caster split. Up until this time, we had raced only on ⅝-mile and smaller tracks, and three degrees of split seemed like a good combination. When I tried to drive on the mile track with three degrees of split, however, I continuously ended up with the left front tire on the apron of the track, unloading the car and having the back end try to come around on me. This didn't amuse the car owner, nor were the NASCAR officials getting any sort of chuckle out if it. I'm not too proud to say that if I did it again, I was going to need new fireproof underwear and a private moment to change. We made the decision to go with two degrees of caster split, and that was the needed change. I was then able to drive the car into the turns and gain valuable time and corner speed with a great reduction of lap times. I was also able to keep my race suit dry cleaning needs down to a minimum.

The last part of caster we need to address is *caster gain*. This happens when the upper and lower control arms are not aligned parallel to the frame. As the car corners, the upper arm pivots up and back and the lower arm goes up and forward. This action increases the degrees of caster, resulting in caster gain. Caster gain lessens driver's feel of the car and may also confuse him or her as to what's really happening.

The relationship between the upper and lower control arms and the mounting points determines when there will be caster gain. Checking for caster gain can be easily done with the caster gauge and moving the wheel up and down in an on track simulation. Check the caster per convention methods in the compressed condition, then again in the extended condition. There should be no difference. If there is, you will need to correct your control arm mounting points. Preventing and correcting caster gain can be done by first making the upper control arms parallel to the frame rails.

Camber: A Top and Bottom Relationship

Camber is the relationship between the top and bottom of the tire, whether it is straight up and down or out or in at the top. Look at the following illustration of wheels that are cambered out on the driver's side. You're thinking, "I have seen that before. When I slid into the curb in the rain, I cambered my wheel, and it cost me a thousand dollars to fix." Race teams camber tires on purpose. And yes, there is a very good reason for it.

On circle tracks, wheels on the left side of the car need to be cambered out, or have positive camber. The wheels on the right side need to have negative camber or be tilted in on the right side. The reason for this is that if the tire were standing straight up, the force of the car leaning over in the turns would lift the left sides of both front tires off of the ground, resulting in poor or no contact with the pavement and no traction. With the wheels tilted at the proper angles, the tires are more flat in the turns, resulting in more traction, and the car also can turn more quickly and in a more controlled fashion at high speeds.

Yellow Flag

Never run a racecar with bad camber settings. The car will never be up to speed, and tires will wear faster, causing them to fail prematurely.

From this view, you can clearly see that the tires are cambered over to the driver's side.

Camber must be set at the race shop and checked at the track by checking tire temperatures and tire wear across the surface of the tire. Crews have the drivers do 20 to 30 laps on the track, and then the crews check temperature and wear on the tires. If wear is even and temperatures are equal across the face of the tire, then the crews know that the camber is set correctly.

Crews typically set the left front tire at one and a half to three degrees positive camber and the right front tire at three to five degrees of negative camber. This camber setting gives the car a funny look. If you were standing at the front of the car and looking at it with the body off, you would think that both front tires were in heavy need of a V8 drink. They would be visibly leaning over to the right on the top. On road courses, crews set the tires to have negative camber so that both tops aim inward. They do this because the cars need traction for left and right turns.

Camber gain is something that happens because the lower control arms are longer than the uppers, as the following figure shows. The arms must be different lengths because just changing the camber of the tires is not enough to turn at high speeds successfully. As the car rolls into the turns, the right side wheel top must pull in to the car, and the top of the left tire must push out from the car to ensure proper tire contact with the track. As the car rolls more, the tires move in and out, keeping up with the movement of the car. Track size, driving style, banking, control arm lengths, and a host of other factors determine what camber is needed for a certain day.

Inside Track

When setting the camber, take temperatures across the face of the tire. A 10-degree difference is about $1/8$-inch shim, or slightly less than $1/2$ degree of camber.)

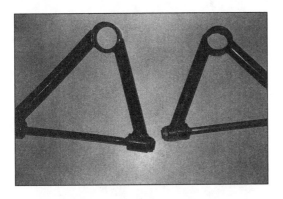

Control arms of different length control the camber gain in the front end of each racecar.

Many times a team misses the proper camber settings and wears tires so unevenly that they shred and burst. We remember one such incident very clearly. Before a race in Loudon, New Hampshire, our team scrambled to repair a worn upper ball joint that had been plaguing us for most of the practice session. The crew opted to remove the arm from the car to ease the replacement of the worn part. When we hurriedly put the car back together, we inadvertently left out a set of shims that sets the degrees of camber.

From the start of the race, it was clear that something wasn't reassembled as it should have been. We opted to stay out on the track running at a slower pace and staying on the lead lap until a caution flag came up and we could take the time to come in, inspect, and fix the problem. Unfortunately for us, there wasn't a caution flag for 35 laps, and that caution flag was for us. By running the car with the improper camber, we prematurely wore out the outside of the right front tire. When the car came off of turn four, the tire shredded, and the car hit the wheel and slid uncontrollably into the outside wall. The entire right side of the car, the front suspension, and both wheels were flattened, our race day was ended, and major repairs were required.

Toe (Not the Big One)

Toe settings are the alignment of the front tires to ensure they travel in the same direction. This adjustment is simple to make, but it is nonetheless important. There are two possible settings:

➤ **Toe out.** The front of the tires are further apart than the rear of the tires.

➤ **Toe in.** The front of the tires are closer together than the rear of the tires.

Adjust the toe with the tie rod ends shown here. No disassembly is needed to make large or small adjustments.

When the racecar is set to be toe out, the car will wander slightly as it goes down the straightaway. As the car enters the turn, it transfers weight to the outside tire, which means the car now follows the direction of that tire. This situation is likely to cause the car to *push* up the track, which causes the driver to turn the car even further to the left. As the car exits the turn, the weight transfers to the inside tire, making the back of the car loose and causing major oversteering. If the driver doesn't recognize this toe out problem immediately, the crew will start making other changes to the car to compensate. Of course, treating the wrong problem results in creating new ones.

Bump Steer (Not the Beefy Kind)

Bump steer is the involuntary steering of the front wheels as the chassis moves up and down. This happens because the connecting and pivoting points of the lower control arms and the steering links are not traveling on the same arc as the suspension moves up and down when the chassis/car moves. If the arcs are different, the links push on the steering arm and steer the car in and out while the steering wheel remains stationary.

Most regular cars have bump steer because of the type of steering and vast amount of suspension travel. You may be able to feel the bump steer by driving over a speed bump slowly on a slight angle. The car feels like it wants to steer to one side then the other. This sensation is what a racecar driver feels in the turns. The driver gets down in the corner, and when the front right suspension is compressed, the wheel turns out and makes a smooth transition into the corner.

The crew adjusts bump steer by raising or lowering the tie rod ends or center link in the car. A gauge is needed for this procedure.

Track Terms

When a car **pushes** up a track, it means as you enter the turn the car will move away from the low side of the track and move toward the outside wall against the directions of the driver.

Inside Track

Bump steer can be a useful adjustment when the car seems loose upon entering a corner. Adjust the bump steer so the outside wheel moves outward slightly; this movement will catch the rear of the car from coming around and causing the car to spin out. This is not a commonly used remedy, however.

Bump steer gauges are easy to use and are a necessary part of the setup procedure.

Ackerman: Which Way to Turn?

When a car goes around a track shaped either in an oval or circle, the inside wheel travels a shorter distance than the outside wheel. Therefore, in most cases, the inside wheel needs to turn slightly more than the outside wheel. Bolting the tie rod on the left/inside closer to the pivot point by about ⅛ to ⅜ inch makes the inside wheel turn more quickly with equal amounts of steering wheel movement. This adjustment is called *Ackerman*. Track size, banking, driver feel, and chassis style all contribute to how much or little Ackerman is needed.

Now you know what adjustments a racecar needs to make it superfast. You know the car needs to be as low as possible without breaking the rules or hitting the track at any point. You know that having a lower center of gravity makes the car more stable, gives the car better handling characteristics, and makes a fullback harder to turn over if a tackler hits his blindside. You know that caster is the feel of a racecar's front suspension. Caster is determined by the speed of the car, the banking, and how much longer the lower control arms are compared to the upper arms. Toe affects the car all the way around the track, and it's the easiest adjustment to make. Make sure your toe is straight before getting out on the track. Finally, you know that bump steer is caused by the misalignment of the lower control arms and tie rod ends and Ackerman is the intentional turning of one wheel more than the other to equal the turning radius of both wheels in a corner.

The Least You Need to Know

➤ A racecar's ride height affects the car's center of gravity, its ground clearance, and its roll centers—all of which help determine how well a car handles corners.

➤ Caster (front suspension feel) and camber (tire tilt) are set together and are used to establish the feel of the car, and tracking of the front end.

➤ Set the toe last, after all the rest of the adjustments are made. Setting the toe affects nothing but toe, but caster, camber, and bump steer settings may affect the toe.

➤ Do these adjustments at the shop; practice time is too precious to waste it fooling with these complicated adjustments.

Chapter 11

Rocking and Rolling

> **In This Chapter**
>
> ➤ Spring your way into the winners' circle
>
> ➤ Some shocking news
>
> ➤ Don't be swayed
>
> ➤ Locating your car

Why do we need springs? Springs are there for one reason only: to keep the car off the ground. Of course, keeping the car off the ground would be easy to do if the springs and suspension were eliminated, because then the car couldn't roll over. However, if the springs and suspension were eliminated, drivers would need dentures because the vibrations would rattle the teeth from their mouths. Springs are needed to suspend the car while outside forces, such as banking, bumps in the track, g-force, and air and wind pressure, work against it.

Shocks and springs are eight of the most important parts of the racecar. Each wheel on the car is allowed to have one spring and one shock. Within these strict limits, crews must make a car comfortable, easy to handle, and most important of all, fast.

Spring Is in the Air

Springs are made from magnetic steel and are heat-treated to keep their tension through years of hard use. Both front and back springs must be no less than $4^3/_4$ inches in diameter and no more than 6 inches in diameter. In addition, front springs are required to have one closed end that is ground flat and one open end. The rear springs must have both ends closed and ground flat.

The spring on the top left is a front coil spring. Note that it is closed on one end and open on the other. The open end installs in the lower control arm, and the closed end sits in the spring saddle. The top right spring is a rear spring; notice that both ends are closed and ground flat.

Inside Track

Springs come in different rates, typically in 25-pound increments. When changing a front spring, change it by 50 pounds; change rear springs by 25 pounds. If you make any less of a change, the driver may not feel it.

Springs are also rated per inch of travel and come in many different rates. They are usually sold in 25-pound increments. If a spring is rated at 500 pounds, it means that for every inch the spring is compressed, it will add another 500 pounds of force. Therefore, a 500-pound spring that is compressed 3 inches has 1,500-pounds of force at that length.

Spring Rubbers

Spring rubbers are round rubber pads with indents that fit into the spring and give it tension, fooling it into thinking it has a stronger spring rate. Spring rubbers are used because of how easily they change the spring rate without changing the spring or height of the car. They can be easily installed or removed during a pit stop. If a driver complains that the car is loose, a crew member can pull a spring rubber out of the right rear spring during a pit stop. With the car now having less spring force against that wheel, the wheel is softer and able to achieve traction easier.

This is a spring rubber installed in a spring.

Our team, as well as other teams, adjusts spring rubbers often. Using spring rubbers makes the springs more adjustable. If you find a 250-pound spring rate works well in the rear of the car, you may want to use a 225-pound spring and add either one whole spring rubber or three pieces of spring rubber to achieve the 250-pound rating. If you need to make a change during the race, you can easily, by pulling one or more pieces of spring rubber from the spring during a pit stop.

Shocks and Springs Together

Shocks soften the blows made by the forces that act on the car. They control the speed at which a particular action may occur. Simply said, springs control how far the suspension travels, and the shocks control how fast or slow the suspension travels. Changing the rate at which the suspension travels changes the way a car transfers weight and turns into a corner or off of a corner.

Springs on a NASCAR racecar need to be just soft enough to hold the car off the ground while being strong enough to keep the car from hitting the ground or causing too much body roll in the corner. They must let the car move to about three inches of suspension travel. If the car travels more in practice, install a stronger spring; if it doesn't travel enough, install a softer spring. This advice is pretty general, but it's a starting point.

Inside Track

Insert the spring rubbers in half or one third pieces. Using pieces instead of whole pads enables you to make finer adjustments when you need to add or subtract some pieces to make the car feel right to the driver.

Under the Hood

If the chassis hits the track at any point, you must install a heavier spring to keep this from happening. But if it hits the track and has less than 3 inches of travel, do not change the spring; raise the chassis height instead. Another thing to keep in mind when choosing springs is that you need to take into account how fast the car is going to be, not how fast it is currently running. Making the car comfortable at slower speeds will result in an incorrect final spring choice. If the car does get up to speed, it will have too much body roll. As the car's speed increases, so does the chance for body roll due to the increased side loads.

The shocks control the spring's speed and let it either compress or extend at the speed you want it to. If you feel the car roll over quickly and hit the suspension hard as it enters a turn, you may want to put stronger shocks in and slow the rate at which the car rolls over. If the car rolls over slowly in the corner, then install a softer set of shocks to allow it to roll more quickly. Keep in mind that this explanation simplifies the issues involving shocks and springs; we would need several more chapters to detail the results of all of the possible adjustments to these parts.

Under the Hood

In most cases, springs in a racecar have three to five times more pressure than the springs in a regular car. But don't install these springs in your regular car, because the increased pressure will make your car perform poorly at slow speeds of 65 miles per hour and less. (And of course you never go more than 65 miles per hour in your regular car.)

Anti-Roll Bars (Sometimes Referred to as Sway Bars)

The anti-roll bars or sway bars in the car also have an effect on the wheel rate started by the main spring. But the great thing about a sway bar is that it has no effect on the car as it runs down the straightaway. An anti-roll bar only works in the corner. As the car rolls over, the bar is stressed and rebounds against the roll. That's how it got its true name: the anti-roll bar. It's not actually a sway bar, it's a part used for anti-sway, but that's the most common name used for it; technically, it's an anti-roll bar.

Anti-roll bars come in various rates and are either solid or tubular. A solid bar holds its rate and springs back less. A tubular bar does the same job as a solid bar and saves you weight in the process, so it would seem to be the better choice, although there is a small driver feel difference between the solid and tubular bars.

The length of the arm connecting the anti-roll bar to the lower control arm plays a vital role in the rate the bar will apply. For example, if you have a typical 36-inch anti-roll bar with arms connecting it with 12-inch centers, and the bar is 1 inch in diameter, the rate will be approximately 350 pounds. If you shorten those arms by 1 inch to 11 inches, the rate changes to approximately 380 pounds. The 30-pound increase can make a noticeable change for a driver and lessen a loose condition exiting a corner.

Shock Settings

Shocks make the car stable and comfortable if they have the correct settings. Most race shocks are adjustable, whether they have an external knob or switch or need to be taken apart and have the valve stacks changed.

Inside Track

Anti-roll bars are great tuning tools. If you have a car that has a slight handling problem, you can easily change the bar or the mounting arm to correct a loose or push condition. A loose condition is having the rear of the car free, and having it come around to meet the front. A push condition is the feeling of turning the wheel and having the car turn slightly but want to continue straight.

Yellow Flag

Never ask other competitors for the spring combination in their cars unless they are using exactly the same chassis and suspension combination as you are. There are too many variables in choosing springs, and different suspensions require different spring rates.

Shocks and Springs Handling the Car

Shocks and springs are the muscles of the car. They control the movement and levels of movement of the car. Most people drive their cars with worn or broken shocks. They bounce down the highway like the little doggy thing in the back window. When the head falls off that little toy doggy, the car's shocks definitely need to be replaced. Installing a new set of shocks can make an old junker feel nearly new. In a racecar, a well-set-up set of shocks will make a good chassis setup great and a bad chassis setup just okay.

Under the Hood

The best analogy for shocks relates to the muscles in and around the knees. For example, a downhill skier's knees take the hit from, regulate, and then absorb all the bumps and turns on the ski slope. The car's shocks do exactly the same thing. When your knees get weak or give out, you fall over. When your car's shocks are too soft or give out, the chassis rolls over, and the driver has no control. The shocks in the car regulate movement. When one of the shocks breaks, you can lose control of your car.

The Good vs. the Bad

A good shock setup enables the driver to drive into a corner, set up the car, and drive out the other side without the car becoming loose, pushing, or doing anything that is uncomfortable or feels weird for a driver. Good shocks give you the confidence to drive up under another competitor knowing that your car will stay under you.

A bad shock setup will make a good racecar a handful for even the best driver. No driver can overcome a bad shock setup. If the shocks are bad enough, a driver will either come in to the pit and get out of the car or put the car in the wall. Bad shock setups either make the car push up the track or make the car loose, causing the rear to come around.

Here are some hints to help you set up your shocks correctly:

➤ If the car is loose on entry, decrease the rebound setting on the left rear or increase compression on the right front.

➤ If the car pushes on entry, decrease compression on the right front and increase rebound on the left rear.

➤ If the car pushes in the middle, increase rebound on the right front and increase the compression on the right rear.

➤ If the car is loose off the corner, decrease compression on the right rear and increase the rebound on the right rear. Or increase the rebound on the left front.

➤ If the car pushes off the turn, increase compression on the right rear and increase the rebound on the left and right front.

Yellow Flag

Never cure a spring problem with a shock change. If the car rolls too much, change the spring before changing the shock. The new shock will mask the problem and cause another one down the road.

Track Locator Bar

The track locator bar (also called the panhard bar) controls the rear roll centers of the car. Raising or lowering the bar will loosen or tighten the car's rear suspension. For example, if you have a car that is pushing going into the turn and runs up the track, then raise the bar. This adjustment raises the roll center, which prevents the car from rolling hard on the rear tires and frees up the back of the car. If you have a car that wants to come around on you going in to the corner, then lower the bar to allow the car to fall over on the rear tires and plant the rear suspension a bit harder.

The length of the bar affects how fast things happen. If the bar is on the short side and the car very reactive, then lengthening the bar will make the car more comfortable for the driver. NASCAR requires the track bar be inside the frame rails, so its length is limited to that maximum, but there is no rule about a minimum length. Another NASCAR rule requires that the mount for the bar be welded to the truck arm.

Inside Track

The length of the track bar affects the way the car handles. The shorter the bar is, the more rear steer the bar puts in the car.

This track bar can be raised or lowered to suit the chassis.

This track locator/panhard bar is short and located off the rear housing; it reacts quickly and needs a soft touch.

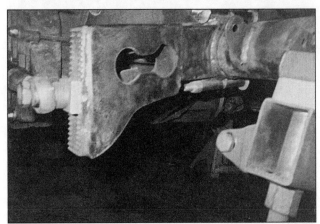

Truck Arms

Truck arms are the rear suspension arms that connect the rear end to the chassis. Truck arms have an adjustment in the front mount. By raising the mounting point, you change the instant center (refer to Chapter 10) and the way the car uses the center of gravity to turn into the corners. The instant center is the intersect point of the upper and lower control arm pivot points.

These arms must be made of magnetic steel and are required by the rules to be one of two types: box or I-beam style. For the box style, you must use 2×3 steel tubing with a wall thickness of $\frac{1}{8}$ inch. I-beam truck arms must be constructed using two C channels with $\frac{1}{8}$-inch wall thickness to complete the required 2×3 dimensions. Each of these truck arms must be connected to the rear end using a minimum of two $\frac{3}{4}$-inch U bolts.

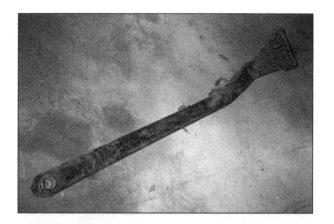

The box truck arm is a durable piece. This one also shows the panhard bar bracket welded on.

These I-beam truck arms are the most commonly used style.

The construction of the truck arms also plays a role in how the car reacts on the track. The more sturdy box style is not as forgiving as the I-beam style. Most teams opt for the I-beam style because the I-beams don't hit the tire as hard when you initiate acceleration. The I-beam design allows some flex, which makes it a more desirable piece and somewhat easier to use. A more versatile suspension is always better.

What Did We Just Say?

In this chapter, you learned that springs are the support of the vehicle. They hold the car upright or as high or low as your suspension needs in order to operate properly. The car's speed definitely affects the spring, as does the shape of the track.

Inside Track

The I-beam truck arm is a more versatile suspension part than the box truck arm. The I-beam's flexibility plays a role in a soft transition from braking and coasting back to acceleration. If your chassis builder gives you a choice between the I-beam and box styles, go with the I-beam.

Spring rubbers can and should be used to adjust the rate of the spring and to fine-tune the spring. Once you think you have the correct springs in the car, leave them and work with the front anti-sway bar. You can correct problems going into or off the corner with this device.

The shocks control the speed of the car's suspension. Stiff shocks slow the suspension movement whereas softer shocks accelerate that movement. Shocks definitely play a big role in how the car handles, and quite often shocks can win or lose you the race. Spend a lot of time on the shocks after you have worked out the other facets of the suspension. There are always gains to be made in the shock valve area.

The panhard bar/track locator can be used to tighten or loosen the chassis, and adjustments can be made during the race. The truck arms are the only links connecting the rear to the chassis. If one of these breaks, or loosens, trouble is around the next corner. So work with your springs and shocks to make the car comfortable. Comfort is the key to giving drivers something they can be confident in, and when drivers are confident, they are usually at their best.

The Least You Need to Know

➤ Choose your springs by how fast you intend to go.

➤ Spring rubbers are a great tuning tool.

➤ Shocks regulate the speed of the spring; the springs control how far the car will roll over.

➤ The track bar/panhard bar controls the rear roll centers.

➤ The rear truck arms are the only links between the rear axle and the chassis.

Chapter 12

A Good Set of Rubbers

In This Chapter

➤ Learning how to measure tires

➤ Determining the front and rear tire stagger

➤ Taking the tire temperature

➤ Checking the air pressure

In this chapter, we are going to talk about tire sizes: how to measure them and why they are important to stockcar racing. We are also going to talk about tire pressures and how they tell you about how your racecar is handling and how you can use them to change the handling of your racecar.

Before we jump right into the racecar tires, let's spend a few pages talking about tires in general to give you a good basic understanding of tires. Once you have this understanding, you'll be ready to dive into the complexities of racecar tires.

How Do Your Tires Measure Up?

Tires are an important part of not only a stock car, but your car as well. The tires carry the weight of the car and its occupants, and allow the car to roll down the road, or track, smoothly. The reason for measuring tires is to ensure the car has the proper size tire. Now you may be asking yourself: What is the right size tire? The answer is that there are several aspects to that question.

Air Pressure and Snow Tires

We all know you can't drive a car for very long on a flat tire. The same is true for a tire that is overinflated. You need to have the correct amount of air in the tire for it to work properly. Air pressure is just one way to measure tires. (We go into air pressure in detail later in this chapter in the section "Tire Temperatures and Air Pressures.")

Another aspect of tires is finding the right type of tire for your type of driving. Many years ago, the coming of winter, cold temperatures, and snow also meant that is was time to replace everyday tires with snow tires. Everyday tires were fairly smooth with some groves in them to allow water to escape from underneath them when you drove through a puddle. Snow tires, while being the same size, were knobbier and had wider groves in them for dealing with the snow. Snow tires are an example of using the right tire for your type of driving.

Track Terms

Aspect ratio is the ratio of tread width to the side wall of the tire. The higher the number, the taller the side wall will be.

Inside Track

When purchasing tires for your car, make sure the size of the tire meets the recommendations for your vehicle. If you are not sure of the tire size for your vehicle, check your owner's manual. When purchasing tires for your race car, make sure you measure them and only buy the sizes that will give you the proper stagger for the track you will be using them on.

Width, Height, and Wheel

The size of a car's tire is determined by three measurements: the width of the tire, the height of the side of the tire, and the width of the rim. For example, 225/70/15 is a typical tire size. The 225 millimeters represents the width of the tire; the 70 millimeters represents *aspect ratio,* which is the height of the side of the tire (also known as the side wall); and 15 inches represents the size of the rim the tire is mounted on. This measurement is determined by measuring the diameter of the wheel. Race tires are measured differently. The typical Goodyear race tire is 27.5 by 12.5 by 15. It is 27.5 inches tall, or in diameter. It has 12.5 inches of tread, or the amount of tire that contacts the track. The diameter of the wheel is 15 inches at the mounting point of the tire.

If you look on the side of the tires on your car, you will see a similar set of numbers. The numbers will vary depending on the type of car you have. For example, rims can vary in size from as small as 13 inches to as large as 18 inches, depending on the vehicle. The important thing to remember is that the rim size of the tire and the rim size of the car must be the same or the tire will not fit.

The same is true for the other two measurements of the tire. The *wheel well,* which is the area on the car where the wheel is mounted, is only so big and can accommodate only a certain size of tires. In our tire size example, the first number, 225, represents the width of the tire. This is the part of the tire that contacts the road. The average family car today has a tire width of 195; more sporty cars have a larger tire width. The wider the tire is, the better the car will handle on the road.

As an example of different tire widths, let's take a look at the tires on a 1999 Chevrolet Corvette and the tires on a 1999 Ford Contour. The Corvette tires are 275/40/18, and the tires on the Contour are 185/70/14. The tires on the Corvette are wider (275 versus 185), taller (40 versus 70), and fit on a bigger rim (18 versus 14). So when the time comes for you to buy new tires for your car, make sure you are buying the right size tire for your car. If you're not sure of what size tire to buy, check your vehicle's owner's manual.

Let's Talk About Racing Tires

Now that we have educated you about the tires on your car, let's talk about the tires on a stock car. First, forget everything we just told you about regular car tires. Most of this information does not apply to racecar tires.

One of the most important aspects of a race tire is its circumference. For those of you that slept through Geometry, the *circumference* of a tire is the distance all the way around the outer circle of the tire. The reason the circumference is so important is because it directly affects the way the car is going to turn. We know what you are thinking, "Wait a minute, the tires do not turn the car; the driver turns the car by turning the steering wheel." That's true, but the tires also can affect the way a car turns.

For an example of what we mean, take a look at a disposable coffee cup. Note that the top of the cup is bigger than the bottom of the cup. Now lay that coffee cup on its side and roll it across a table. The coffee cup does not roll in a straight line. It turns toward the small part of the cup. Tires work the same way. If you put tires on the right side of a car with larger circumferences than the tires on the left side of the car, the car will turn to the left when you roll the car forward. Because the cars go counterclockwise and make left turns on most stock car tracks, a racecar should have a larger

Track Terms

Circumference is all the way round the outer edge of a circle.

Inside Track

A larger right front tire will cause the car to pull to the left under braking. Many teams will use this method to lead the car into the turn. Having larger sized tires on the right side of the racecar makes the racecar turn to the left easier. If you put the larger sized tires on the left side of the racecar, the racecar will turn to the right easier.

circumference tire on the right side of the car. This difference in tire circumference helps the car turn left better, and the better the car turns in the corners of the track, the faster the car will go.

Taking Stock in the Tires

When most race teams go to the track, they buy new tires at the track for that race. The tires are brought to the track by the manufacturer (or a reseller) in a trailer and unmounted. Each race team has at least one member (some teams have more) whose sole responsibility is to pick out and set up the tires for that race. Upon arriving at the track, that team member heads directly for the tire trailer to begin the search for the best tires available. The tools they use to determine a tire size can vary from a simple tape measure to a more complex slide rule. Most teams opt of the less advanced, but more accurate tape measure. Tape measures are more accurate because they provide the exact size of the tire.

To determine the circumference of a tire, the team members search through piles of tires, measuring each one until they find a tire that measures in size to what they are looking for. When they find a tire they think will work, they pull the tire off to the side and bounce it on the ground a few times. The reason for bouncing the tire on the ground is to get the tire back to its *unstressed* size. You probably didn't realize that tires get stressed just like the rest of us. When tires are piled one on top of another, the bottom tire is *stressed* because it is carrying the weight of all of the tires on top of it. The bottom tire can become squished by this weight, and if you measure this tire right away, you will get an inaccurate circumference size. Bouncing the tire on the ground returns the tire to its unstressed condition.

Because the tire is not mounted on a wheel and has no air pressure in it, the center of the tire cannot be measured to determine its circumference. Instead of measuring the center of a tire, team members measure the *crown* (the edge between the top and the side) of the tire to determine the circumference of the tire. Although this measurement does not represent the size the tire will be when the tire is mounted and with filled with air, it gives them enough information to determine which tires they will mount on the wheels. This measurement is referred to as *dry size* and is written down in a logbook that contains the tire sizes of all the tires a team purchases during the racing season unless a different stagger is needed.

Track Terms

A **stressed tire** is a tire that is being compressed or stretched from its normal shape. An **unstressed tire** is a tire that is in its normal shape and not being compressed or stretched.

The correct way to measure a new tire on the tire truck.

Tracking Tire Information

Recordkeeping is not something that the average person may think of as being an important aspect of stock car racing. However, it is one of the most important things a race team can do. Because most of the races are held at the same venues (or tracks) year after year, it is vitally important for the race team to document as much information as possible while at the track. One of the many items a team keeps track of are the tires.

Most teams spend a small fortune over the entire race season on tires. A single race tire can cost as much as $375. It is not unheard of for a race team to purchase 120 sets (or 480 tires) during a 30-race season, which adds up to as much as $180,000 per year just in tires. Keeping track of all of these tires is not a small task and requires a large amount of recordkeeping.

Teams track the following information about their tires:

➤ The number of tires purchased at a track

➤ A tire's *dry size* (the size of a race tire before it is mounted on a rim and filled with air)

➤ A tire's *at pressure size* (the size of the race tire after it has been mounted on a rim and filled with air)

➤ A tire's *scuffed size* (the size of the tire after it has been driven on for a few laps)

➤ The number of laps run on a particular set of tires

➤ The number of laps run on an individual tire

➤ Which tires are part of which set

Keeping track of all of this information helps the team determine what worked well and what did not.

Measure It Again

After a team member selects a set of tires, the tires are mounted and brought up to the recommended air pressure. The next step is to remeasure the tires to ensure that the desired tire size is being achieved.

As stated earlier, team members first measure the crown of the unmounted tire to determine the tire's circumference. After the tire is mounted and filled with air, the tire is measured in a different location. Because the tire is now pressurized, the largest part of the tire is in the center of the tread width. The team member places the end of tape measure in the center of the tread width and moves all the way around the tread until the reaching the end of the tape measure. This measurement represents the circumference of the tire *at pressure*. This measurement is also added to the tire logbook for future reference.

This is the correct way to measure the circumference of a tire after it has been mounted on a rim and filled with air.

Under the Hood

Instead of regular compressed air, some teams use nitrogen to help eliminate water in the tires. Water causes the circumference of a tire to increase in size. This is due to the extra expansion due to heat.

After all of the tires have been mounted, pressurized, and remeasured, team members decide which tires they will keep and which tires they need to replace. The key factor in making this decision is the initial tire growth. *Tire growth* is the difference between a tire's dry size and a tire's at pressure size. Tires are like people: some tires grow more than others, and some tires grow faster than others do. The ideal situation would be the tires would stay at the exact sizes as installed on the car. This would completely eliminate the variations in growth, and cause the car to react differently as the race goes on. If the tires don't all grow the same, at the same rate, the chassis will react differently. You may have heard a report from a driver after a pit stop that the set of tires just put on the car are not as fast as the last set, this maybe be due to one tire growing or not, and affecting the original set up.

Stagger Without Drinking

You have a bunch of tires mounted up on the race wheels, pressurized to the recommended air pressure, measured, and logged into your tire logbook. Now what? Now comes the task of choosing a set of tires to use.

Match Maker

Several factors are considered to determine tire sets. The first factor is the circumference of each tire. Ideally, you want to have the larger tires on the right side of the car to help the car make left turns when it goes around the track. (Remember the coffee cup example from earlier in the chapter?)

Next, you need to determine which of those larger tires will go on the right front and which will go on the right rear. To start out, the larger of the two tires should be on the right rear of the car. As far as the left side of the car is concerned, put the larger of the left side tires on the left front and the smaller tire on the left rear. Now that you have selected the four tires for the car and where they should go, you need to make sure you made the right choice. The way to determine whether you have selected a good set of tires for your racecar is to determine the *stagger* of the front and rear tires.

Track Terms

Stagger is the term for the difference in size from the left side tires to the right side tires.

How Can I Get More?

Stagger is the difference in size between the right side tires and the left side tires. Stagger is only determined from the left and right side of the car; it is never determined from the front of the car to the back of the car. Suppose that the right rear tire has a circumference of 86 inches, and the left rear tire has a circumference of

84 inches. The rear of the car would then have 2 inches of stagger. If the right front tire has a circumference of $85^1/_2$ inches and the left front tire has a circumference of $84^1/_2$ inches, the front stagger would be 1 inch.

As a general rule, you always want to have more rear stagger than front stagger. Why? When a driver turns the steering wheel of a car to the left, the front of the car starts to move to the left before the rear of the car moves left. Stagger in the front allows the wheel speed to stay consistent during the course of the turn. It also allows the car to pull slightly during braking. With the inside tire being shorter, it will slow faster and pull the front end into the turns. Different stagger on the front will affect this. So less stagger is needed. NASCAR rules prevent the use of a brake bias device for side-to-side control, so this is a way of achieving bias without breaking the rules.

If the front stagger is larger than the rear stagger, the team members need to change the tires or move one or more tires to another spot on the racecar until they come up with a good set of tires. This whole thought process is done for every set of tires at every race a team wants to compete in. Most teams prepare several sets of tires to use during a race weekend because a team needs tires to practice on, tires to qualify on, and several sets of tires to race on. Because picking the right tires is an involved process, many teams have crew members who do nothing but prepare tires for the racecar.

Track Terms

Loose condition is the term used to describe the feeling in the racecar when the back of the car wants to spin around the front of the car.

Track Terms

Push condition is a term used to describe the feeling that the racecar does not want to turn. The car would rather continue straight.

When Is Too Much Enough?

You may be asking yourself, is there such a thing as too much stagger? The answer is yes. When a racecar has too much stagger, it gives the driver the feeling of driving on ice. If you have ever driven your car in the snow and ice and you feel the back of the car sliding back and forth on you as you drive, this feeling is called having a *loose condition*. When you turn the car to the left, it feels as though the back of the car is going to slide to the right and spin the car around in the opposite direction.

As we are sure you can imagine, a loose condition is not a comfortable feeling for the driver. Racecar drivers are just like you: they like to be pointed in the direction they are going, especially when they are traveling in excess of 100 miles per hour. Too much stagger results in a very unhappy racecar driver.

Is there such a thing as too little stagger? There sure is. Having too little stagger in the car creates a *push condition*. A push condition is when the car wants to continue in a straight path instead of turning. Most stock car racetracks are ovals or have some type of turn in them, so this condition can cause major problems for the driver.

Imagine that you are a racecar driver speeding down the front straightaway of the track at over 100 miles per hour. You are about to enter into the turn. You turn the steering wheel to start turning the car, but the car wants to go straight. You look in front of you, and all you can see is a big, white, 12-inch thick concrete wall that you know is tougher than you are. As each second goes by, you get closer and closer to the wall; you turn the steering wheel even more to avoid the wall, but your car is in love with the wall and wants to give it a big, fat kiss. If you think driving on ice and snow is scary, it is nothing compared to driving a racecar that is smooching a concrete wall at over 100 miles per hour. Racecar drivers do not like this experience at all.

With too much stagger, the racecar will be loose and will want to spin around. With too little stagger, the racecar will push up the track and hit the wall. Neither situation is good. So how do you know what is too much stagger or too little stagger? Most teams determine how much stagger they want to use at a particular track by practicing. The driver drives a few laps on the track with a certain set of tires to get a feeling for how the car is set up. After a few laps of practice, the driver calls the crew chief on the radio and tells him how the car is handling. If the car is not right or the driver is not comfortable, the crew will make the necessary changes until the car is set up correctly and the driver is comfortable. The crew logs all of the changes made to the car, including the amount of front and rear stagger, so that the next time the team competes at that track, it knows how to set up the car, including how much front and rear stagger is needed.

Tire Temperatures and Air Pressures

To assess how the racecar is performing, the crew needs to know how the tire contacts the surface of the track. Looking closely at tire temperatures tells the crew more about how the car is working than most drivers can.

Taking Tire Temperatures— Now Bend Over!

To take tire temperatures, you need a *pyrometer.* There are several different types of pyrometers; the easiest to use is the digital probe type. To read the tire's surface temperature, you stick this small device directly into the surface of the tire. Another type of pyrometer is the laser gun type. Both types give very accurate readings instantaneously.

Track Terms

A **pyrometer** is a device that measures the amount of heat on the surface of an object.

This is a digital pyrometer.

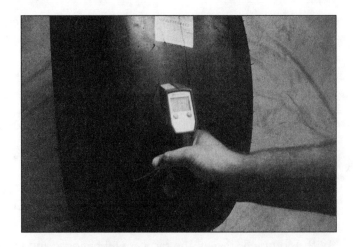

This is a laser pyrometer.

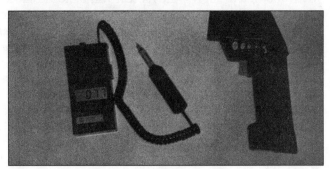

Where Do You Take the Temperature?

After a driver makes several very fast laps in practice, he or she comes off the track, and the crew goes to work quickly to take the tire temperatures. The crew needs the hottest temperatures possible to ensure that it gets the most accurate readings. Like most other materials, tires cool by spreading the heat across the face and dissipating heat, so the crew must take the tire temperature before that happens.

When taking tire temperatures, the crew must check three different locations on each tire:

➤ Outside the tread (O)

➤ Middle of the tread (M)

➤ Inside the tread (I)

The examples of tire temperatures in the following tables show temperatures from these three locations on each tire. The locations on the racecar are referred to as the right front (RF), right rear (RR), left front (LF), and the left rear (LR). Look at the following example of tire temperatures:

	O	M	I			I	M	O
LF	170	171	170		RF	195	200	205
LR	185	185	185		RR	195	195	195

Notice the right front tire has a growth in temperature along the face of the tire. This growth indicates that the tire does not hit flat on the track in the turn. Notice also that the right front tire is an average of 5 degrees hotter than the right rear tire. This difference is directly related to the fact that the right front tire doesn't hit flat along the track. It slides along the ground, rather than gripping the ground, making the tire hotter. This condition is a cause of understeer or a *tight*.

Let's look at the next set of tires:

	O	M	I			I	M	O
LF	170	171	170		RF	195	195	195
LR	190	190	190		RR	205	205	205

Notice that the rear tires are hotter than the front. This difference comes from the rear of the car sliding around in the turns, a condition known as over steer, or *loose*. You may have experienced this feeling in your own car. In wet weather, you drive up to a corner, turn the car like normal, and have the back of the car swing around, causing the car to spin out. Racecar drivers experience this feeling many times during a race. Sometimes drivers cause damage to tires by overheating them or by over-driving the car.

Track Terms

Tight is a term that describes how the racecar is handling. It refers to the front tires sliding across the track. The front end doesn't grip.

You now understand the basics, so let's go a little further. Take a look at the following tire temperatures:

	O	M	I			I	M	O
LF	170	175	170		RF	195	200	195
LR	190	190	190		RR	195	195	195

Notice that the middle temperatures are 5 degrees hotter in the center of the front tires. Two things can cause this difference. One is a chassis that has push in it that causes the tires to slide across the ground and heat up. This heat causes an unacceptable growth in air pressure. You may have had this happen to you in your own car: You turn the steering wheel, but the car continues going straight. The other reason for this condition is too much air pressure in the front tires. You may be asking

145

yourself, "Don't all tires have the correct pressure printed on the side of the tires?" No, race tires do not have this information. Goodyear, the manufacturer of the racing tires, provides a recommended pressure setting, but this recommendation is not set in stone.

Track Terms

Loose is the term that describes how the car handles when the rear tires slide across the track instead of gripping the track.

Inside Track

Lowering the air pressure of the rear tires helps the car grip. Raising the air pressures in the front tires can result in a more positive feel for the driver, but it can also make the car understeer, or push. If the tires become over inflated they don't have a flat tread width to ride on.

When to Pump It Up

Air pressure may not seem that important, but it directly relates to how the car handles. Normally, a race-car on a circle track has lower air pressure on the left side of the car than on the right side. This difference is because most of the weight of the car is applied to the right side tires in the turn. Having lower pressure in the left tires allows the tires to sit flatter and have more grip. The reason you can't run the lower pressures on the right side is that the tires, with all that weight applied, would fold over, having less than all of its tread surface flat to the ground. A folded-over tire is not good for traction.

Having low air pressure also gives the driver a mushy feeling, or the feeling of having a flat. If you have ever gotten a flat, you know the feeling that the car gives you just before it goes completely flat. You know something is wrong and that your car isn't driving the same. Air pressure can also be adjusted to help the handling of a car. When we talk about handling, we are referring to the push or loose condition we talked about earlier in the chapter.

So you can see, air pressure is more important than you may think. It's also important in your own car; keeping the proper air pressure in your tires can improve your car's feel and greatly improve gas mileage.

Let's look at some examples of tire pressures during race situations.

Example 1:

Before the race		After the race	
LF 14	RF 24	LF 20	RF 30
LR 14	RR 24	LR 20	RR 30

Example 1 shows good air pressure growth; the car is probably working well.

Example 2:

Before the race		After the race	
LF 14	RF 24	LF 21	RF 34
LR 14	RR 24	LR 20	RR 30

Example 2 shows too much front air pressure, especially right front pressure growth. This car probably has an under steer condition. This shows the right front tire was being used more than any other. Chassis adjustments are needed.

Example 3:

Before the race		After the race	
LF 14	RF 24	LF 20	RF 30
LR 14	RR 24	LR 23	RR 34

Example 3 shows too much rear tire pressure growth, indicating an over steer condition. Running the car like this will burn the tires off the car. Adjusting the chassis so the weight will be distributed more evenly, or more to the rear tires. Softer rear, or stiffer front springs will help correct this problem.

As you can see, air pressures and tire temperatures are important. These crucial measurements enable the crew to fine-tune the racecar.

Inside Track

Always check the air pressures in your tires. Too much or too little air pressure affects the handling of your racecar. Avoid problems before you go out on the racetrack by checking the air pressures.

Inside Track

Good air pressure growth is when both right side and left side tires grow evenly. If one tire's air pressure grows more than any other tire, the car has a problem.

The Least You Need to Know

➤ Always measure each tire in the same place on the tire.

➤ Tires have a direct effect on the handling of the car.

➤ Always measure tires before and after each practice session and race.

➤ Know the approximate stagger for each track before picking tires.

➤ Take at least three temperatures across the tread of the tire.

➤ Reset your air pressures before each practice session.

➤ Keep an accurate logbook about your tires.

Chapter 13

Shaking It Down

In This Chapter

➤ Knowing the importance of testing

➤ Setting and reaching testing goals

➤ Learning from test sessions

➤ Practicing for the pit stop

With any track, a number of factors can and do affect the performance of a racecar. The best way to determine how to set up a racecar for a given track is to practice at that track. Practice sessions, or *test sessions* as they are more commonly called, are the ideal time to tune the racecar for maximum performance.

As with any endeavor, the more you practice in stock car racing, the better you become. In the race shops and around the tracks, you may hear people talking about the amount of seat time (driving experience) a driver has in the racecar. In the next few pages, we talk in more detail about why seat time is important. During this time, a team finds out what works and what doesn't, finds the quickest line around the racetrack, and works out the kinks in the pit crew. The rest of the chapter talks about what goals the team should set for the test session and what the test session should teach the team.

Why Testing Is So Important

The first time you try something new, it usually takes some time to get it right. The same is true for stock car racing. Each track is different either in size or banking, each racecar can be different in how it was built or set up, and each driver has his or her own style of driving. These are just some of the major factors that can affect the performance of a racecar.

Eliminating Variables

In order to eliminate as many variables as possible, the best thing a race team can do is practice or test its racecars. Because it is illegal to drive a racecar on public streets, race teams need to test their racecars on the track. (Anyway, driving a racecar on public roads cannot simulate the conditions of driving on a racetrack.)

Race teams with big-dollar sponsorships or deep-pocketed car owners rent a track at which they compete for a day or two in order to test their racecars. Testing the racecar at a track where the team competes is a good idea because the team learns how to set up the racecar for that track and what the quickest way around that particular track is.

Inside Track

The goals for a test session are 1) learn how the racecar will perform at that track, and 2) learn about the track, including the quickest way or line around it.

Shake It Down

If a race team is new or has purchased or built a new racecar, the team needs to shake down the car before the team can be competitive in a race. Shaking down a car is like taking a test drive. You want to make sure everything on the racecar is working properly before you start pushing its limits. In other words, do not try to go 150 miles per hour down the front straightway until you're certain that the brakes and the steering are working properly. If they are not, the driver will be very unhappy, and the racecar will be very bent.

We talked briefly about how well-financed teams practice, but how do the unsponsored or weekend racers practice or test their racecars? Although all of these teams would love to have the financing to rent a track for a day or two, the harsh reality is that most of the small teams cannot afford to do this. If a team does not have the money to rent a track for a test session, the only other alternative is to use the hour or two before the race to practice or test the car. Although practicing at a track the day of the race is important, this time is usually used for making minor adjustments to the car and is not the time to find out if anything is broken or does not work.

Planning Is Everything

As we said earlier in this chapter, the goal of a test session is to determine the best setup for your racecar at that particular racetrack. However, this should not be your only goal. Many other things need to be done, and the first time to try these is not during a race. You will spend a lot of time and money getting into a race. When you get into a race, the driver, the racecar, the pit crew, and the crew chief all need to be ready for the race and for any situation that may arise during that race.

Before you go to a test session, put together a checklist of things you want to test as well as things you want to practice. For example, the critical part of any race is the pit stops. Racecars can gain positions and lose positions on the racetrack based on how quickly they can get into and out of the pits. You do not want the first time your crew performs a pit stop to be in a race. Many races are won or lost by the performance of the pit crew. Just look at Jeff Gordon and the Rainbow Warriors, as his pit crew is called. Jeff's pit crew was a major factor in all three of his Winston Cup championships.

Before the driver even gets into the racecar to do a practice run, the crew and the driver must look the car over and make sure all of the necessary components of the racecar are working properly. For example, a driver might simply start the engine to make sure that the engine is not leaking fluids and that the engine sounds good. When the driver steps on the gas, does the engine rev or is there a slight delay before the engine revs? If there is a delay, you may have a problem, which will need to be investigated. Do the lug nuts holding on the tires need to be tightened? Don't laugh; it does happen. (In fact, it has happened to one race team who shall remain anonymous.) Are the brakes working properly? Is the steering working properly? Is the racecar filled with fuel? We know these issues seem simple, but it is easy to forget to check the basics.

Inside Track

Use a pre-testing session checklist to ensure you did not forget to do something on the racecar before you go out on the track.

Going out on the Track

After you have checked and double-checked all of the basics, it is time to climb into your racecar and take it out on the track. Use the first few laps to warm up the racecar. Check to make sure that all of your gauges are working properly and your oil pressure is in the normal range. Check the brakes to get a feel as to how much pressure you need to apply to stop the racecar.

The goal of the first few laps of a test session is to ensure that the racecar is working properly and to get the driver comfortable with the racecar. These laps are often referred to as shaking down the racecar. These first few laps should be at a low speed. After you have checked to ensure that everything in the racecar is working, start to increase your speed to see how the racecar handles at a higher speed. As your speed increases, you will notice a change in how the racecar handles.

When the car first goes out on the racetrack, the tires are cold, which affects the handling of the racecar. After you make a few laps under higher speeds, the temperature of the tires increases, which changes the handling of the racecar. When the tires are cold, they do not grip the racetrack as well as when the tires are hot and sticky. Until the tires heat up, the racecar may be a little bit loose in the corners, but after the car gets some heat in the tires, it will grip the racetrack better.

How Does It Feel?

After the racecar has turned a few laps under higher speeds, the team can start to assess how it is performing. There are several ways to determine how the racecar is performing. The first and most important way is to ask the driver. The driver can tell the crew many things about how the car is performing.

The first thing to check is that the engine is accelerating when the driver steps on the accelerator. The crew wants to make sure that there is no delay from the time the accelerator is pressed to when the racecar accelerates. If there is a slight delay, the engine may have a problem and should be checked immediately. You need a perfect engine to test with.

Yellow Flag

If the engine does not accelerate as soon as the driver steps on the accelerator, the engine may have a problem. The driver should pull off the track so that the crew can check the car immediately.

Don't Push Me

If the engine is accelerating properly and sounds strong, the driver should then check how the racecar is handling in the turns. If the racecar wants to go straight when entering a turn, it has a push condition. A racecar with a push condition is very difficult to handle. To make the racecar turn, the driver must turn the steering wheel more than usual and lift off the accelerator, or slow down the racecar. Slowing down a racecar in order to make the racecar turn is not the optimal handling condition. Doing this will allow your competitors an opportunity to pass you in the turns.

It's a Loose One, Isn't It?

The opposite of a push condition is called a loose condition. A loose condition is when the racecar is turning too much when entering a turn and the back of the racecar loses traction and starts to slide around the front of the racecar. The condition gives the driver the feeling that the racecar is going to spin around in the turn. To prevent this from happening, the driver must lift off of the accelerator, or slow down the car, in order for the back of the racecar to regain traction. As with the push condition, slowing down will give your competitors an opportunity to pass you, which is not a good thing.

During a test session, you want to find out if your racecar is loose or pushing in the turns. Although we have explained these handling conditions as occurring when entering a turn, these conditions can also occur in the middle of the turn or when exiting a turn. The crew chief can watch the racecar to see whether these conditions exist, but the best person to tell you if these conditions are happening is the driver.

How can a driver tell whether these conditions are occurring? The short answer is by the seat of his or her pants. When a driver climbs into a racecar and straps in, he or she becomes part of the racecar. A driver is able to feel if the racecar is loose or if the racecar is pushing to the outside wall.

How Hot Is It?

Another way to find out how a racecar is performing is to check its tire temperatures. Tire temperatures provide a lot of information about how the racecar is performing. For example, if the tire temperature on the right front tire is much hotter than any other tire on the racecar, chances are that the car has a push and a cross weight condition. Change the cross weight and check camber on that tire.

Chances are that your racecar will have either a push condition or a loose condition the first time you go out on the racetrack. Do not worry about it. There are ways to correct both conditions. There are times is has neither. This is called being neutral. Most drivers like this since the car is smooth and easier to drive.

Inside Track

If the temperatures of a racecar's front tires are higher than the temperatures of the rear tires, it has a push condition. If only one tire shows increased and excessive growth, then check the camber and camber curve on that tire.

Changes: What Works and What Does Not

The goal of any test session is to find the best setup for the racecar at that particular track. This process of finding the best setup is not an easy or quick process. It involves a large amount of trial and error. You may make a change to your racecar to correct one problem only to find that you now have another problem to correct. Be patient. When making a change to a racecar, only make one change at a time. If you change multiple things at once, you will not be able to tell which change to

Inside Track

When making changes to the setup of your racecar, make only one change at a time and then go back out on the racetrack to see the effect of that change.

the racecar caused the change in the handling. Make one change, and then go back out on the racetrack for a few laps to see what effect that change has on the racecar.

The primary goal of any practice session is to determine what works and what does not work. It would be very difficult for us to explain in detail every possible change you could make on a racecar, but the following sections review some of the more common changes you could make on the racecar and how they effect its performance.

Tires

In Chapter 12, "A Good Set of Rubbers," we talked extensively about tires, tire temperatures, and tire stagger. When you are watching a Winston Cup race on television, you may hear the announcers saying that a particular team is making an air pressure adjustment. Air pressure adjustments change the stagger, or size of the tires, which in turn changes the handling of the racecar. Increasing the stagger or air pressure makes the racecar feel loose; decreasing the stagger or air pressure tightens up or creates a push condition in the racecar. Although increasing or decreasing the air pressure is an option for changing how the racecar handles, there are parameters for each tire and the amount of air pressure you can use.

Springs and Rubbers

Another way to change the handling of the racecar is to change the *spring rate* of the springs in the racecar. Because it would be rather difficult to change the springs in a racecar during a 17-second pit stop, pit crews change the spring rate with a spring rubber. A *spring rubber* is a piece of rubber, which is shaped to fit in between the bars of the spring. (Chapter 11, "Rocking and Rolling," explains the ins and outs of springs.)

Track Terms

Spring rate is the term used to identify the strength of a spring. Spring rates are measured in terms of pounds per inch of travel.

By adding a spring rubber to a spring, you are increasing the spring rate of that spring, or making the spring stronger. Increasing the spring rate of the right rear spring will help loosen the condition of the rear suspension of the racecar. Decreasing the spring rate, or removing a spring rubber, will help tighten the racecar. Because it is easier and quicker to remove a spring rubber than to add one, most race teams start out with spring rubbers in and then remove them if the racecar is not handling to their satisfaction.

In addition to adding or removing spring rubbers, another technique used is to compress or decompress a spring that is already in the racecar. The way this is accomplished is by turning a jacking bolt up or down, which is mounted above the spring. Turning down on the right rear bolt loosens up the racecar; loosening the bolt tightens up the racecar. The opposite is true for the left rear, turning down on the bolt will help tighten up the car, and turning out on the bolt will help loosen it up. The next time you are watching a NASCAR race pit stop, see if one of the pit crew members puts a long bar into a hole in the rear windshield and turns the bar once or twice. What that person is doing is turning the jacking bolt, which compresses or decompresses the spring and changes the handling of the racecar.

All of these methods are different ways in which a pit crew can change the handling of a racecar. Although there is no set rule for determining the best setup for a racecar, there is a rule of thumb: Change one thing at a time, test how it works, and then make another change. What you are doing is determining how a particular change will affect the racecar. The last thing you want to do is make a change to the racecar with no idea how that change is going to affect the racecar. Although you cannot predict with precision how a change will affect a racecar, you should basically know what effects that change would have. You want to eliminate as much guesswork as possible.

Things You Should Learn at a Test Session

So far in this chapter we have talked about why testing is so important, what goals should be set for a test session, and how to find out what works on your racecar. Now we need to talk about what you need to learn about the track during a test session.

Different Strokes for Different Tracks

Because every track is different in terms of size, shape, and banking, you cannot use what you learned about a ½-mile flat track on a 2-mile, high-banked superspeedway. Each track has its own personality and characteristics.

In order to be successful at stock car racing, you need to be familiar with the racetracks you race on. You must know how the racetrack is laid out. Is the surface smooth or bumpy? Does the track become narrow at any point? Does one turn have a tighter radius than the others? Is the outer edge of the racetrack surface faster than the inner edge? Knowing the answers to questions like these helps you be competitive in the race.

Track Lines

Each racetrack has at least one line around it that is the fastest line for your particular racecar. The line another racecar driver uses may not be the best line around the track for you. Finding out which line works best for you and your racecar is one of the things you need to learn at a test session. The *track line,* as most race teams refer it to, is different at every track, and some tracks may even be wide enough to have two lines.

One way to determine the track line for a particular track is to look for a black line on the track. At high speeds, the tires on the racecar wear away and leave rubber on the racetrack. That black line on the racetrack is the rubber left behind from other racecars. This line will give you an idea of the track line that some of the other racecars have been running. See how your racecar performs when it follows this line around the racetrack. You probably will have to adjust your line slightly, but this line is a good starting point.

Inside Track

When the tires on a racecar are going any direction but straight, they create friction, which slows down a racecar. This is not a good thing.

Handling the Turns

Most racetracks consist of two turns and two straightaways, an oval for the most part. The straightaways are pretty easy to figure out. The turns, however, are another matter. Because you want to maintain your speed for as long as possible before entering the turn, you need to figure out where or how you want to enter the turns. If you enter a turn from the inside of the straightaway, you will have to turn the steering wheel a large amount in order to complete the turn. However, if you enter the turn from the outside of the straightaway, close to the wall, you will not have to turn the steering wheel as much to complete the turn.

The ideal approach to entering a turn is to start from the outside of the racetrack and then drive the racecar across the racetrack. By the time you reach the middle of the turn, you want to have your racecar on the inside or bottom of the racetrack. Then as you complete the turn, you want to drive across the racetrack so that as you are back to the outside or top of the racetrack. This is the ideal track line for most racetracks. It allows you to maintain as much speed as possible and to turn the steering wheel as little as possible and puts you in the ideal position for going down the other straightaway. Keep the racecar close to the outside wall as you go down the straightaway and prepare yourself to enter the next turn. Remember this way: outside, inside, outside. You want to start a turn from the outside, be on the inside in the middle, and finish on the outside again. Try this a few times, and you will get the hang of it.

Inside Track

Keep good records on everything about your racecar and the racetrack. When you go to that racetrack, you will have notes to look back upon to see what worked and what did not work. This will also help for other tracks having the same conditions, whether it be the track surface, layout, or weather. Referring to notes is much easier than trying to remember everything about every track.

Although we can give you many ways to look for the ideal racetrack line, the only way to find it is to get out on the racetrack and see how your racecar performs. Be sure to have your crew chief or someone else on the crew taking lap times to see how fast your racecar is performing. It is also a good idea to have your crew tell you over the radio what your lap times are. Sometimes what you, the driver, may think was a bad or slow lap was actually a pretty good lap according to the stopwatch. This information will let you know what was not a good lap as well. Keep records of your lap times and of the line you were running.

What Would I Do?

Once you have the track line figured out, start thinking about scenarios. What would I do if this happened? What would I do if that happened? You want to be prepared for any and every situation you and your pit crew may face during a race.

Suppose you blow a tire and hit the outside wall. What are you and your pit crew going to do? Because this is a possible situation, you need to be prepared for it. The first thing you as the driver should do is try to get the racecar under control and off the wall. Check to make sure that there is no traffic coming up behind you, and then get to the bottom of the racetrack as quickly as possible. Hopefully, by this time, your crew chief has radioed you to make sure you are okay. If he hasn't, then fire him. He probably was a lousy crew chief anyway.

Now that you are on the bottom of the racetrack and out of the way of the other racecars on the tracks, head to pit road to have the tire changed and the rest of the racecar checked for additional damage. As you are heading back to pit road, see if your spotter can give your pit crew an idea of the damage to the car. This will give your pit crew a few extra seconds to get things ready for when you reach the pits.

The moment you hit the wall, your pit crew should have sprung into action. Crew members know that because the car blew a tire, they are going to have to change at least two tires, probably all four. That means your pit crew should be on the wall with all of the equipment needed to change four tires. The other pit crew members should be getting the equipment together needed to repair any body damage to the racecar. This equipment usually consists of one or more large hammers, duct tape, and a saw. With these tools, any body damage to a racecar can be repaired. It may not look pretty, but it will get you back on the racetrack.

As you approach your *pit box,* your pit crew should be ready to go. The first thing to do is to change the tires. Then do a very quick assessment of any other damage to the racecar. If everything looks basically okay, with the exception of the racecar having a flat side, get back out on the racetrack and see how the racecar is performing with the new tires. You may have another problem, which would require you to return to pit road.

Inside Track

Pit box, also know as a pit stall, are the terms used to identify the location on pit road where you are allowed to service your racecar.

This process sounds like a lot to do in a short period of time, and it is, which is why it is so important for you and your pit crew to be prepared for any situation you may encounter during a race. Imagine if the flat-tire scenario occurred and no one on your pit crew knew what to do. Crew members would be bumping into each other or grabbing for the same tool. You would pull into your pit box, and no one would know what to do. Practice, and be prepared. Make sure everyone on your race team knows what his or her job is at all times and in any circumstance. If you know this and practice this, you will be able to overcome almost any situation that can arise.

An additional benefit of running through possible scenarios that could occur on the racetrack is the practice your pit crew will get. The more practice a pit crew has servicing the racecar, the faster they will be able to perform that service. If your pit crew can get you serviced and back on the track in a shorter time than the other pit crews can get their racecars back on the track, you can gain track position without even being on the track. The only problem is that every other pit crew is working just as hard as you are for that advantage. Regardless, giving the pit crew practice at working on the racecar uncovers any kinks or problems that exist and gives the team the opportunity to resolve these issues before a race. By the time the pit crew goes to the racetrack, you want to make sure everything is resolved, and everyone knows exactly what needs to be done. So when you go to a test session, be sure to also test your pit crew. They are just as important as the racecar itself.

As you can see, test sessions are a very important part of being a successful race team. You need to test your equipment, learn about the tracks, and find out how to fine-tune your race setup, and test your pit crew. Each of these things is critical to being a successful race team and needs to be practiced on a regular basis. And we don't mean during a race.

The Least You Need to Know

➤ Use a checklist to prepare your racecar for a race or test session.

➤ Make one change at a time to your racecar. Then go out on the track and test that change.

➤ Try different things when searching for the best setup for your racecar.

➤ Find the track line that works best for you and your racecar.

➤ Keep good records about everything during a test session.

➤ Practice pit stops.

➤ Make sure everyone on the pit crew knows what his or her job is.

Part 4

Showing Your Stuff

In this next part, you will read about the reason behind qualifying for a race. In addition, you will learn how to set up your racecar to let it all hang out *during the qualifying run.*

Before you can race 500 miles, you need to be able to turn a good qualifying time. It is your first chance to show your stuff on the racetrack, so make sure that you do a good job. After all, you don't get the chance to make a first impression again, at least not at that race. Last, but not least, you will learn how racecar drivers prepare themselves for a qualifying run.

Chapter 14

Why Is There a Need to Qualify?

In This Chapter

➤ Who races and who goes home early

➤ Provisional starting positions

➤ Championship points and what they get you

➤ Deciding who goes first

➤ The pros and cons of qualifying

What is the purpose of qualifying? If all stock car drivers are professionals, why then do they need to qualify in order to compete in a stock car race? Qualifying, which takes place at stock car races, does not involve checking your qualifications, like when you are applying for a job. Qualifying at stock car races involves seeing how fast your racecar can go. The faster you go, the closer you start to the front; the slower you go, the closer to the back you start. The primary purpose of qualifying is to determine the starting order for the race.

Qualifying in a stock car race is just one of NASCAR's attempts to keep things as fair as possible. The idea behind qualifying is that any and every race team has an equal chance to start on the front row. If a race team has a bad performance in one race, it does not affect the team's starting position at the next race. At each race, every race team has an equal chance of starting on the front row based on how the teams qualify their racecars.

Qualifying: Who Gets In?

The purpose of qualifying is to determine who gets into the race and who has to go home early. In most cases, only the top 44 racecars get to compete in the race. But in some cases, championship points and even the postmark on the entry form may determine who has the opportunity to race.

Second Chance to Race

In addition to the top 40 racecars, there are usually four additional racecars allowed to compete even though they did not qualify in the top 40. These last four positions are called provisional starting positions or just *provisionals*. Provisionals are awarded to racecars that did not qualify for the race and are in the top 35 in championship points. But this will vary from one series to another.

The idea behind provisional starting positions is simple. Anyone can have a bad day, even the best racecar driver. If a racecar driver has a bad qualifying effort, then that driver is unable to compete in the race. Provisionals are like forgiving someone for doing something bad. Even if a racecar driver has a bad qualifying effort, he or she can still get into the race by taking a provisional starting position.

Inside Track

The fastest racecar during qualifying starts the race in the best spot, called the pole position. Being fastest in qualifying is called "winning the pole."

Provisional starting positions will get drivers into the race, but there is a penalty for taking a provisional starting position. Remember we said earlier that the fastest racecar starts in the first starting position? Racecar drivers who take provisional starting positions aren't that lucky. The penalty for taking a provisional starting position is that the driver must start the race in one of the last four positions. That means the driver will have at least 40 racecars starting in front of him or her. In order to win the race, the driver will have to pass all of these racecars. This position is obviously not the best place to start a race from.

Track Terms

Championship points are the points awarded to a race team for competing in a stock car race.

Although provisionals are available at every race, they are not available to every race team that attends a race. Provisional starting positions are only available to race teams who are in the top 35 in *championship points*. At the conclusion of every stock car race, each race team is awarded a certain number of championship points. The higher you finish in the race, the more championship points you are awarded. Therefore, the more races you attend and compete in, the more points you will be awarded.

Because stock car racing is so competitive and so expensive, not every race team is able to attend every race. If a team does not attend and compete in enough races to accumulate enough championship points to stay in the top 35 in points standing, then that team will not be eligible for a provisional starting position. Provisionals are basically a benefit to the race teams who attend every race, but have a bad day and need some forgiveness.

Even if a team does not qualify for a race, it may still be awarded championship points for attempting to qualify. In some NASCAR racing series, it is possible to accumulate enough points by attempting to qualify in every race to end the year in the top 35 in points. Doing this will make a team eligible for a provisional starting position in the first few races of the following season.

Rain Outs

Even though the NASCAR racing season is during the spring and summer months when the weather is nice, occasionally the weather does not cooperate, and qualifying can be delayed or even cancelled. When qualifying is cancelled, how are the starting positions for a race determined?

When qualifying is rained out, the starting positions for a race are determined by the championship points standing. Number one in the points standing starts in the number one starting position, number two in points, starts in the number two starting position, and so on back to the thirty-fifth starting position. That covers the first 35 starting positions, but what about the remaining positions? How are they determined?

The remaining starting positions are determined by the date of the postmark on the race entry form that is mailed to NASCAR. That's right—whoever mailed his entry form into NASCAR first and is not already in the top 35 in championship points gets the thirty-sixth position and so on. This is another way NASCAR gives every race team the opportunity to compete in a race. So if your racecar is not fast enough to qualify or if qualifying is rained out, you still have an opportunity to compete in the race.

Inside Track

Fill out and mail your race entry forms into NASCAR as soon as you get them. It could mean the difference between racing and going home. One way to ensure your entry form is postmarked correctly is to bring it to the post office yourself and ask for a copy of the postmarked letter. This way you have proof of when you mailed the entry form.

The Lottery

Now you know why all stock car races have qualifying. The next question is how the order of qualifying is determined. In an effort to keep things as fair as possible and to avoid showing favoritism, the order in which racecars qualify for a race is determined by a lottery. For example, if 75 racecars show up for a race, the NASCAR officials will put numbers 1 to 75 in a hat. One member from each race team then picks a number from the hat, without looking, of course, and whatever number is picked is the qualifying position for that team. In some cases, the officials really use a hat, or in most cases, they use a bingo wheel with the numbers in it. A team member turns the wheel to mix up the numbers and then picks a number. Either way, this is the fairest way for determining the qualifying order for a race.

Now you may be wondering, what difference does it make if you qualify first or if you qualify last? If you were to ask five different crew chiefs this question, you would probably get five different answers. Some race teams prefer to qualify last because then they will know how fast they need to go in order to get into the race. Others may want to qualify first so that they can start working on their race setup right away.

Inside Track

For a qualifying attempt, use lightweight oils in your engine, transmission, and rear end to make your car faster. Lightweight oils flow easier than heavyweight oils and will increase horsepower.

Most teams set up their racecars differently from qualifying to the race. After all, the goal of qualifying is to go as fast as possible for only two laps, but the goal of winning the race is to go as fast as possible for 500 miles and win the race. There are things race teams can do to the setup of a racecar that will make it faster over a few laps but will not last for an entire race.

After a race team completes its qualifying laps, the pit crew has to go to work to change the racecar from a qualifying setup to a race setup. This change takes time, and some teams are more concerned about the race setup and want to start working on it as soon as possible. By qualifying first and getting back to the garage area, a team will have more time to work on its race setup than a team that is qualifying last.

Pros and Cons of Qualifying Positions

As with anything in racing, there are both pros and cons to qualifying positions. In the previous section, we talked briefly about qualifying first versus qualifying last. The following sections provide more details on this issue.

Why Qualifying First Is Good

By qualifying first, you are setting the benchmark that every other team must beat. You have the opportunity to spend more time working on your race setup, and you will be qualifying under the current weather conditions, which affects the racecar performance and track conditions. As each racecar attempts to qualify, more rubber is put down on the racetrack, which also affects the performance of the racecar.

Why Qualifying First Is Bad

By qualifying first, you need to have your racecar setup completed with the pre-qualifying inspections and be on line and ready to go before any one else does. This means that you will have less time to prepare your racecar for qualifying than a team that is qualifying much later.

Another down side to qualifying first is that you will be qualifying on what is referred to as a green track. A *green track* is when there has been very little if any new rubber put down on the track surface by other racecars in your series. As each racecar makes a lap on the racetrack a certain amount of rubber is left on the track. Most green racetracks are tight and make it difficult for the driver to turn the racecar.

Why Qualifying Last Is Good

If you qualify last or toward the back of the field, then you have the opportunity to know how fast you must go in order to get into the race. You also have more time to work on your qualifying setup and have the benefit of seeing which track line other racecar drivers are following and how that line worked for them. Most drivers and teams prefer to attempt their qualifying runs after most of the other drivers have already gone.

Inside Track

Each different series, NASCAR Winston Cup Series, Busch North Series, and Featherlite Modified Series, uses different tires. These tires have different tire compounds (refer to Chapter 12). Each of these series may race on the same weekend, and qualify on the same day. The mixture of compounds affects the next style of tire that is used on the track. The most commonly affected tires are radials against a bias ply tire.

Why Qualifying Last Is Bad

The downside of qualifying last is that the weather can change from the time you set up your racecar to the time you attempt to qualify. Once your racecar has been inspected, you cannot make any changes to the racecar until after you qualify. This means that if you set up your racecar in anticipation for a late-afternoon qualifying attempt, when the temperatures are cooler, and the weather remains hot into the afternoon, your racecar will not perform as well.

Another issue is that if someone qualifying in front of you crashes and breaks something in their engine and puts oil on the track, the track will be slippery, which will reduce your qualifying speed. You can see that many factors can affect the performance of the racecar and how you qualify. The only thing you can do is set up your racecar for what you think the conditions will be and hope you guessed correctly.

Race Position

Why is it so important to start a race up front? The most obvious reason is that if you are starting up front or on the front row, you are that much closer to the finish line and winning the race. Another reason is that you have 43 other racecars that you do not have to worry about trying to pass to get to the front because. you are already in the front. The down side of starting up front, if there is such a thing, is that you have 43 other racecars all trying to catch and pass you. Is it better to be the chaser or the car being chased? Personally, we would rather be chased.

Starting in the Rear

Qualifying poorly and having to start the race in the back of the field also has its pros and cons. The first pro is that at least you are in the race and did not have to go home early. The worst thing for a race team is to work hard all week long back at the shop, work even harder at the racetrack, and then find out that all that work was for nothing because the team did not qualify. So given the choice between starting last in a race and going home early, any race team would rather start last. So be happy you made it into the race, regardless of how you made it there. Either way, qualifying is better than packing up and going home early.

The cons to starting in the back of the field are fairly obvious. Having 43 racecars between you and the finish line is no small obstacle to overcome. Passing another racecar is not an easy task, especially at 190 miles per hour.

Another disadvantage of starting the race in the back is the location of your *pit stall*. Pit stalls are assigned, for the most part, based on qualifying position. If you qualify up front, then you will have a pit stall closer to the end of pit road. If you qualify in the back of the field, then your pit stall will be closer to the beginning of pit road.

The goal of a good pit stop is to spend as little time on pit road as possible. If your pit stall is located at the end of pit road, then you will be able to get back out on the track quicker and unobstructed by another racecar. If your pit stall is at the beginning of pit road, you may be slowed by other racecars exiting their pit stalls when you pull out of your pit stall to get back on the racetrack. Many races have been won and lost by what happens on pit road. A pit stall closer to the end of pit road will allow you to get back on the track quicker than a pit stall at the beginning of pit road.

Track Terms

A **pit stall** is the assigned position on pit road for teams to perform their pit road duties.

I Can't See

Imagine that you are starting dead last in the race. At about lap 40, you see that two cars up toward the front of the pack got together and hit the outside wall. Now all of the racecars behind them slow down to avoid the crash. The driver of a racecar in front of you decides to intentionally spin his car around to avoid the accident because he would not be able to stop in time. Spinning the racecar around creates a wall of tire smoke across the track, which blinds you from seeing where the crash is and which way the other racecars are going to avoid the crash.

You look down at the tachometer, because there are no speedometers in racecars; you are going 150 miles per hour. You cannot see through the smoke, and you are not sure if the crashed racecars are still up against the wall. If you take your foot off of the accelerator, you will lose valuable speed and possibly track position. If you go low on the track to avoid where the crash happened, you may get hit by the crashed racecars sliding down the racetrack. If you stay high and try to drive through the tire smoke, you are risking a crash with the racecars up against the wall.

If you are a racing fan, you know this is a very possible scenario. If you saw the movie *Days of Thunder* with Tom Cruise, you know how he handled it. He drove directly at the crash, expecting the cars to slide out of the way by the time he got there, as would typically happen. But that didn't happen. A more serious crash took place. No matter what decision you make in this scenario, if you had qualified up front, then all of this would be happening behind you and to someone else. By the time you would go around the track, the caution flag would be out, and you would not have to worry about the crash, in most cases.

The major disadvantage to starting in the back of the field is that not only do you have to worry about how to get to the front of the pack, but you also are at a greater risk of getting caught up in a crash in front of you. All it takes is one racecar with a poor setup, an overly aggressive driver, or simply being in the wrong place at the wrong time, and your day can be done in an instant.

Yellow Flag

You are at greater risk of being involved in a crash when starting a race in the back of the field than when starting the race in the front.

An "A" for Effort

In this chapter, we have talked to a large extent about qualifying: why there is qualifying at a stock car race, how the qualifying order is determined, and what happens if or when qualifying is cancelled because of rain. We also talked about what a provisional starting position is and the benefits and disadvantages of starting a race from the front and from the rear.

As you can now see, there are other benefits to a good qualifying effort besides starting on the front row. One benefit we have not talked about so far is how a good qualifying effort can benefit the team over a period of time. Everyone knows that the winner of a race receives the most prize money, championship points, and general media attention. What most people do not know is that a consistent qualifying effort, even if you do not win or even finish the race, also draws attention to the team. Qualifying for a race is the first time that the team can show its stuff.

In the early years of stock car racing, qualifying did not mean much. The only one who received attention from stock car racing was the winner. Today that has all changed. Stock car racing has become so popular that even the qualifying sessions are broadcasted on national television. Pole winners, the top qualifiers, are interviewed by television, radio, and newspaper reporters. All of this attention given to the driver, the team, and the racecar helps race teams attract sponsors.

Sponsors and Fans

As stock car racing becomes more competitive, the cost of running a competitive race team goes up. The way race teams keep up with these expenses is by attracting and keeping corporate sponsors. Corporate sponsors are drawn to the sport of stock car racing because of its increase in popularity in recent years, its brand-loyal fans, and its increased television coverage.

Under the Hood

Marketing studies have shown that NASCAR fans buy products just because the company that makes the product is the sponsor of their favorite racecar driver.

Everyone wants to be a part of or a fan of the winning team. Corporate sponsors are no exception to this. With big-name teams practically having their choice of big-name corporate sponsors, that does not leave much for the mid-size corporate sponsor to choose from. Many small- to mid-size corporations would like to be involved in stock car racing. However, they do not have enough money to spend on sponsorships to put their name on the racecar of someone like a Jeff Gordon or Dale Earnhardt.

Even if you have not won a race yet, but you have a track record of good qualifying efforts, you can use this record to attract one of the small- to mid-size corporate sponsors to your team. Corporations are willing to spend money as long as they feel it is money well spent. In regards to stock car racing, money well spent means lots of exposure. Remember that the reason the sponsor signed on with you is because the company wants to get the greatest exposure possible.

A top qualifier gets just as much exposure as the winner of a race. Be sure to use the qualifying sessions not only as your attempt to get into the race, but to also promote your sponsor as well. Remember qualifying is the opportunity for you to show your stuff. That stuff includes your racing ability, team effort, and promoting your sponsor. Qualifying is the first step toward victory lane, so be sure not to spin your tires and hit the wall.

The Least You Need to Know

➤ Qualifying determines the starting order for the race.

➤ Provisional starting positions are taken by drivers who are in the top 35 in championship points and failed to qualify.

➤ If you do not qualify for a race, you will still be awarded some championship points.

➤ Send your race entry form in right away. It could mean the difference between racing and going home early.

➤ A pit stall closer to the end of pit road enables a driver to get back on the track quicker.

➤ Qualifying is your first chance to show off at a race. Be sure to give it your best effort, and qualifying last will enable that team to know exactly how fast they need to go to get in the race.

Chapter 15

Putting It on the Edge

In This Chapter

➤ Understanding shock pressures

➤ Taping the grills: down force 101

➤ Dealing with the weather

In Chapter 11, "Rocking and Rolling," you learned that shocks can and do have different effects on the car by having various pressures. You can achieve different pressures by changing valve stacks in adjustable shocks or by purchasing many different preset, valve-stacked, nonadjustable shocks.

This chapter covers shock valves, jetting, and pressures. It also explains how weather affects racing by describing how different weather conditions affect the tracks, the car and engine, and the racing crews. You will also learn about taping the front grills, including how taping works, why less is more, and why more may be needed.

How Do They Work?

You need to learn how the shock works in order to learn how to use it to adjust the car for racing or qualifying. The shock is made up basically of a body, a shaft piston with valve stacks, and nitrogen-packed oil. It has many more parts, but these are the working parts of the shock. As the piston travels up and down inside the body, the resistance is regulated by how slowly or quickly the oil can pass through the piston, thus allowing the piston to travel up or down in the body.

Under the Hood

Teams always have more than the four shocks they have on the car. There is always a back-up set, a set for qualifying, and another set to change the personality of the car. By having these extra shocks, teams can make changes very quickly and take advantage of all the practice time given for a race.

The compression stroke is the shortening of the shock or when the car rolls over onto the shock. The rebound stroke is the action of the shock extending or getting longer. Each of these actions has a valve stack to control the speed of the motion. The stack is made up of four shims, all of different diameters. The thickness of each of these shims determines the strength of the stack and how much resistance it will put on the piston traveling through the oil. In addition, different pistons require different valve stacks to do the same thing.

Inside Track

Running your shocks on a shock dyno with a specialized operator will ensure you have exactly the valve and pressure combinations you desire. You can revalve your own shocks, but make sure that at some point you check them on the dyno.

There is also a jet in the top of the shaft, which allows oil to go through and around the valve stack. By changing this jet (referred to as *jetting*), you can change the way both sides of the piston will pass, compress, and rebound. Jetting softens the valve stacks equally.

With so many variables and so many choices, teams must have a specialized shock person to ensure proper choices are made. Teams also purchase or rent the services of a shock *dyno*. This computerized machine tests the performance of shocks so that the smallest of changes can be made and recorded for future use. By testing each shock, teams also can be sure that the valving they have chosen is the resistance they need or want. This testing also gives teams a baseline to refer to while making changes in practice or the race.

Vince Valeriano goes to every race on the Busch North Series Tour and assists teams with shock valving and jetting. He assists in shock assembly and suggests changes teams can make to quicken lap times. He brings a truck full of parts and a computerized shock dyno. Vince Valeriano says, "the shocks are similar to the timing in the motor. You can slow or quicken the roll and attitude of the car by valving or jetting your shocks. Shocks carry the car into the corner, hold it smooth, and softly bring it off the corner onto the straightaway."

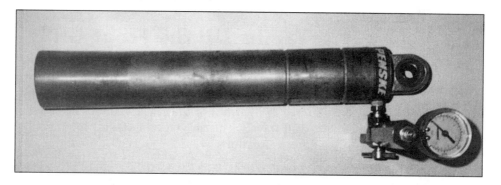

This gauge allows accurate pressure changes and is small enough to attach with the shock still on the car.

Why Different Shock Pressures Are Necessary

The track surface, the speed of the car, track shape, and track size all have an effect on the shocks. As the car goes through the corner, it changes where the weight is applied, and the shocks regulate this change and make it a smooth transition. If the car doesn't transfer weight soon enough as it enters the corner, then making a change to the left rear rebound and right front compression pressure will help transfer weight more quickly. If the weight transfers too quickly, the opposite changes will be required. Adjusting shocks takes time and experience. Basic tuning skills apply, but hands-on experience is needed to be a professional.

Shocks are pressurized with nitrogen, which is clean, dry air. The amount of nitrogen is determined by the manufacturer first and then the crew chief. Adding nitrogen changes the spring rate in the car. The more nitrogen pressure the crew adds,

Yellow Flag

Always use nitrogen in your shocks. Never use compressed air to pressurize your shocks. Compressed air is prone to water contamination, and that will alter the performance of the shock.

the higher the spring rate becomes. Teams adjust the nitrogen pressure as they need to, for example, when qualifying. Many teams raise the pressure in the front shocks 25 pounds or more to compensate for the extra front down force of the taped front grills. The rear shocks may be increased 10 pounds or more to help in heating the tires more quickly for qualifying.

Inside Track

For qualifying, pump up the pressure in the front shocks about 25 pounds. This increased pressure overcomes the increased down force you get from taping up the front grills and allows the car to be more free in the air (but keeps it under the driver's control). The increase in front down force loosens up the rear of the car and makes it faster, but more difficult to drive.

Yellow Flag

By taping up the front grills, teams can make the car faster through the air, but taping can also heat up the motor and cause race-ending damage. Be sure to tape enough of the grill to free up the back of the car, but not too much to make the engine overheat.

Taping Up the Front Grills

Teams use duct tape in different colors to cover some or all of the grills and front valance. With all the grills open and front brake ducts and cooling holes uncovered in the front of the car, the car absorbs a lot of air as it travels. This air gives the racecar too much lift for most situations.

Why and When to Tape

Taping the grills and front ducts allows race teams to direct the air going over the top of the car. Keep in mind that air is not moving over the car, the car is moving through the air. Air travels at about 5 to 30 miles per hour, and the car is going 100 to over 200 miles per hour. This speed gives the car the right of way. As the air is pushed out of the way and flows around the car, it forces the car to the ground. This force helps the tires get a firm grip on the track.

Letting the air into the grills and brake ducts not only cools the radiator, oil, and brakes, but it also removes down force on the car and creates lift. The lift we are talking about is the air getting scooped up by the open holes and pushed up against the parts using this air. Sometimes this lift makes the car push or creates an understeer condition because the front of the car is lifted slightly, which causes the front tires to lose traction.

The Effects of Taping

Taping some of the grills allows less air inside the car, forcing it around the car or over the top of it. This air pushes down on the car allowing more traction, more turning, and faster corner speeds. Taping different portions of the front grills lets you control how you want the air to travel over or through the car and puts you in control over Mother Nature, or as close to it as possible.

Air is free, and the correct use of it is imperative to going fast. By taping up almost all the vents and grills in the front of the car, you can harness the power of all the air the car travels through. Taping all the grills puts maximum down force on the front of the car, making all the front turning available to the driver.

Keep in mind that taping the grills does have an affect on the rear of the car. The rear of the car loosens quite a bit, making the rear end of the car come around on you. By controlling this action, you get maximum speed from the car. Extensive taping is usually used only for qualifying because making the car this loose in the rear is detrimental to good tire wear and makes the car harder to drive. You can't race like this. But you can make two laps this way. You also need to adjust shock pressures by increasing about 25 pounds. This will compensate for the increased down force due to taping the front grills.

Taping for qualifying is time consuming, because the tape must be very smooth and free of bumps, tears, and other imperfections. The crew tapes the grills closed or nearly closed. The crew also tapes any cooling ducts, such as those for the oil coolers or for the brakes. For one or two laps, this taping will have no affect on the performance of these parts because the crew disconnects the oil coolers completely anyway, and brakes can operate without cooling for several laps.

But keep in mind that closing the main grills that cool the radiator can be very dangerous because the water temperature in the motor rises quickly. You may have seen this situation many times during qualifying when the car shuts down and you can see a trail of steam or water being pumped out the back. This trail means the car heated up in only one or two laps and couldn't run at extended periods of time with the grills completely covered.

Inside Track

Teams also use a clear tape made by Dupont to cover the entire front section of the car. This tape allows all the sponsors' paint color and stickers to be seen clearly and smoothes out any imperfections and transitions from the grill covers to the bumper cover. This tape also keeps the track debris from harming the extensive paint schemes seen on racecars.

Inside Track

Disconnect the oil cooler during the qualifying laps. It's not necessary for this short of a time, and disconnecting it will add to your horsepower by causing the oil to heat up and thin more quickly. Disconnecting the cooler also allows you to close any openings in the grill for the cooler, which will add to down force.

Engine damage can happen very quickly if the engine is overheated. Cracked blocks and heads, blown head gaskets, or burnt pistons can cause a major crash by dropping water or oil on the track.

How Weather Affects the Track

Weather affects everything from racecars to crews to the track surface. The track surface is susceptible to temperature and moisture content. Even on a regular day with the sun shining, the track has some moisture on it from the overnight temperature change. It is also porous and holds water from rain. If it rained yesterday, the track would still be somewhat wet today. The cars running on it eventually dry the track out, and that in turn changes the surface once again. A wet surface reduces traction, and as the track dries, you will have to loosen the car to make it turn.

A cloudy day reduces the track temperature and allows for some quicker lap times due to better traction. As the sun comes out and the track heats up, the track in turn heats the tires. Most tracks are made form asphalt, and asphalt is made of an oil base. As the sunny day progresses and the track starts to hold the heat, the oily base comes up and affects traction. Track crews use the best possible sealant to reduce the affect of this base, but nothing works 100 percent in this situation.

Under the Hood

Overcast days are the biggest problem for racers because these days are sometimes cloudy and sometimes sunny. Cloudy moments cool the track and cause the racecars to be tight or understeer, and sunny moments make the track too hot and cause the racecars to be loose or oversteer. The track is very unpredictable, so most crew chiefs pick a setup that may not be the quickest, but is more adjustable. The smartest crews and drivers can be front row qualifiers often, some one time pole winners may have guessed right for the current conditions.

On extremely hot days, the track also compresses slightly, giving a soft feeling to drivers and making the track come apart. Chunks of asphalt sometimes break away and create holes in the track, creating another obstacle for drivers and crews. This happens quite frequently with new tracks or tracks that haven't had heavy cars race on them. The track is also affected by wind blowing dirt, sand, and debris onto the track;

this debris affects traction. If the track is anything but clean, warm, and dry, the tires won't adhere to the track. It's like having a wet package and trying to apply tape; the tape kind of stays on the package, but it is easily pulled off. Tires react the same, due largely in part to the weather.

Some crews watch and adjust the car right up until it is their time for the qualifying laps. As cars are qualifying, the clouds move over the track to cool the track and then move off, allowing the sun to shine and heat the track. This movement happens many times, and crews scramble to adjust tire pressure and tape for the changing conditions.

The worst thing that could happen is that the crew puts on some tape because of cloudy skies, and when the car pulls out onto the track, the sun appears, making the car too loose to drive and the qualifying effort not up to par with where the team was running. This happens often, and crews must suck it up and either accept the time they get or run in the second round of qualifications and hope they choose more wisely. Use of weather stations can help greatly during qualifying. Crews can make closely calculated changes to the jetting of the fuel curve in the engine to produce maximum horsepower.

This weather station gives the air temperature, the relative humidity, a barometer reading, and the air density; it is a good basic system.

How Weather Affects the Car

Weather also affects the jetting of the engine and how much fuel can be given to the engine. The more oxygen-packed the air is, the more fuel the engine can use efficiently to produce horsepower. As the air thins out, the ability for making horsepower does, too. Engines need air and fuel to produce maximum power, and when one or both of these are eliminated, so is your horsepower. Engine builders walk the fine line between too much and too little fuel. A step over the line on the rich side means the car will go slow; a step over on the lean side burns up the engine. Teams have an engine tuning specialist for just this reason.

As the weather changes, the engine tuner adjusts the jets and timing in the engine. There are many ways to do this: the crew can change main jets in the carburetor or change air bleeds to make small adjustments. *Air bleeds* control the mixture of air during different speed ranges of the motor.

The crew can also change the ignition timing by moving the distributor and making the spark advance change as weather conditions permit. Most race engines can use spark advances of 28 to 55 degrees advance. Most stock car engines perform best between 36 and 44 degrees advanced timing. This means that at about 40 degrees, before the piston reaches "top dead center" (this being its furthest travel upward before starting its rotation down the cylinder), the spark plug fires and starts to ignite the air and gas in that chamber. Maximum compression then occurs at the time of complete ignition and produces the most power, forcing the piston downward as fast as is possible in the current conditions.

When conditions are good, timing can be reduced slightly, and better power can be obtained with less chance of detonation. *Detonation* is the knocking you hear in your engine when you use bad gas or when you're trying to drive an engine that's ready to overheat. Detonation is caused by gases rapidly combusting from more than one place in the cylinder or chamber and meeting, causing the sound you hear. This greatly reduces power output and can do terrible damage to your engine.

Weather affects the crew, too. Much research has been done on how weather affects the human mind and what the state of weather can do to the state of the mind. Simply put, bad weather results in bad attitudes; good weather results in good attitudes. Of course, this blanket statement doesn't apply to all people, but it does apply to the majority. We have found that on a rainy or rain-threatened day crews in the garage area are negative and down. On sunny, warm days, the teams are more apt to be positive and happy. And a happy crew is a hard-working crew. After all, who wants to run around in the rain and lay under a car getting wet?

Yellow Flag

When tuning your engine, be sure not to lean out the main jets too much, or you will burn the pistons. Leaning out the mixture creates horsepower, but it also creates a lot of heat.

Yellow Flag

Beware of detonation inside your engine. The name alone should scare you. Detonation causes severe engine failure, burning pistons, valves, and cylinder heads. It's caused by excessive heat, too much timing, or bad gas.

This basic timing light works well and is easy to use.

This chapter explained the need for exacting shock pressures and an expert to adjust them. Shocks are more than comfort pieces on the car. They are precise tuning tools and can be an integral part of a great setup.

Taping the car can give you more front down force, but you must compensate with shock adjustments. Taping gives you control of the front area because you can adjust as much as you need to create the desired feel for the driver. However, if you tape too much of the grill, you can cook your engine; taping too little could hurt the front turning force.

Weather changes affect the track dramatically and can change the outcome of a race. The track changes due to sun and heat and can go from loose to tight in a matter of minutes. Weather also changes engine tune-ups. *Fuel curve* and timing can have a great deal to do with horsepower, and they both need to be adjusted according to the weather.

Track Terms

Fuel curve refers to the volume of fuel needed by an engine during the course of the RPM (revolutions per minute) of the engine. The engine will "pull" more fuel per RPM during higher torque loads.

179

The Least You Need to Know

➤ Shocks need to be adjusted to the springs and track.

➤ The wrong shocks can make for a slow ride around the track.

➤ Taping the front grill can give you much-needed down force.

➤ Adjust the shocks and springs when you tape the front grill.

➤ Weather changes the track: Heat makes it slippery, and cold gives it more traction.

➤ Weather differences cause the need for engine tuning changes.

Chapter 16

Foot to the Floor

In This Chapter

➤ Thinking with your head, not your foot

➤ Driving into the corners too fast

➤ Driving with your left foot

Before you get into the car, you need to be prepared mentally. We don't mean you need to have your head examined, although the more we race, the more we believe that needs to be an off-season requirement for qualified drivers! We mean you need to have peace of mind and focus. You need to have a plan, and you also need to be thinking clearly. Getting onto a racecar with anger will make you either a hazard to the other competitors or a statistic in the record book for cautions and wrecks. In this chapter, we talk about things a driver should think about and some of the things he or she shouldn't think about. We also explain how to drive the car in the corner, apply the throttle, and brake.

Mental Preparation

More than half the current drivers will admit to having either some nervousness or butterflies before the start of each race. If more than half will admit to it, one has to wonder what the true percentage is. We would bet it is about 75 percent. Some drivers need the encouragement of a little high blood pressure to get the best out of them; these drivers get focused only after something pressures them into this state of mind.

Of course, every driver is different. From my experience, there are five different types of drivers:

➤ **The angry driver.** If your car handles well, it's very easy to dispose of angry drivers. They are usually driving in over their heads and always on the edge. It's easy to get them to make a mistake or nudge them off their edge. A little self-control can go a long way against this type of driver.

➤ **The happy driver.** This driver talks and jokes with the crew throughout the race.

➤ **The clueless driver.** This driver scares me the most. Clueless drivers act as if they have no idea they are even in the car, nor do they remember driving in the race. Clueless drivers come down on you when you're under them entering the corner. This type of driver is also likely to pin you against the wall without ever knowing you're there.

➤ **The just-another-day driver.** This driver has no change in attitude at any time before during or after, has no apprehensions about being in the car. The size of the track nor the drivers around them have any affect on them.

Inside Track

Clear your mind of all unnecessary thoughts before a race. Don't take for granted that you can drive while not fully concentrating on the job at hand. Stock car racing needs your full attention.

➤ **The scared-to-be-in-the-car driver.** This type of driver is scared or always apprehensive to be in the car. They have great fear of what could happen to them, and are nervous to be around other cars. This doesn't always make them dangerous or bad drivers. In fact there are some very good and winning drivers who still fear getting into the car. Most will not admit they are scared at all, but show signs of it before, during, and after the race. Like the nervous and jumpy way before the race, and sigh of relief and jovial demeanor right after the race.

No matter what kind of driver you are, you need to prepare yourself mentally to be successful in racing.

The Importance of Focus

We have all had to focus on one thing or another, and driving a racecar is something to focus on very intensely. But don't make yourself nervous. You need to develop skills to attain pre-race focus.

Most drivers have a routine or ritual they do before every race. Most drivers don't admit to being superstitious, but many of them certainly engage in superstitious behavior. They always have to put their shoes on the same way, put on their gloves before their helmets, eat the same thing every race day morning, talk to the same people before every race, or even wear the same underwear to every race (ugh!). These activities help drivers focus on the race, and focus is needed to perform at your best.

Things to Remember

When preparing yourself to get in the car, remember that you will be in the car for a long time, and getting out is not an option, unless you are sick or feel that your participation in the event will cause a dangerous condition. Upon entering the car and strapping in, make sure your radio works. Check that you have communication between you and your crew and establish communication with the spotter.

Look around the inside of the car to ensure all tools and equipment have been removed. Test any device your going to need during the race, such as the fans, pumps, or driver cooling systems. You won't get a chance to do this while out on the track. If the cooling system doesn't work, you will fry.

Get comfortable and collect your thoughts about the start of the race. Know what you want to do. Talk to yourself out loud if you have to. This will make it more real to you. Don't think yourself into tunnel vision. You need to focus, but not to the point of daydreaming. Stay clear and in the present—don't imagine accepting the winner's trophy before you even start the engine.

One of the most important things to remember is to breathe. Don't sweat before it gets hot in the car; when the heat does get in the car, you will feel that heat more than if you were in the desert with a snowsuit on. To understand how hot it is, sit in your car with the heat on in the dead of summer and wear your warmest jacket, ski gloves, and hat. Drive on the most wicked road in town and make sure you keep the windows closed. Do this for a couple of hours, and you will get the feeling of what it's like inside a racecar.

> **Yellow Flag**
>
> Being inside that stock car may be the hottest place you will ever be. The driver compartment can be typically 140 degrees. A good cooling system is not only recommended, but required.

Things Not to Concern Yourself With

There are many things not to concern yourself with before the race. One of the key things is the crew. Let the crew chief do his or her job. No matter what happens in the pit area, it should have no effect on you as the driver. The crew members have a job to do as well as you do, so let them do it. They are nervous, too. They know they have pit stops coming up, and they want to perform as well as they can. Don't look at them as they prepare the pit area. They may be doing something you don't like, but it's their pit area, and they will do it their way. Remember, they are working in the pits, not you.

When getting in the car, I (John) developed a bad habit of asking the crew, "Are the wheels tight?" The crew members have come to hate this question so much that they repeat it to me as I say it now. As I slip into the car window, I hear a chorus of "Are the wheels tight?" I'm thinking of making it a song. The other thing I ask when I am strapping in is: "Has anyone topped the fuel?" I know the crew members have done it, but I just can't keep myself from asking. Asking questions like these comes from past mistakes from past crew members. It's stuff that bothers me, but I shouldn't be thinking about it.

I am notorious for thinking about issues that are unrelated to the race. When my mother was sick, I couldn't help but wonder if she was okay. When my friend was sick for a couple of years, I couldn't go a few minutes without thinking about her. It got to the point where I would be sitting in the car in the qualifying line and I wouldn't be aware of anything that was going on around me. I was there physically, but no one was home inside me. These distractions hurt my driving, until I came to the realization that I couldn't do anything about these illnesses. In addition, my friend told me that if I didn't do well, then I couldn't come see her, so I had better get my head on straight and concentrate on what I was doing. I soon did, and my driving improved greatly. Peter would be on pit road and often ask during the race was anything wrong, and I would say no, but there always was. He could tell by the moves I made during the race and my lack of talking that something was amiss.

When you're in the racecar, don't think about bills, whether your stocks went up, whether Potsie on *Happy Days* was really singing those songs, and for God's sake, what the hell is a Pokémon? During a race is not the time to be pondering the cost of pork rinds; it's the time to be driving. Clear your mind of that extraneous stuff. Think about practice: Who was fast? Who wasn't? Who can be passed and where? Don't think about anything else but what needs to happen in the next 500 laps.

To clear your mind before a race, try not to concern yourself with things that are going on around you, such as pre-race ceremonies—unless, of course, you're involved in them! Don't let yourself get distracted by other drivers either; they like to play mind games. Drivers will say things before the start to either startle you or scare you. One of our favorites is when a driver who is starting in front of our team says, "We had to put new brakes in the car; I'm not sure what's going

Yellow Flag

Do not concern yourself with the crew. The crew chief is responsible for directing the crew, which takes that pressure off the driver.

Inside Track

Some drivers do mind clearing and building techniques such as yoga or sense control. Using these techniques helps them think of nothing but driving and helps make them better drivers.

to happen on the start, so just hang back for a few laps." Yeah, sure, why don't we just pull in the pits and watch until you think your car is okay? If another team has a problem, don't make it yours.

A guy who's starting behind you may come up to you before the race and say, "We found some real speed in the last practice; we are going right to the front." This comment is supposed to scare you. It makes us laugh and makes a good story to tell the crew. But we can't say that we don't do it, too. I walk by the line as I am walking to my car and pass a comment to one of my guys like, "I can't believe we found all that metal in the oil filter; I hope this thing will start." Then you can hear the chatter from the other teams: "Did you hear that?" "Watch out! He might blow up right in front of you." This comment makes other drivers hesitant to come up behind you and try to pass. Try to keep such comments out of your mind, but realize that no one can be that focused all the time. So develop skills to balance your thinking.

Driving It in Deep

I'm not sure whether it's because of my drag racing background or all the welding and race gas fumes I've been exposed to, but I have a bad habit of driving into the corners way too fast sometimes called over driving the car. It has become an issue for our team and a hard habit to break. Leaning on the gas and driving the car on into the corner is not always the best thing to do. Many times letting the car coast into the turns a little easier sets it up for a much smoother transition from the middle of the corner and a faster lap time. But easing off the gas is not so easy for drivers to do. Drivers want to lean on the gas and go faster then the lap before.

Inside Track

Don't go wheeling off into the corner unless the track can take an action like that. Doing this will only upset the car, force it up the track, and make you vulnerable to being passed.

Corner Speed

There are reasons for backing off the throttle going into a corner. One of them is *corner speed*. Racecars have a maximum speed they can corner with, and that speed is regulated by the grip of the tires. Of course, tire traction has so many determining factors: track type, track surface, heat, aerodynamics, suspension, and so much more. But corner speed is essential to exit speed, and exit speed leads to speed on the straightaway and the resulting lap times.

Practice is a good time to determine what kind of speed your car gives you in the corners. You can

Track Terms

Corner speed is the action of the car from the entrance to the exit of the turn. It's the rate a car can sustain in a turn without loosing traction.

185

keep increasing the speed of the car until it breaks loose or pushes up the track. If the car breaks loose, the back of the car will come around on you, either spinning you out or forcing you to chase the back of the car up the track. If the car pushes, it will automatically move up the track due to too much corner speed, leaving the tires with less traction.

So it's not how fast you can go, it's how fast you can make the car go without exceeding the speed of the car's traction ability. That's what makes a good driver different from a fearless one. A fearless driver just goes full throttle and whatever happens, happens. A good driver tests how fast his car will go and runs it to the limit every lap, not past it. The fearless driver goes fast, but the good driver goes fast more consistently.

Picking Up the Throttle Faster

One of the resulting factors of corner speed and a controlled entry is being able to pick up the throttle faster. Picking up the throttle faster is paramount to going fast. Of course, the fastest way around a track is to never lift off the throttle, but that's not possible on any track, except Daytona International Speedway and Talladega Speedway. These speedways are so large with wide sweeping turns that the cars can track through the turns with wide-open throttles.

Being able to pick up the throttle faster enables a driver to position himself or herself up on the car in front of him or her, making it possible to pass. And the name of the game in racing is going to the front. Following all the techniques we have talked about in this chapter leaves you with a car that gets into the corner well, reacts better in the middle of the turns, and exits turns ready to be throttled up. These are the important things a driver looks for in a racecar. Such a car gives a driver a chance to win.

Yellow Flag

When choosing a brake system, make sure you choose a system big enough to meet the needs of your racecar. Making the wrong choice will make for a long day at the track

Braking

The last thing needed for driving a car in deep is a good set of brakes. There is no use driving the car on into the turn if you can't slow it down. Brakes are incredibly important items. Some tracks require more brakes than others, so the variety of brakes rivals the variety of cereals on the grocery store shelves. There are two-, four-, and six-piston calipers, for example. Each brake system is designed to do something different.

Short track brakes, for example, are typically the biggest brakes of all. Short tracks not only require fast braking, but also require extended amounts of hard, hot breaking. In this situation, brakes are tested to their limits. Crews are often sent scrambling for fire extinguishers to put out fires caused by overheated, abused brakes. That's right; your brakes can ignite and go up in flames.

This braking system is the large style used in stock car racing. With a very thick pad and good cooling characteristics, it's a proven combination.

One the toughest tracks on brakes is Martinsville, Virginia. Teams install one set of brakes to practice on, and a brand-new set to race on. The long straightaway and short tight turns make for exciting racing and headache-causing brake problems if you make a mistake in choosing the wrong caliper, rotor, or pad compound.

Picking the Proper Pad Compound

When you go to an auto parts store and ask for a set of brakes for your particular car, there is usually only one type of brake pad for your car, and this pad sometimes fits as many as three or four other different cars. In racing, you maybe have as many as five different pad compounds. The pad compound determines how soft or hard the pad material is, and that determines the pedal feel, operating temperatures, and braking distances.

The softer compounds allow quick, cold braking with positive pedal feel. These brakes work well very quickly into the race and give confidence in the short term, but they fade in long race situations and won't give positive braking toward the end of the race. Softer pads grip better than harder pads and provide incredible braking, but they cause more heat and are therefore more prone to overheat the system and greater pad wear.

The harder compounds provide better braking longer into the race, but require more heat to

Inside Track

Three typical brake pad compounds are available from most manufacturers: soft, medium, and hard. Choosing the right compound can put you another step closer to the winners' circle.

Inside Track

Start your brake bias with about 60 percent of the braking power to the front brakes. This is a good starting point for most cars and will ensure that you don't spin out from having too little front brakes.

operate. These compounds are good for drivers and teams that run long races with hard braking or teams that can't afford to change their brakes often, because this pad provides long-term braking without parts service. The harder pads also cause less heat to go to the rotors, which provides a more positive feel to the driver.

Notice how the stock brake pads on the left compare to the beefy race units on the right.

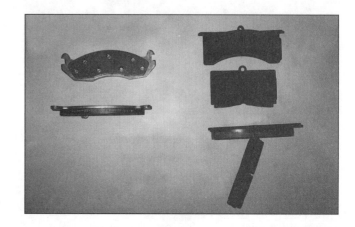

Adjusting Brake Bias

If you ever watched a driver compartment-mounted camera and saw the driver reach over and turn a knob while underway, that driver was probably adjusting the brakes. The pedal system is fitted with a cockpit-mounted adjuster in reach of the driver so he or she can make break adjustments while out on the track. Asphalt racing like NASCAR usually requires 60 percent braking up front and 40 percent in the rear. This is a good starting point for most cars, but it will require adjustments.

Yellow Flag

Only make changes to the brake bias adjuster if the car reacts to braking. Don't be fooled into thinking the problem *is* always the brakes; the problem could be in the chassis.

If the car is underbreaking, the car runs up the track and forces a push condition. This condition means that too much front brake is being used. The brakes are not slowing the rear of the car, and it's running over the front end. If there is too much rear brake, the back end will loosen up and seemingly want to spin out the car. In this case, you have to adjust the brake bias controller and use more front brake. Note that these conditions happen only during breaking; if they happen at any other time, the problem is not in the brake adjustment.

Choosing the Master Cylinders

Normal cars have one master cylinder. This cylinder, called a double master cylinder, controls both the front and rear brakes. A racecar has three master cylinders: one for each of the front and rear brakes and another for the clutch. With three master cylinders, the driver can control the pressure given to each of the front and rear brakes with the brake bias adjuster we already talked about.

These master cylinders have different bore sizes. The popular bore sizes are $^3/_4$-inch, $^7/_8$-inch, and 1-inch. Auto parts manufacturers make them larger and smaller, but these three sizes make up the stock car typical choices. The larger bore sizes provide more controlled braking pressure, but the smaller sizes provide more braking pressure.

Inside Track

Install a master cylinder in the front brakes one bore size smaller than the rear brakes. This will help in reducing rear brake pressure and make the 60 percent front brake percentage easier to achieve.

Drivers can adjust the balance of the front to rear brakes by turning this knob and changing the pedal to master cylinder configuration.

This car has three separate master cylinders. On the left is the front brakes unit, the middle one controls the rear brakes, and the far right one controls the clutch.

Cooling the Brakes

Racecar brakes require some things that regular car brakes don't. They require a very high boiling point fluid, a fluid not prone to moisture contamination and not prone to breakdown. Another very important thing they require is air. With the incredible heat buildup and continued use, they need air to cool them and lots of it.

The difference in these fluids is their boiling points.

Years ago, crews would aim a couple of hoses toward the brakes and forget about them. With today's increased braking abilities, heat has become a major concern and a thorn in some teams' sides. In the past few years, braking engineers have introduced huge air inlet ducts. The more air you can get into the brakes, the better and longer they will perform. In some cases, NASCAR allows small fans to be installed in the cooling lines connecting the air ducts to the brake systems. These fans help a lot under caution periods to cool the brakes and get them ready to go under green flag racing. Not all series will allow fans in the cooling lines due to regulation restraints.

Another heat-fighting product is the brake fluid return system. Brake fluid travels only about $1/2$ inch during pedal depression. This means that the same break fluid is inside the brake caliper for the entire race. With the return system, the fluid is pushed through the caliper and sent back up to the master cylinder, allowing it to cool somewhat and be reused at a more acceptable temperature later on in the race.

Inside Track

Always use the most air cooling to the brakes that the rules allow. Never cut corners on the quality or quantity of your brake cooling system. Doing this may cost you more in broken or burnt parts.

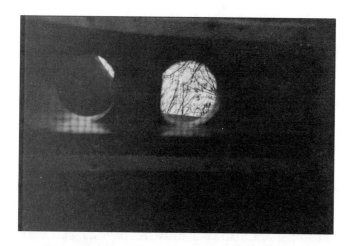

These ducts carry air to the brakes to cool the rotors, calipers, and fluid. With temperatures of 500 degrees or more, cooling brakes is no easy task.

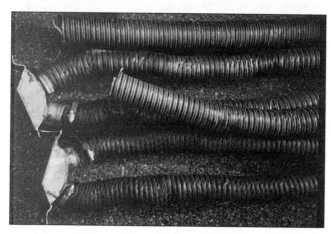

These hoses carry cool air to cool the brakes. Note the fabricated aluminum ends. These ends are bolted to the spindle and direct the air to the associated parts.

This system incorporates a return system. Fluid travels from the master cylinder to the caliper, and back again.

191

Saving the Brakes

Saving your brakes is an important part of finishing the race. In order to win, you must first finish. One technique in saving breaks is easing off the gas sooner into the corner. Don't slam the breaks going into the corner; squeeze them instead. Try to let off sooner and let the car coast more through the corner. Use a brake pad suited to your driving style. If you are easy on the brakes, then a soft pad may accommodate your driving. If you are rough on the brakes, choose the more durable, harder pad compound. No two drivers hit the brakes alike, and no two will wear them the same either.

Some of the things we have learned in this chapter have been to think before acting. Even in the most critical of situations, you need to think. Don't react without thinking first. Watch your speed into the turns; your entry speed affects your corner speed and exit speed, which is more important than your entry speed. Picking up the throttle sooner will affect your lap times in a positive way as long as your corner speed isn't affected in a negative way by an overzealous entry. Driving is more of a control effort than it is a test of courage. You can bomb the lap if you like, but thinking and controlling the car will almost always be the faster way around for a longer length of time.

The Least You Need to Know

➤ Be mentally prepared for every race; don't be beaten before you even get into the car.

➤ Never worry about things the crew members are doing. That's not your job, and it's not your concern.

➤ Corner speed is more important than driving deep into the corner; choose the correct speed for the car, and don't overdrive it.

➤ Pick up the throttle as fast as the car will allow; this will ensure the fastest exit speed and good lap times.

➤ Choose the correct brakes for the car and track designs. Don't get caught with too small of a brake system because it saved you a couple of pounds on the weight of the car.

➤ Use all the brake cooling you can get. Less heat is better than having your brakes on fire.

Part 5

Gentlemen, Start Your Engines

You have finally made it to the show. Now the trick is surviving the experience. In this part, we will talk about racing strategies, getting past the first lap, moving to the front of the pack, and using driving techniques such as drafting.

After you have read the chapters in this part, you will have a better understanding and insight into the sport of stock car racing. So climb into that racecar, strap yourself in, and get ready to go.

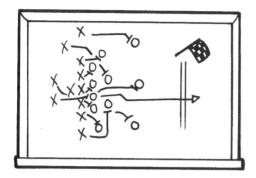

Chapter 17

Strategy and Victory Lane

In This Chapter

➤ Knowing when to save tires, and when to burn them up

➤ Making fuel last

➤ Passing your way to victory lane

➤ Gaining in the pit stops

There are many ways to victory lane. In this chapter, we will discuss some winning strategies. We will talk about when to use tires and when to save them, how to save fuel and why, how to pass cars, and how to make the most of pit stops.

Saving Tires

Tires play the biggest part of how a car will perform and how long it will last out front. Saving your tires can be frustrating, because when that green flag drops, the first thing you want to do is run to the front! You need to conduct yourself as if you were running the race instead of driving it. You must know how far, how fast, and how long your legs can carry you, so you can pace yourself. Tires need the same care.

Suppose you started the race and decided to drive conservatively, running average lap times of 30 seconds for the first 25 laps. In the next 25 laps, you average 30.2 seconds. The average lap time of the next 25 laps is 30.4, and your last 25 laps average at 30.6. You finish with a 100-lap average of 30.3 seconds. You didn't experience a dramatic drop off in lap times. Your tires wore evenly, and you didn't abuse them, which left you with good rubber to race on later in the race with the proper air pressure built up.

Suppose another driver was more aggressive and drove hard; he ran his first 25 laps at 29.8 seconds, the second set at 30.3 seconds, the third set of 25 at 30.5, and the last set at 30.7. His average for 100 laps would be 30.325. Although his lap times during the first 25 laps looked great, the next three sets of 25 fell off his initial aggressive pace. He wore the tires too quickly and didn't leave himself any good rubber to race on, and his lap times suffered for it later on in the race.

As you can see, running a more conservative pace allowed you to be .025 seconds in front of the driver who abused his tires and caused them to deteriorate prematurely. So although it may have looked like the other driver was flying right along, he was actually hurting his long-term goal of winning!

Tire-Saving Techniques

There are many ways to save your tires. Of course, you need to save your tires while staying close to the *race pace,* so you can be in position to win at the end. Taking notes and closely watching tire wear in practice helps a team learn what chassis changes and driving style changes can maximize tire use.

For example, drivers can save tire wear if they drive into the turns slightly easier; let the car coast easily through the turns, not with great side loads to the tire; and ease into the throttle, allowing the car an easy transition from the turn to the straightaway. Of course, it's hard to hold your position, keep competitors behind you, and pass, all while doing this.

Another way a driver can save tires is to let the car *diamond* the turns. When a driver does this, he allows the car to run faster into the corners and run up the middle of the turn. The driver then slows down by using the brake, turns, and comes off the turn fairly straight.

Another driving technique is to make the track as wide as possible. In order to do this, the driver must turn the steering wheel as little as possible. To use this technique, stay out close to the wall, don't drop to the bottom of the track when in the turns, and stay higher in the *first and second groove.* However, this technique does leave you open to being passed.

Inside Track

Take good notes and record lap times in your practice or hot lap session. This record gives you an advantage in knowing how long your tires will last. Then you will know how fast a pace you can run and keep your tires in winning condition.

Track Terms

The **race pace** is the average lap times of the front-running cars. The race pace is usually considerably slower than the qualifying times. The cars are set up for long-term runs, not for the one- or two-lap qualifying runs, which slows the lap times and makes for closer racing.

One easy way to save tires is to just slow down, but that's not very conducive to winning, is it? What we mean by slowing down is to run a more comfortable pace, stay out of trouble, don't pressure the guy in front of you, keep close to the leaders, and leave enough time for a charge to the front at the end. Let the leaders fight it out and waste rubber and traction, leaving you with car that handles well for the end. The problem with this technique is that it works only on long races with tire limits.

Why Tires Need to Be Saved

There are many factors in determining how you can save your tires. But you do need to do so. In NASCAR's Winston Cup Series, there is no limit on how many tires you can use. If you need to pit more often, you can do so. But in the Busch Series, Craftsmen Truck Series, and all of NASCAR's touring series, there is a limit to the number of tires.

Drivers and teams must regulate and determine when and how many tires will be used. Teams sometimes risk losing positions to keep from pitting early in a race so that they can have fresh tires for the second half. Other teams would rather have the best tires at the beginning, gain as much track position as possible, and try to hold off charging competitors with better rubber toward the end. This strategy sometimes works with great results on *one-groove tracks* where it's hard to pass.

Yellow Flag

Diamonding the corners leaves you open to the driver behind you pulling up under the left rear of the car and making you take a higher and maybe less advantageous line off the corner. This move allows the other driver to pass you, leaving you out of position and open to getting passed again.

Fuel Mileage Needs to Go a Long Way

Another factor to consider is fuel mileage. We know you're thinking, "This is a racecar, why would we care how much fuel mileage it gets?" There are several reasons. The first is that better fuel mileage means one less stop for fuel. If your racecar can run a 400- or 500-mile race on one less stop, you can win by a wide margin. Michigan Speedway is the prime example of this. Many races have been won at that track not by the fastest or best handling car, but by the car with the best fuel mileage.

Track Terms

The **first groove** is usually the most used groove and fastest groove, the **second groove** would be the groove used to pass when the first groove is being used, or blocking occurs.

Fuel Mileage in Racecars vs. Regular Cars

A regular car may get mileage ranging from 20 to 35 miles to the gallon. The typical racecar may get 5 miles to the gallon. The stockcar carries 22 gallons of fuel, and a regular car carries about 18 gallons. Therefore, a regular car can go about 500 miles on a tank of gas, whereas a racecar can only go about 100 miles. That's some difference.

The automotive industry works very hard to gain valuable fuel mileage for your car to make the car not only more appealing, but also within the guidelines of the federal government's regulations. With the introduction of fuel injection, the automotive industry enjoyed the benefits of highly efficient, computer-regulated engine management systems. With these systems, fuel management has become more controlled and less a burden to manufacturers. The engine's fuel curve is adjusted to engine heat, air temperature, engine vacuum, and throttle response, and the system also adjusts the timing in the engine, using all fuel and expending less unburned, toxic fuel into the atmosphere.

However, NASCAR doesn't allow the use of fuel injection. Instead, stock cars must use carburetors. Cars with carburetors just don't have the complete control of all aspects of the engine like their fuel-injected counterparts. But the use of carburetors is mandatory in stock car racing.

Track Terms

One-groove tracks are racetracks with a preferred place on the track to race on. If you are not in the groove, you are not going to be up to speed.)

The Carburetor: Drink Less

There are a few different ways to obtain better fuel mileage with a carburetor. The simplest way is to lean out the fuel mixture in the carburetor by reducing the size of the main fuel jets. But this change takes away from long-term horsepower and engine longevity. Leaning out the force curve like that will put more heat in the engine, and heat is the enemy.

The second way is to build an engine specifically designed with small intake ports, the smallest cubic inch allowed, and a slightly smaller camshaft. The problem with this setup is that the engine makes less horsepower. And you can't win with less horsepower, can you? Sometimes you can, but it depends on the track. On short tracks with sweeping turns and short front and back straight sections where throttle usage is at a

Yellow Flag

Be careful leaning out the fuel curve. Race engines have high internal cylinder pressures and exhaust temperatures of 1,400 degrees or more. Removing fuel might help fuel economy, but it may also cause extreme engine failure.

minimum, the driver can roll the car through the turns faster using less engine power to propel the car down the straight portions of the track. Tracks with long straight portions require more throttle usage, thus using more fuel.

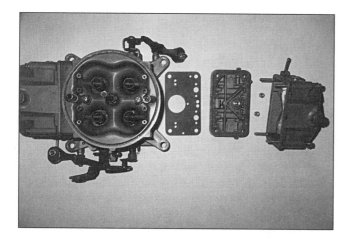

This is where the main jets of the typical Holley Carburetor.

Change Gears

Another way to save fuel is to change rear gears of the car to limit the RPM (revolutions per minute) of the engine. This change slows the engine speed without completely sacrificing performance. Of course, whenever you save fuel, you do give up a little performance. But saving fuel over a long race can be worth sacrificing a slightly faster track speed.

The driver can also save fuel. Many drivers run the car very hard, using up fuel. By feathering the throttle and running close to the cars in front of you, saving fuel becomes a factor you can control.

Under the Hood

Running closely behind the car in front of you will help you save fuel. The car in front of you tows you along from the vacuum effect caused by both cars being so close. This also allows both cars to share the drag affect of the air.

While driving at high speeds with the desire to pass, many drivers find themselves torn between running up front or having the patience and control to hold back and run a slightly slower pace. This doesn't sound like racing now, does it? But control is all part of the big picture, which is being in a position to win at the end. And if you're out of fuel at the end, you're out of luck, too.

Track Terms

Chrome horn is a reference from the 1960s and 1970s, when stock cars had stock bumpers. Drivers would run up behind the car in front of them and tap it with the bumper, letting the driver know they wanted to go by.

Track Terms

Restrictor plate tracks are currently Daytona, Florida, and Talladega, Alabama. These tracks are 2½ miles or longer in length and if restrictor plates weren't used, current stock cars would exceed safe speeds for closed course circle track racing.

Passing to Victory Lane

Passing in a stock car race is harder than it looks. Trying to pass another racer when he doesn't want you to is more than a frustrating experience. When attempting a pass, you need to have a plan. First, make your moves in your head, know the possibilities, and have alternate moves to counter blocks made by the car in front of you. Thinking ahead will gain you not only the position, but also help you in future moves.

You can relate this experience to driving on the freeway with all three lanes blocked, and no one wants to let you in front of them. The difference is that there are no police officers to ticket you for tailgating, weaving back and forth, and using the *chrome horn*.

Passing on the Big Tracks: Don't Try It Alone

Passing has become more difficult on *restrictor plate tracks*, such as Daytona and Talladega. These tracks have very close racing, closely matched cars, and three-wide, 200 miles per hour racing. At these tracks, it's not uncommon to have 44 cars on the lead lap and racing in one big pack.

Passing at these tracks must be set up with two or three cars at a time. They must get together, work as a team, and pass together. But this strategy doesn't always work. Sometimes one car gets hung out of the draft; that car may lose 10 or 15 positions before it can get back in line and try to pass all over again.

Not every pass needs to be that well thought out. There are chances to pass when the car in front of you makes a mistake. To capitalize on those situations, you need to be ready and have the nerve and quick re-actions to make that kind of pass. You can try to pressure your competition into a mistake by riding them hard until you can get the *fast groove* and go on by.

Passing in the Corners

Our favorite way to pass is to run up on car in front of us just off the corner, drop to the inside, and take the more desirable line into the next corner. The passed car will almost always give you the line in and drop behind you in fear of getting passed by the car behind you. It's the easiest way to pass if you have good power and a fair handling car. The only problem with this type of pass is that you need to get in the corner first, but not so fast that you run up the track and let the passed car get under you, getting that same run you just did and putting you in the vulnerable situation of being passed by that car and others.

Our second favorite way to pass is on the outside of cars that pile up in the corner or *check up*. This means they all have to hit the brakes, turning the usually slower groove into the faster groove for a few seconds. Taking advantage of this situation can gain you one position, maybe two. But don't get caught on the outside of a track with one groove, or you can lose positions very quickly.

A very popular way of passing, but not for the one being passed, is to bump the car in front of you right in the middle of the turn and upset the back of his car. While he chases the back of his car up the track, you run up under and alongside him, gaining the preferred line.

Track Terms

The **fast groove** is the place on the track where the most traction can be obtained. This place results in the fastest lap times and is the best passing zone.

Track Terms

To **check up** is to back off the throttle, allowing following cars to close up quickly on your back bumper. It usually causes problems for the cars just behind you. This is sometimes used as a defense move to keep closing competition from getting a run on you off the corner. It takes away from their momentum.

Running in a pack like this makes passing difficult, so choose your line and passes wisely.

When Getting Passed Is Smarter Than Passing

Although this may sound unusual, there are times when getting passed is better than passing. When you're in the middle of a run, sometimes a faster car behind you will do anything to get by you. The car may be *using up its tires* and trying to run from the back to the front. Instead of getting pressured and maybe bumped up the track and passed by more than one car, it's smarter to let the car go by early. You can easily pass this car later in the race when tire wear becomes an issue.

This same car may also be a problem to competitors in front of you. Pressure for both of them makes each run harder and use up tires. This situation makes it difficult for both of them to hold you off later in the race because your car will handle better.

Track Terms

Using up the tires means you're running on the edge as fast as the tires will allow, making them hot and slick. This is not a good idea for long races.

Under the Hood

Lifting off the gas earlier in your entry into the corner and getting on the throttle earlier off the corner is easier on the tires.

Fighting for Position

The worse thing you can do in a race is fight for position with a car that's considerably faster. Do this only at the end of a race when position is of great importance. Doing this early in the race is a recipe for disaster. Frustrating a fast, hot-headed driver who is running to the front can only put both of you in the wall, especially if the race requires more than one pit stop. Many times it is more prudent to give up the position and gain it back later when time permits. This strategy, of course, does not apply to short races with no pit stops. If this situation applies to you, then run the preferred line and give enough room to race with the competition.

In racing, everyone wants to win, but only one driver pulls into victory lane at the end of the race. You have to know when you're either in position to win, can be in position to win, or are in the position to take second place. Most drivers won't hear of second place, but championship drivers know when second place is better than crashing out to last.

Even though each individual race has a winner, the series championship is the crown all racers seek. Winning a race is great; winning the championship makes you a great driver. Go for the win, but take what your car will give you and be in position to take what others give up to you.

Inside Track

When entering the pit road, make sure your speed is not exceeding the preset pit road speed, or NASCAR will bring you back in for a penalty stop. Competitors regulate their pit road speed by using the tachometer in a predetermined gear to tell how fast they are going. After running speeds of 150 to 200 miles per hour, pit road speed of 35 to 50 miles per hour may seem like a crawl.

Pit Stops

On the road to victory lane, you need to pit. Pit stops are required to run long races in order to change tires, get fuel, and make adjustments to the car. Remember when that faster car went by you before? Now you are going to pit and make chassis or tire changes that will allow you to pass that car and hopefully a few more!

Pit stops give teams a chance to change many aspects of the car: aerodynamics, chassis, springs, weight transfer, tire pressure, and more. In a couple of pit stops, you can make a twentieth place car a top five contender.

Inside Track

In entering your pit stall, make sure to stay away from the inside pit wall and position your car so you are not blocked in by the car in front of you.

Pit stops can also make or break your *track position*. Coming in to pit under caution in tenth place, getting a fast pit stop, and returning to the track in seventh can greatly improve your race. Doing this allows your crew to help you pass cars; you won't have to use up the car getting by those three competitors, which keeps the car in better shape to race for the win.

Getting to victory lane is difficult. The weather, tire wear, fuel economy, and other cars to pass all have an effect on the outcome of the race. You need to know when to pass and when to be passed, when to pit, how many tires to take, and when to lean on it and go to the front. Racing is a team sport needing quick-thinking team members and good decision-makers. Always place your car in position to win and have a good car for the end of the race.

Track Terms

Track position is your current place in the race. Track position is very important for one-groove racetracks.

The Least You Need to Know

➤ Make sure you have enough rubber left on your tires to race for the win.

➤ Take good notes and keep good lap time records to find out how long your tires will last.

➤ Lean your fuel curve only as much as your engine will allow, exceeding this amount will cause long-term damage.

➤ Sometimes getting passed is smarter than passing, work with your crew to determine what kind of pace is best.

➤ Running in a pack can help you save fuel.

➤ Pass with your head, not with your attitude.

Chapter 18

Getting Past the First Lap

In This Chapter

➤ Smokin' up the tires

➤ The pitfalls of burning up the rubber

➤ Getting down on the gas

➤ Moving into position

This chapter covers the start of the race. The first lap of the race is going to set the pace for you and the cars around you. We are going to talk about heating the tires and what can happen if you don't. We will also describe what your mental state should be when you approach the first lap and how to position yourself in the start of the race to gain an advantage.

Heating the Tires

Tires operate best at a predetermined temperature set by the manufacturer and dependent on the compound of the rubber. The only way to reach this temperature is to run the tire at the speed for which it was built. The hardness and thickness of the rubber determines how much heat the tire will withstand and at what temperature the best traction can be obtained. It's almost impossible to heat the tires while under caution or at the start of the race. You can heat them slightly, but be careful of hitting the brakes or spinning the car sideways while doing it. Flat spots could occur, or overspinning the rear tires could prematurely wear valuable rubber.

Under the Hood

Weaving the car back and forth does not necessarily heat the tires so much as it cleans off the loose rubber, tar, debris, and track surface that lays on the track during cautions. This debris is sometimes called the *loose stuff,* and you see it on the outside of the track or places on the track where the cars don't run. Announcers sometimes refer to this debris as the gray areas of the track, because it tends to lighten the color of the blacktop on television.

Why Tire Heating Is So Important

At the start of a race, the tires are cold. They haven't been refrigerated or anything, but they are at the temperature of the day plus the track surface temperature. This temperature doesn't exactly make them race ready, but they are asked to get up to speed and give traction immediately so the driver can accelerate upon the drop of the green flag.

Under the Hood

Race tires are underinflated for the start of the race, but they are precisely measured, and exact amounts of nitrogen are pressured into them so that during the race, and under extreme conditions, they will grow to the proper operating pressures. Before they do, the tires feel flat or soft. Racers adjust their speeds until the tires reach the correct pressure.

Another wrench in the works is the removal of a small amount of air pressure, making the tires unstable at the start. But this is done to allow for the extended heat cycles that the tire is asked to endure while under race conditions. As you learned in

Chapter 12, "A Good Set of Rubbers," tire pressure increases with usage of the tire and the effects of heat and the force of the car. Preparing for this increase takes an experienced driver and care for the tires in the opening laps.

Not preparing your tires can cause you undue stress and agony as you suffer through worn and uncooperative tires until you can pit and take on another set. This can make for a very long day, loss of positions on the track, and a diminished chance of winning. If you wear the tires or damage one early, you will have to abuse the car or the rest of your sets trying to play catch up.

What Can Happen If You Don't

Not heating the tires can result in many different problems. One of them, and maybe the most important one, is no traction. Traveling into a turn at over 190 miles per hour with no traction can result in catastrophic results.

Imagine how you felt driving on a rainy or snowy day along the freeway in heavy traffic. You need to make a lane change, so you turn your wheel. Much to your dismay, the car continues to go straight. A stock car driver gets this same feeling going into the first turn at top speed. The driver must finesse the car into turning in the middle of 40 other cars doing exactly the same thing.

Most of the time, cooperation is asked for and given during the opening laps of a race, but it is never expected. There is always one guy looking to gain valuable positions and win the race in the first lap. In a race held at Thompson Speedway in Connecticut some years ago for the Modified Tour Cars, we witnessed just such a driver. When the green flag dropped, and the field of cars ran into turn one, he immediately ran his car low and down on the inside lane, gaining 10 positions before entering turn three. The field was still as tight as the start, and the cars entered three wide on a two-lane track with cold and underinflated tires. Of course, the driver couldn't hold the car low, and he drifted up. When the smoke cleared, and all the cars were visible, we counted 12 victims. One car was on its side against the wall and on top of another competitor. If this doesn't make a case for heating your tires, then what will?

Yellow Flag

Failure to heat your tires will result in either prematurely worn tires or a car that handles poorly. Always make sure your tires are at the proper operating temperature or close to it before running deep in the corner.

Yellow Flag

Running in the loose stuff or gray areas of the track with hot tires under race conditions almost always results in a flat. Race tires have no grooves to clean debris off them and are too soft to repel foreign objects.

How about just abusing your tires before they are hot and up to pressure? You can drive on them and even race on them, but will you be as competitive as if you followed general procedure and treated them correctly? Probably not. In most cases, you will fall back in the later laps, lose ground, and frustrate yourself trying to keep up.

Tires are kind to the drivers in most cases. They ask only to be prepared correctly and driven to the limits of their performance. Overinflating tires can help on the start and on restarts, but on extended runs, you can have a condition of *crowning*. This means a tire is rounding in the middle and holding the edges of the ground. This results in less rubber to use and considerably less traction.

Underinflating tires can result in a soft feeling in the car; this feeling is due to the tires getting a concaved look to them. The car uses only the edges of the tires and again loses traction. Underinflation also causes the sidewall of the tire to fold over, making the car feel unstable and taking concentration and confidence from the driver.

However, slight underinflation helps on long runs. It allows the driver to build up tire pressure and reach a more comfortable racing pressure over an extended period of time, giving that driver an advantage at the end of the race. This advantage only holds if the race stays under green flag conditions and cars with over inflated tires are not allowed to cool them and reduce the tire pressure under the caution flag. This is called having the race come to you.

Crew chiefs take this factor into consideration when they are preparing for a race. If a particular race or track has a history of long green-flag conditions, then the crew may set the tires up a bit soft. If it has a history of many cautions, tires that are more fully inflated may be a more effective setup for that race.

When the Green Flag Drops

After the dropping of the green flag, most drivers want to run to the front. Very few have the patience and self-restraint to run the race in a smart and educated way. If you find a driver with total self-control, good driving ability, and a good car, you will see a winner.

Get on the Throttle

The green flag drops, and you run the car up through the gears until you get into fourth or high gear. Now you have to get into that first turn. You lean down into that turn, hoping the car will stick to the track and allow you time to get back on the throttle and come up out of the other side.

You were able to negotiate the first turn. Now you have to do it all over again, this time at an even faster speed for turn three. This is where most problems occur. Your speed is up, the car is still a little uncooperative, and you're unsure of what your surrounding drivers will do.

You hit the gas again and run up on the car in front of you. Gaining a line of sight ahead of him, you can see where you want to be, but you just can't get there. You have to know at this point what your car will do, because 20 of those 40 drivers want ahead of the cars in front of them. And 20 moves will be made or attempted before the pack returns to turn one.

Inside Track

Watch a driver who gets himself in trouble early; this incident may be an indication of someone who is not capable of controlling his emotions.

Sorting Out Things

You have an idea of where you want to be and when you would like to get there, but depending on where you start the race and who is around you, your plan may or may not work. Keep apprised of who is around you and what type of drivers they are. Knowing this will help you make smart decisions as to passing and pit strategy. Make sure your crew knows your plan before the race and knows if you change it mid-race.

The first lap is always the worst. You never know what the cars around you are going to do. You can only speculate as to their actions. Most of the time everyone just tries to get through the first lap; when they get up enough confidence and tire heat, they head to the front.

We never make a beeline for the front. As a team, we always decide what we are going to do and have a plan as to when we will pit, who we will run with, and what cars we want to be ahead of. We try to stay to that plan as much as possible.

Inside Track

Have a plan when starting a race. Never go to a race and just wing it. You may have to alter your plan slightly during the race, but you will benefit from already being prepared, having scheduled pit stops, and organizing emergency solutions.

Of course, this plan may change as the race progresses, but now we are still talking about lap one.

Starting a race on a large track with lots of space is much easier than trying to push your way through the pack. There is room to move around and dodge racers who insist on running it into the corner and slamming on the brakes, making the back of their cars swerve from side to side.

It's difficult to see this from the bleachers, but from our seats, it sometimes looks like a dog ran on the highway during rush-hour traffic in New York City. It amazes us that drivers with such talent and experience can be so excited to start another race. If you ever get the chance to see drivers up close before the start of a race, you will be surprised at the glazed looks and blank expressions they have. As soon as the race starts, these racers seem to wake up and come to life. Some are more animated in the cars than even they think.

Yellow Flag

Clear your mind for qualifying. You can't get out there to run you car as fast as it will go and be thinking of the broken hinge on the garage door at home. You must have total concentration and give 110 percent.

If you watch television qualifying coverage, you can see some of the most talented professionals almost losing their lunch. Some others look as though they want to beat up the interviewer because they are so nervous. Still others hang around joking with the crew, as if they are not concerned at all. A good example of this last type of driver is Kenny Wallace. In the middle of what seems like a standup routine for pit road, he jumps in the car, knocks out a top-five qualifying spot, gets out of the car, and finishes the joke. Everyone deals with the pressure of the start of races a little differently.

The start of the race is the most stressful part of racing for some drivers, although they won't admit it. We like to talk to the drivers starting the race in the rows around us. We let them know that we will be on soft tires or brakes that need a lap or so to come in.

Turn One

Imagine that you're strapped into a 3,400-pound stock car with more than 40 other competitors. All the drivers are weaving their cars back and forth trying to clean the tires. The sound of more than 32,000 horsepower surrounds you. The seat harness is tight, and you're already hot from the fire suit, gloves, boots, and helmet you're wearing. Beads of sweat run down your face as your heart races faster than it ever has before. You grip the wheel and try to clear your mind to concentrate. All you can think about is that guy in the stand above the start line. He's showing you one wrapped flag and pointing directly at you! He's telling you that there is only one more lap until the flag goes green.

You look at the gauges; everything seems fine. You start to panic because you can't get the car into second gear. You're jamming the stick rearward as hard as you can, and then you notice you haven't pressed the clutch. Embarrassment sets in, but lucky for you, no one can see you. So now you start to talk to yourself, and you're answering, too! No, you're not crazy; you're just nervous about what is going to happen.

The car is in gear, you have cleaned your helmet shield 20 times, and the belts are so tight that numbness is about to set in. Your spotter tells you, "One to go, one to go." You're ready to go. You think, "I have done this a hundred times; this is no big deal."

Then you round turn four, you look up, and the flagman is nearly hanging completely out of the stand. All of a sudden, there it is! It's green! Your spotter is yelling, "Green, green, green!" You smash down on the throttle, the rear tires break loose, and you're on your way! Almost unconsciously, you shift gears and run up on the car in front of you. The pack is tight, and sweat runs down your face. The roar of 40 racecar engines speeding along the track is nearly deafening; dust and debris are flying through the car like a tornado as you see the leaders going into turn one. This is it! Your first turn of the race. With both hands on the wheel, your right foot on the throttle, and your left foot ready to work the brake, you run quickly with the field into turn one. The speeding pack of cars looks like a herd of wild horses being stabled. You can feel the g-forces pushing you out to the right; it almost feels like you are trying to hold up your 300-pound Uncle Joe after a three-martini lunch.

As you enter turn one, your heart rate slows. You're moving the steering wheel less, and your gloves feel as if they actually fit now. Your face mask is no longer fogged, and you can see past the car in front of you. That wasn't so bad now was it? You are in turn one, and you're still in one piece.

Holding Your Line

Holding your line in the first turn is very important. This means stay in one lane, hold that lane, and let the dust settle from 40 plus cars getting underway. It's the sportsmanlike thing to do. Of course, not all racers think this way. They see the first turn as an opportunity to gain valuable positions, but many times a turn one move on the first lap has bad results.

One of the first stock car races I participated in had just such results. It was a modified race in Flemington, New Jersey. This odd-shaped track had almost no straightaway. Drivers were constantly turning and accelerating. I started the race in row 14, in 27th place. When the green flag waved,

Inside Track

Starting closer to the rear of the field puts you more at risk of first turn incidents. But starting there often will better prepare you for restarts and racing in heavy traffic.

36 tour-type modified stock cars took off for turn one. The car directly in front of me went low and tried to run it in hard; the racer in front of him tried to block the move. They went wheel to wheel, and the next thing I was looking at was the bottom side of the two cars. Although both cars ended right side up, neither one could continue because of the heavy damage. I am sure both drivers would have liked a chance to act and react differently.

You can see how important it is to hold your line and stay patient. We can't recall one time when the race was won on the first lap.

Jockeying for Position

Although holding your line is important, it is equally as important to plan your strategy. The crew predetermines your plan, but when opportunity knocks, you better be ready to open that door. Most drivers feel they can jockey for position after two laps. These drivers dart inside and out looking for a hole and a quick position or two. This is a good time to pick up positions because many drivers are not so racey yet. Most are willing to give up a spot rather than tangle with an opponent. Other drivers will definitely try to block you, but if you can get the line they wanted, they will back off a bit at this stage of the race.

Sometimes it's best at this point to gain a spot and look for clear openings. If the opportunity arises, take another spot. One thing you want to look for is someone who runs up front, but didn't have a good qualifying effort. This driver is going to be making holes that can benefit you. Stay close and fill every gap this driver makes.

Another way to position yourself is to know the track. Some tracks are one-groove tracks. If you're on a one-groove track, make sure you're in the groove and capitalize on every mistake the cars in front of you make. If a driver takes a high line into the corner, stuff your nose under him. Just make sure he knows you're there, or he could come down on you, touch your bumper, and spin out.

If a driver tries to block you by running into the corner low, stay close. That driver may run up the corner and present you with a passing opportunity in the middle of the corner, where you would like it. When entering the corner low, the car will usually want to drift up a bit from the middle off the corner. If you enter the corner high, you can get a run on someone

Yellow Flag

Blocking is done to keep an opponent behind you, but racers are not very patient people for the most part. Blocking is positioning your car in order to take up all the racing space, making a competitor run on the apron of the track, or in the loose stuff to pass. Which of course makes it very difficult. Most drivers allow some liberties with lane jumping, but if you push the issue, some will move you via the bump-and-go method. The bump-and-go method is using your bumper to push a car out of the groove and make the car check up so you can pass with little or no resistance.

who does this, because you can run a straighter line in the middle and run lower off the corner, getting the preferred line down the straightaway.

Another way to position yourself is to watch the cars in front of you, and notice who is having trouble. Some cars are slow into the turns, but fast off the turns. These cars provide a good outside passing opportunity if you can run in the corner and around them. But make sure you get around them before the middle of the turn; otherwise, their exit speed will allow them to beat you.

Under the Hood

One-groove racetracks generally have the fastest part of the racetrack along the inside or around the white line on the track. Two exceptions to this are Darlington Raceway and Indianapolis Raceway Park, where the faster groove is high along the outside wall. The design and shape of these tracks makes this oddity possible.

If certain cars are fast into the corner, but slow off the corner, try to figure out why. Do they lack power or have a bad push? If so, passing them on the outside is a good option. Be careful they don't push into you and make sure you have the room. Getting leaned on and nudged into loose stuff will only cause you to lose position or end up flat-siding the wall. Flat siding the wall is when you hit the wall coming off the corner with the whole side of the car. It usually bends the wheels or suspension parts as well as scuffing up the side of your car. When you are behind a car with a bad push, you can lean on it a little and move it up the track. The bad push makes it very difficult for the driver to counteract this move because he will have great difficulty turning down into you because of his push.

I tried a move like this at a race in Jennerstown, Pennsylvania. I was following a car up through the field until it came up on a blocker. For a few laps, we both tried different ways to pass the blocking

Yellow Flag

When starting the race, be careful not to miss a shift or shift too hard. More transmissions and rear gears are broken at the start than at any other time during the race. Only exiting from a pit stop can rival the start for transmission problems.

car. Because none of my low attempts made any headway, I went to the outside in turn three and made it stick all the way through to where the blocking car pushed up and leaned on me. I was caught between him and the wall. The damage was extensive: bent shock, flattened side, and bent wheels and lower control arm. The only thing I didn't get was a flat. My car limped around the track for the next 50 laps, losing many positions. This kind of thing happens when you jockey for position. Many times you think you have something clear, and when you get there, the door closes, usually on your toes.

Getting past the first lap isn't very hard to do, if you follow a few good rules. Make sure you concentrate and have a clear head. Getting nervous or having butterflies is fine; just don't let nervousness prevent you from making good decisions and capitalizing on others' bad decisions. Always make sure that you have clean tires and that you have heated them as much as possible, without causing flat spots. When the green flag drops and you get up to speed, make sure you hit every gear and have positive throttle response. Sort out the competition and react to what's going on around you. When you do have opportunities, go for the position, but not if it means tangling with another competitor. It's way too early in the race to bang up the car.

The Least You Need to Know

➤ Heat your tires to operating temperatures, or they will not have the proper grip.

➤ Keep your tires clean for the start and restarts of the race. Make sure they are clean of debris.

➤ Avoid running your car into the gray areas of the track. These areas can lead to flat tires and poor traction.

➤ Be prepared for the start of the race. Do not daydream, and keep your mind clear of all non-race-related issues.

➤ Have a plan going into the race and keep to that plan until circumstance forces you to change it.

➤ Hold your line going into turn one; don't swerve back and forth. Getting past the first lap is the gateway to the rest of the race.

➤ When jockeying for position, make sure you can fit into the hole or space you are shooting for. Always know where you want to be long before you attempt to get there.

Chapter 19

In the Spotlight

In This Chapter

➤ Smile, you're on camera

➤ Interviews: Don't say anything you might regret

➤ Radio communications: "Roger, 10-4"

➤ Appearances: How's my hair?

Now that NASCAR has become the fastest-growing spectator sport in America today, the level of exposure for the drivers and teams has greatly increased. Fans want to know everything possible about their favorite drivers. They want autographs and team merchandise, and most of all, they want to experience what it is like to drive a racecar at over 150 miles per hour.

Fueling the public demand is the coverage provided by the media for all NASCAR Winston Cup races. In the early days of NASCAR, there was a limited amount of media coverage, and television coverage of the races was unheard of. In the mid-1980s, all of that changed, and NASCAR started to be regularly covered by the media. It was becoming so popular at the time that Ronald Reagan, president of the United States, attended the Daytona 500 in Daytona Beach, Florida. After this, stock car racing was no longer just for "good ole boys"; it became a mainstream-sporting event.

Under the Hood

In 1979, CBS was the first network television station to broadcast flag-to-flag coverage of the Daytona 500 nationwide. During that race, after two racecars crashed, the drivers got out of their racecars and had a fistfight on national television. As unfortunate as this incident was, it helped draw attention to the sport of stock car racing.

Television Coverage

To give you an idea of how popular NASCAR racing has become, just recently NASCAR announced that it would be negotiating the television rights for all NASCAR Winston Cup races starting with the 2001 season. Prior to this announcement, each racetrack negotiated the television rights for its race.

Under the Hood

In 1985, NASCAR received a total of $3 million for the television broadcast rights to all 28 NASCAR Winston Cup races.

According to a recent press release from the Associated Press, the new television contract, which was awarded to the NBC, FOX, and TBS networks, is reported to be worth $400 million per year for the next three years. Part of the reason for the high price is that during the last decade, NASCAR is the only sport whose television ratings have increased every year. This fact proves that the popularity of the sport is not showing any sign of slowing down. Sponsors love this attention, and many companies are looking to get involved with a team.

Cameras

Over the years, as NASCAR's popularity increased, so did the quality of coverage provided by the media. At first, television coverage was limited to a few cameras located high above the racetrack. Today, television coverage has expanded to include in-car cameras, bumper cameras, pit road cameras, cameras mounted in the outside wall of the racetrack, and even small cameras mounted on the side of the helmet worn by a tire changer on the pit crew. Each of these cameras allows the viewer to get closer to the action and to experience what it is like to be a part of the racing. Not everyone has the skill or ability to be a racecar driver. But with the increased coverage by television media, anyone, regardless of age, skill, or ability, can see what it is like to be a part of a race team.

Under the Hood

Television stations covering NASCAR races are coming up with more unusual camera locations in order to give the viewer a better perspective of what is involved in a NASCAR race. Maybe the internal engine camera is next.

In the movie *Days of Thunder,* the main character, Cole Trickle, is interviewed by his potential crew chief about how much driving experience he has had in Winston Cup racecar. Cole's response is that he has never driven a racecar before, but that he has seen it on television and the coverage provided by ESPN was amazing. He goes on to say that there is a lot you can learn from watching a race on television and that based on what he has seen on television, he is sure that he could drive a racecar.

Although this answer would never get you the job in a real-life interview, it has a certain amount of truth. Television cameras are mounted everywhere in a racecar: on the roof of the racecars to see down the racetrack, inside the racecar to allow the viewer to see what the driver sees out of the windshield, inside the racecar aimed at the driver so the viewers can watch how the driver drives the racecar, in the rear bumper of the racecar to let the viewer see exactly how close these guys get to one another at over 150 miles per hour, and along the side of the racetrack to give the viewer the sensation of what it is like to have 30 or more racecars passing you at over 150 miles per hour. This camera position shows the viewers just how fast these racecars are traveling around the racetrack.

In-Car Camera

All of these camera locations not only help bring the viewer closer to the sport, but they also help the viewer understand and experience what it is like to be in a racecar. Two of our favorite camera locations are the in-car camera aimed out the front window and the rear bumper camera. The in-car camera is our favorite because it gives you the driver's perspective.

Yellow Flag

With television cameras mounted just about everywhere in a racecar, teams need to be careful about what they say and do during a race. You do not want you or your crew to say something in the heat of the moment that might get you in trouble with your sponsor.

From the in-car camera, you can see what it looks like when a crash happens in front of you, and you get to see what it looks like from the inside, when a racecar goes spinning across the infield. When you see a crash or a spin happening from the bleachers, you may be wondering, "What is it like to be in the racecar right now?" These in-car cameras allow you to have that sensation without the risk of getting injured. We would all love to be in the racecar ourselves, but during a crash, the safest place to be is watching what happens from that little camera mounted in the racecar.

Another benefit to the in-car camera is the increased exposure the teams can offer their sponsors. All race teams use any chance they can get to promote their sponsors. When a race team knows that it will have an in-car camera, the team places stickers with its sponsor's name on it anywhere the camera is pointing. These cameras use wide-angle lenses, allowing the viewer to see most of the dashboard on the inside of the racecar. Therefore, the dashboard is an excellent location for promoting a sponsor on national television.

A great example of promoting a sponsor took place when one of our competitors had an in-car camera mounted in his racecar. The camera was pointed at the driver, so the viewers could see him during the race. His sponsor was Little Trees Air Fresheners. You know, the air fresheners that look like little Christmas trees? Instead of doing the usual thing and just putting a sticker on the dashboard, one of his crew members came up with a great idea. Because most people hang the air fresheners from the rear view mirror, the crew member did something similar. He took one of the air fresheners and hung it right in front of the in-car camera, so when the television station turned on the in-car camera during the race, all the viewers could see was the air freshener flapping in the wind in the racecar. It was such a great idea that the race announcers talked about it all race long. Everyone just kept laughing and talking about it. The sponsor was so happy with the idea and the coverage it generated that it signed on with the race team for an additional three years. All the rest of the teams were envious that we had not thought of something like that.

Rear Bumper Camera

Our other favorite camera location is the rear bumper camera. The rear bumper camera is mounted inside the trunk of the racecar, and a small hole is cut out of the bumper for the camera lens. This camera uses a wide-angle lens, which enables you to see what is going on behind the racecar. Although the other camera locations are also interesting, the rear bumper camera allows you to see just how often racecars bump one another.

You know how you feel when you are driving down the highway at 60 miles per hour and someone starts to tailgate you? You become anxious or even angry with the other driver, and that driver is probably no less than 10 feet from you. Racecar drivers are traveling at three times that speed and getting bumped in the back. Imagine how that must feel! It takes a lot of nerve to drive two inches behind someone at top speed.

The rear bumper camera also gives you the sensation of just how close racecars get to one another during a pass. Watching the view from the rear bumper camera, you quickly realize that there is a lot more action and intensity going on in the race than you notice from the stands.

Inside Track

It is a good idea for a race team to have an in-car camera in its racecar. This camera helps promote the sponsor, the driver, and the race team. The more exposure you can offer a potential sponsor, the better your chances are of signing on that sponsor.

The Helmet Camera

In addition to the action on the racetrack, the pit stop is an exciting aspect of races. Changing four tires and adding 22 gallons of fuel in less than 17 seconds makes for quite a bit action on pit road. For several years now, television crews have realized this and have been trying to figure out a way to get the viewer closer to the action on pit road. They broadcast in split-screen mode to show the viewer multiple pit stops at one time. They have reporters stationed on pit road to cover the pit stops and interview the crew chiefs after the stop, all in an attempt to get closer to the action.

Then television crews finally came up with a way to provide a shoulder-side view of what a pit crew does during a pit stop: They mount a small camera on the shoulder of a tire changer for one of the teams. This small remote camera gives the viewers the sensation of doing a pit stop without leaving the comfort of their La-Z-Boy chair. The helmet camera is aimed directly at the tire so that when the tire changer is changing the tire, the audience sees exactly how fast these guys can do their jobs. You can't get this view from the grandstands.

Interviews: Don't Say Anything You Might Regret

This chapter covers the exposure drivers and teams face as a result of being in the sport of stock car racing. These drivers and teams are usually not prepared for the level of exposure thrust upon them or the level of access fans want to them. We have heard several drivers say that they could not believe the extent some fans would go to just to get an autograph from them or photo with them. Racecar drivers have the same level of media exposure as many of the more traditional mainstream sport athletes, such as baseball players or basketball players.

Inside Track

Make sure your driver, crew chief, and anyone else who might be interviewed by the media is prepared for it. The last thing any of you want to do is say something negative that will come back to hurt the team. Believe it or not, this happens more often than you might think.

Double-Edged Sword

Media and fan attention is both good and bad for the drivers and the teams. It is good because the attention helps draw more fans and more sponsors to the sport. The downsides to this attention are the continued pressure on the team to win and the loss of the driver's privacy. Drivers face enough pressure to win races. Having a reporter stick a camera and microphone in your face every race and ask, "Why aren't you winning anymore?" can get on your nerves pretty quickly.

Racing is a sport of both skill and luck. If you have the skill to take advantage of opportunities and you are lucky enough not to be involved in any crashes on the track, you just might be able to win the race. However, you can have the fastest racecar on the racetrack, but if you get caught up in an incident on the racetrack, you could be going out early. What most of the media seem to forget is that even though there are 40 racecars on the track, only one can win the race, and becoming that one is pretty tough to do.

Inside Track

If by chance you happen to see drivers out in public, say in a restaurant, remember to respect their privacy. Don't go up to them in the middle of their dinner to ask for an autograph. Wait until after dinner, and then go to their table and politely ask them for their autographs. Trust me, they will greatly appreciate it. Don't you hate it when your dinner is interrupted?

A Quiet Night out (Yeah, Right)

The other downside to media exposure is the driver's loss of privacy. We're not talking about people looking into your bedroom windows, but we are talking about things like going out for a quiet dinner with your wife or girlfriend. When you are as exposed to the media as the top NASCAR drivers are, it becomes almost impossible to continue to do the simple things in life such as going out to dinner. Can you imagine what it would be like if Jeff Gordon tried to take his wife Brooke out for a quiet candlelight dinner and all of Jeff's racing fans showed up at the restaurant for an autograph? The poor guy would not even have a chance to say two words to his wife.

One night, I was in a restaurant in New Hampshire during one of the Winston Cup races. I was sitting there with my team enjoying a quiet dinner after a very long and hot day at the track. In between bits of Fettuccini Alfredo, I noticed that Chad Little had slipped into the restaurant for a bite to eat with a few of his team members. My first reaction was to go over and say hello and talk to him about how practice went for him, but then I caught myself and decided to wait a minute. I thought, "This guy is probably just as tired as I am, and all he probably wants to do is sit down to a good meal and relax, just as I wanted to when I first walked in." So I sat back down and decided to leave Chad alone to enjoy his meal.

Not two minutes later, a few people from the bar noticed him sitting there. (Mistake number one Chad: Always sit with your back to the bar and door when you don't want to be recognized or bothered.) The next thing you know here comes what seemed like the entire bar over to his table for autographs. What is the guy supposed to do? All he wanted was a nice dinner, and instead it turned into an autograph session. He couldn't just get up and walk out; after all, the entire bar of people was standing between him and the door. It took about 20 minutes, but Chad signed every autograph and shook every hand that wanted to be shaken. Then he finally received his dinner. He was probably more exhausted after dinner than he was when he first walked into the restaurant.

Some may say that is the price you pay for fame and fortune, but we think it stinks. Just because you are a popular and successful NASCAR driver does not mean you should have to give up things like a quiet dinner with your spouse.

Driver Promotions

Part of the responsibility of being a NASCAR driver is to help promote your sponsor and the sport itself. Driver promotions are very popular because they allow the sponsors to leverage the popularity of a particular driver. NASCAR fans will buy anything and everything that their favorite driver is endorsing. It does not matter what the product is, as long as the driver says he likes it or uses it.

For example, drivers Kyle Petty and his son Adam Petty are currently in a television commercial promoting their use of Goodyear's Gatorback belts. The Petty name has been in racing since the early

Inside Track

Your reputation as a driver goes a long way in determining how valuable you are to a sponsor. Make sure you earn your reputation, because it will follow you for your entire career.

days of NASCAR. Adam is the fourth-generation Petty to be involved in NASCAR racing. His grandfather, Richard, is commonly referred to as the king of NASCAR racing. No one has accumulated or broken more records than King Richard did during his racing career; he is a legend in the sport of NASCAR racing. This type of fan following and name recognition makes sponsors drool. They know that anything associated with the Petty name will be a success.

Television Commercials

Jeff Burton, who drives the number 99 Exide Batteries racecar in the NASCAR Winston Cup Series, is currently featured in a commercial that compares his Ford Taurus racecar against a production Ford Taurus driven by an average person. At first, the commercial compares the cars, talking about the amount of horsepower and how fast each car can go. Then Jeff says that his racecar is started from a powerful Exide battery, and the woman driving the regular car says hers is, too. Then the woman in the production Ford Taurus pulls out in front of Jeff, causing him to lock up the breaks on his racecar.

The message in this commercial is that you can have the same powerful battery that is used in a NASCAR Winston Cup racecar. People love this kind of stuff. The thought of driving a car with the same components that are in a racecar fuels people's egos. They think that if the parts are good enough for a racecar, they have to be good enough for them. This thought is exactly what the sponsors are after. Who says speed does not sell products?

Under the Hood

Television commercials are a great way for sponsors to promote their products and their relationship with NASCAR. Unfortunately, this type of advertising is limited to the NASCAR Winston Cup drivers, certain NASCAR Busch Series drivers, and the new NASCAR Craftsman Series drivers.

Commercial Crew Chiefs

In addition to the drivers promoting a sponsor's products, crew chiefs are also getting into the act. The crew chief is person with the knowledge and experience to get the racecars to go as fast as possible. They are the ones with secrets and the answers on how to win races. They are the people you go to when you need advice on your racecar.

Sponsors are using this image of crew chiefs to help sell products. Although the crew chief may not be as well known as the driver, the crew chief takes the credit for making the call that allows a driver the opportunity to win a race. After winning enough races, the crew chief can be just as popular as the driver can. For example, Ray Evernham, former crew chief for Jeff Gordon, and his crew, known as the Rainbow Warriors, became popular for giving Jeff the opportunity to win races. Just a few years ago, it was unheard of for the crew chief to become as popular as the driver was. The increased exposure from the media and the increased popularity of the sport has opened up a whole new world of product promotions for NASCAR race teams.

Under the Hood

Drivers are not the only ones getting all of the media attention. Car owners, such as Jack Roush and Joe Gibbs, are getting some the media attention as well. You never know, the crew may be next.

Personal Appearances

Personal appearances are probably the most favorite form of exposure for sponsors and race teams. They attract fans and promote the products. When a driver takes the time to stop and sign an autograph or take a picture with a fan, the fans feel closer to the drivers. The drivers become real people to them, not just someone behind the wheel of a racecar.

The more successful a driver becomes, the more fans cheer for him or her. All of this exposure forces drivers to be more like politicians. They need to be able to speak well in front of the camera, and they need to possess a certain amount of charm and likeability.

If a driver does not speak well in front of the camera, it can hurt his career. Team owners know this, and in order to ensure that their drivers present themselves well in front of the camera, some drivers attend speaking classes to help refine this skill. We know of several Winston Cup drivers, who we will not name, who have attended a

Dale Carnegie seminar on public speaking. Although at first it may be tough for them to realize that they do not speak well in front of the camera, after they attend a public speaking seminar, they realize how much better they look and sound. All of this training is part of becoming a successful racecar driver. Although the primary skills of driving are learned on the racetrack, the secondary skills of public speaking become more important as a driver moves up into the professional ranks of racing.

Some examples of driver appearances include trade show appearances, autograph signings, new location openings, press conferences, and corporate functions. Each of these events is geared toward increasing attention to the sponsor. These events can be aimed at increasing public awareness of the company or used as an incentive bonus for its internal employees. Because only certain people have what it takes to drive a racecar professionally, they are a rare breed, and everyone wants to be around someone special.

Trade Shows

Trade shows are a normal part of the business of selling products to the general public. The goal of a company attending a trade show is to attract as many people to its booth as possible. One of the more popular ways of doing this is to have a celebrity appearance at the booth. Having a celebrity at a trade show booth attracts more people to the booth who are trying to meet that celebrity. While the people are waiting to meet the celebrity, salespeople present their products to the people waiting in line.

Yellow Flag

Personal appearances are a great way for the public to meet a driver. However, if a driver is rude to a fan that has been waiting in line for an autograph, that person probably will not be a fan for very long. Some drivers (we won't mention any names) need to remember that the fans who come to the races make this sport as successful as it is.

Now depending on the type of products a sponsor makes, using a NASCAR racecar driver for a celebrity appearance at a trade show may or may not be an effective tool to draw people to the booth. If the company creates products for the automotive industry, a NASCAR driver will draw a good crowd.

In addition to having the driver in the trade show booth signing autographs, the company will also usually have what is called a *show car* in the booth as well. A show car is a racecar that is used specifically for promoting the sponsor at events such as trade shows or corporate functions. These show cars are racecars that for one reason or another are no longer used in competition. These racecars are kept cleaned and polished and are transported from trade show to trade show around the country.

Having a racecar at a trade show along with the driver can be a great attraction for the sponsoring company. How often does the general public have a chance to see a real NASCAR racecar up close? The answer is not very often. Giving the public a chance to see one in person is a great attention getter.

Location Openings

Beside trade show appearances, another good way for companies to use race teams for increasing corporate exposure is to have them attend a new location opening. When a company opens a new store location, it spends a large amount of money on advertising in an attempt to draw people to the new location. An excellent way to help draw people to the location is to advertise that a particular racecar driver will be at the location for a period of time to meet visitors.

The popularity of the driver helps draw attention to the store and helps increase the popularity of the driver and the sport. Fans are more likely to cheer for a driver they have met in person than for one they have never met. The next time that driver is on television, the fans will remember that they met that driver and will cheer for them. It is nice to say, "Hey, I met him. He's a really nice guy." This type of promotion builds the racing fan base.

Some companies may even request that the entire team, racecar, and hauler attend a location opening. Imagine driving down the road and seeing a NASCAR Winston Cup tractor-trailer parked in the lot of a new store. Chances are good that this is not an everyday occurrence in your local neighborhood. Your curiosity will make you wonder what is going on, and you will probably stop or at least drive by to see what's up. Having a race team attend a new location opening is an attention getter, and with the popularity of NASCAR on the rise, nothing works better.

Corporate Functions

Besides promoting the sponsor at events such as trade shows and new location openings, race teams are used for corporate functions and employee incentive programs. Teams and drivers are invited to attend corporate functions such as business dinners or annual meetings to show employees or customers what the company is doing to advertise the business. These types of functions draw people to the meetings, show the seriousness of the investment to promote the business, and are used to help bring new customers to the business. Companies use their sponsorship in NASCAR to do business with one another. Sponsoring a NASCAR racecar means that a company is almost guaranteed a certain amount of exposure that may otherwise be out of its financial reach. Sponsoring a NASCAR race team gives businesses an avenue to potential customers and partners that may otherwise have been unobtainable.

NASCAR is hot right now, and everyone wants to be in on what is hot. The public cannot get enough of it. The new breed of drivers like Jeff Gordon and Tony Stewart, who possess a certain amount of charisma and charm, attract all kinds of media attention. Companies are finding ways to use NASCAR to promote their businesses regardless of the products they produce; NASCAR racing is seen in all types of advertising and promotional events. NASCAR is definitely in the spotlight of today's business and media companies. So if you are thinking about starting a race team, make sure you also consider this side of the sport. Before you go to the races, polish up the racecar, comb your hair, and make sure you have your acceptance speech ready. The cameras will be rolling, and you never know who will be watching.

The Least You Need to Know

➤ Fans want to know everything possible about their favorite drivers.

➤ NASCAR is not a "good old boy" sport anymore.

➤ During a NASCAR race, television cameras are everywhere. Watch closely: You just might learn something new.

➤ Drivers and team members need to be prepared for an interview. If they say something wrong to a reporter, it will haunt them for quite a while.

➤ Drivers need to be charismatic, charming, and good public speakers. Speaking in public is more important than you think and even harder than you can imagine.

➤ Team owners and crew chiefs can be just as popular as their drivers are. They also need to be prepared for the increased exposure to the media.

➤ Respect the privacy of drivers. Don't assume that they are obligated to give you an autograph. They are regular people and need some personal time.

Chapter 20

More Than One Way to the Front

In This Chapter

➤ Is horsepower really the answer?

➤ Torque and horsepower: friends or foes?

➤ Can you pass with compassion?

➤ Do you need a bodyguard to pass?

To get to the front of the pack, a driver must pass. In this chapter, we discuss how to pass and whether horsepower plays the role everyone thinks. We talk about the different ways to pass: some are friendly and sportsman like; others may be unfair and downright dangerous. But each is effective and used by nearly every racer in NASCAR.

Speed and Power

Wouldn't it be so nice to be able to hit the gas and power on by anyone you like? Most racers don't have this advantage, and most would like it.

Handling Down the Straightaway

During a race, you will hear the announcer say, "Look at that car handle down the straightaway." This comment refers to the way the car powers past an opponent. Using superior horsepower, of course, is the easiest way to pass. It's very much like trying to get on a highway: If the car in front of you is slowly getting up to speed and you have a more powerful car, you can kick it down a gear and motor on past. Some racers have a similar advantage. Although horsepower doesn't vary that much in the professional ranks, it is a factor in the sportsman and entry levels.

Yellow Flag

Having more horsepower will make your car go faster, but be sure to adjust the car. The extra speed will need accommodating chassis changes.

Having more horsepower is like being the muscle guy on the beach. At any time, you can kick sand in the face of all the little skinny horsepowered guys. But watch out! Horsepower is available to everyone who can afford it. More horsepower can make a good racer into a great one, or it can bulk up that skinny horsepower guy into a steroid monster. Having lots of power can make things a bit easier for you. For example, you have the luxury of passing in more advantageous parts of the track, such as the straightaway.

Just as speed is a result of power, so are worn tires. Having big power and passing frequently can result in worn and blistered tires, and all the power in the world can't help you after your tires are gone. So remember to save those tires!

There have been situations on short tracks where we have outpowered opponents but didn't have the tires to finish going to the front. Being careless with newfound power can make for a very frustrating race. We have passed other racers down the straightaway, got into the corner, faded up the track with worn tires, and been passed again. I continued this lap after lap, until excessive tire spin from tire-abusing power left us chasing an opponent with a better handling, but less powered vehicle. So power can be a detriment as well as a benefit.

Regulating drivers with lots of power can be like taming a lion. All they want to do is lean on the gas and show previously more powerful opponents that they can hang with them now. Nothing makes a driver more confident than powering down a straightaway and waving goodbye to slower cars.

Under the Hood

Never sacrifice engine longevity for the addition of a few horsepower. We have learned in our many years of building race engines that it's much wiser to use a more durable part than a severely lightened one in its place. NASCAR race engines need to run for long periods of time at high RPMs. The internal parts must be of the best quality and have highest stress ratings. Save those "trick" lightened parts for the qualifying engines.

Torque vs. Horsepower

With the introduction of new motor designs, cylinder head and manifold designs have given greater power gains than any other two parts of the motor. Working with both these parts can alter the torque and horsepower of the engine. Torque and horsepower come hand in hand.

First, you need to know what torque is. *Torque* is the result of applied mechanical power to move and turn an object, and torque is how a racecar is propelled forward. The amount of torque that is applied determines how fast the car will go. Basically speaking, torque is what you feel in the seat of your pants when you step down on the accelerator, that incapacitating feeling of helplessness when you slam the gas pedal down on your mom's four-cylinder Toyota Tercel. Okay, so you will need more car than that to make you understand. But any sports car will give you an idea of what racers have under their foot and what a feeling of security torque gives them out on the track.

Yellow Flag

Horsepower is a great thing, but with a lot of power, you must be careful not to spin the tires off the corners and burn up the tires.

Horsepower is the result of torque. *Horsepower* is what you feel when you slam down on the accelerator and the RPMs rise. Torque feels like it's pushing you, and horsepower is the feeling of being pulled down the track. Horsepower is the most desired item by any driver, because most drivers think they can drive well. They figure that all they need to succeed is big power. Of course, we're not going to be the ones to stick a pin in that balloon. Horsepower is only one part of being successful, a driver also needs proper torque, good driving and decision-making skills, a car that handles well, and a great crew. Then, of course, there's luck, if you believe in that.

Inside Track

Torque is used for exiting the corners, and horsepower is used for getting down the straight-away.

Bump-and-Go

The bump-and-go method is one of the greatest ways to pass and look like a star. This method may be the most popular short-track method of passing. It requires precise moves and steady calculations. You must calculate the speed of the car in front of you and adjust your speed and timing to meet the car exactly in the middle of the corner. The instant before your opponent touches the accelerator, you put the nose of your car into the rear bumper of that car, which upsets its handling, it frees up the rear of their car forces it up the track, and allows you to pass it on the inside. In a perfect world, this is the way the method would work. In the racing world, a driver often runs a car in the corner, sets up his opponent as if he were a sitting duck, and slams him hard enough to loosen his teeth. We know this sounds a little harsh, but it does happen (all too often, we might add). The most successful racers are specialists at the bump-and-go method.

Where Should You Bump-and-Go?

The bump-and-go method works just about anywhere. You can work this method running into the turns, but you take the chance of spinning out the other car. By bumping into the corner, you remove static weight from the rear of the car, which makes the rear end to come around on you and may put you in the wall. Buddy Baker, former Winston Cup champion and winner of multiple races on the NASCAR circuit, often refers to this situation as "missing the accident." "Seeing the accident" is driving into the wall front first.

Yellow Flag

If a car bumps you and sends you up the track, never turn down and try to block it. That car is probably already inside you and has taken the position.

Another bump-and-go opportunity is off of the corner. As your opponent exits the turn, you bump his rear bumper slightly, making his car loose or light in the rear and giving you more room and a better line off the corner. With this technique, passing your opponent is inevitable, unless you spin the other car. In most cases, a car spinning off the corner comes around and crosses the track, either in front of you or, if you're lucky, behind you, collecting many of your opponents. This won't make you popular with the other teams, but it may clear out a few healthy runners and make winning a little easier. But as clean, honest racers, we wouldn't want that, would we?

Track Terms

The **infield care center** is a miniature hospital. It is equipped with all the necessary tools and instruments a doctor needs to care for injuries sustained on the track or in the pit area.

Another way to bump-and-go is to maneuver your car on the inside of your opponent and lean on the inside quarter panel, which slides the other car up the track and clears a lane for passing. The worst way to bump-and-go is to position yourself on the outside and lean on the right rear of an opponent's car. This causes the other car to turn right and aim at the wall. Usually, the other driver overcorrects, and more times than not, the incident ends in a spin and a trip to the *infield care center*.

When Is Not Safe to Bump-and-Go?

The bump-and-go method is not without its faults. It most definitely makes your opponent angry and many times vindictive. You need to be sure you can bump, go, and get away with it, because once you do it, your opponent will try to bump you back if given the opportunity. If the racer now doing the bumping is not as skilled in the art of forced maneuvers, he or she may have you spinning like a top or ending the race with a crumpled wad of metal on the business end of the track tow truck. This kind of thing almost never gets a smile from the car owner—not your car owner, anyway.

There are other types of contact passes. For example, while you're on the outside of an opponent, you can lean your car on the right front of an opponent's car to loosen up the rear of the car and allow you to power on by. This type of pass doesn't always work because the inside car has the preferred line and will in most cases use you as leverage to regain control. Another type is to run into the corner under the opponent and use that car as a cushion to keep your car from coming out from under you, because most racers will run you in low and force you to hit the *apron* of the track.

The bump-and-go method is very popular at the end of a race. You will see it more in the last 10 laps than at any other point in the race. We can recall several times where the second-place car won using this very maneuver.

Track Terms

The **apron** of the track is the flat area connecting to the banked part of the track. Hitting this area with the left front tire results in unloading the rear suspension and spinning the car. Avoid doing this.

Under the Hood

Driving into the right front of an opponent can turn him down the track and make an outside pass possible on a one-groove track. But be careful that he doesn't use you as a backboard to bounce off of and regain control. The car on the inside already has the advantage of using your car and tires to gain traction.

Dale Earnhardt used it with good success at the second Bristol race in 1999 against Terry Labonte. On the last lap of the race, going into turn one, Dale ran up on Terry and bumped him slightly harder than he wanted to, resulting in an overreaction by Labonte, who used too much throttle and spun the car. After the spin, Labonte went from first to fifth, and Earnhardt won the race. But Earnhardt paid dearly for that win through weeks of ribbing from other teams and answering for it in the press.

Another example took place in the early 1999 race at the Busch Race in Milwaukee, Wisconsin. Rookie Casey Atwood, eager for a win, used the bump-and-go technique to pass Jeff Green in turn four on the last lap. This last-ditch effort made Atwood a first-time winner and Jeff Green a disappointed and frustrated driver with no recourse but to take second place. Both Labonte and Green showed great restraint and gentlemanly attitudes in post-race interviews; they're true NASCAR racers.

Knowing when it is safe to bump and go is important to your safety as well as your opponent's. Spinning out your opponent can cause great physical harm to him or her or another helpless victim who may be collected by the crash. The safe places to bump-and-go are in the middle of the corner or just off the corner. These two places are also the most common. Doing it in these places gives your opponent a chance to recover and continue to race instead of crashing his car. You might call it fair play; others just call it racing.

Yellow Flag

After bumping another competitor, make sure you have room to get back up the track. Most drivers will crowd you after being passed in this manner.

I can recall a time (one of many) when I used the bump-and-go during a qualifying race, and I was not in the best mood. A rules infraction started me at the end of the line. At the drop of the flag, I was on a mission. When I approached a racer who was notorious for blocking (and he was blocking), I lost my patience and bumped him from behind. After turning him sideways, I tried to get on the inside and pass only to tag him again, removing the front end of his car and most of mine. I did manage to make the race, but not without a lot of damage to my car and plenty of harsh looks. The damage to my car rendered me barely competitive, and for the feature race, I struggled for 300 laps of competition. I learned the hard way that some situations call for a more subdued passing alternative, not such an aggressive move.

Brute Force

Surely every race fan has seen a racer brutalize another car in order to pass. From firsthand experience, we can assure you that being passed this way is no picnic. Some of the most brutal passes we have witnessed have come in qualifying races. Racers find themselves either getting into the *transfer position* or heading back to the trailer to go home.

One of the most brutal passes we have witnessed came in a qualifying race. Three laps from the end of the race, a racer was two cars out of transfer, and he tried the bump-and-go move three times. When that didn't work, he went to the outside and leaned on the right rear of his opponent's car, turning the car sideways to the right and into the back of the car in third place. All three cars tangled with the second-place car, which flipped violently and ended up on top of the pit road wall. The perpetrator of this crash hit both the inside and outside walls, making junk of his car. The third-place car landed on its side in the grass. All three victims had much to say to the passer.

Bully Your Way to the Front

There are many ways to bully your way to the front. This kind of driving is called *rough riding,* and it has become more prevalent in races in recent years. Anyone who has watched a NASCAR race can recall at least a few times where a favorite driver has been either called for rough riding or has been the victim of it.

With the cars and competition drawing closer together, it's becoming increasingly harder to pass without some form of contact, unless a driver gives up the position. Drivers like Mark Martin give up positions early in the race, knowing their cars will come around later in the race and be in position to win.

Being bullied is no fun. It's almost like grammar school, where the big guy tried to take your milk money. But this time, you're equipped with some muscle of your own: a 700-horsepower 3,400-pound car that makes you as big as he. Your will to succeed and desire to win can help you persevere even when the most brutal bullies are banging their way to the front.

Inside Track

The **transfer position** is the last eligible position from a qualifying or last chance race. If six of 20 cars in a last chance race will qualify for the main feature race, then the sixth spot is the last transfer position.

Track Terms

Rough riding is when two or more cars engage in considerable or heavy bumping expressly to pass or crash a competitor. This is not acceptable by NASCAR and will often result in a penalty stop, or loss of a lap by the perpetrator.

Some of the ways to bully your way to a win are to force your opponent to make a mistake, even a small one, and capitalize on it with a push or shove to make a small mistake a big one. Some of the biggest bullies out there are the first to point fingers when they are moved intentionally or roughed up a bit.

In the September 1999 Busch North Race held in Loudon, New Hampshire, two drivers, Dale Shaw and Tom Carey, were fighting for position. They traded places a few times over the course of 10 laps. From my vantage point directly behind them, I could see tempers were flaring, and patience was giving out. Although both drivers were given racing room, time was running out to make it to the front. Both drivers fought for fifth place. For the third time, Shaw ran into turn one, a car checked up in front of him, and he was caught on the outside, but he was running well and holding his line. Carey saw a chance to pass and leaned on the gas to get up along side Shaw. Getting in there a little to hot, Carey got into him once, then again, a third time, and then a forth. They battled for position all the way through turns one and two.

As they exited turn two and headed down the back straightaway, Carey tried to pull in front of Shaw by pulling to the right. After such a brutal banging off that corner, Shaw would have none of that and held his line high to the wall. Carey turned right, and Shaw turned left. The results were catastrophic for Carey. His car slammed the back stretch wall head on and nearly flipped over. I darted to the inside in a very aggressive move along with several other cars to avoid contact with Carey's car, which was now spinning and shredding parts. As luck would have it, I was able to avoid major contact.

Yellow Flag

Rough riding almost always gets you in trouble. Most racers won't sit quietly after being shoved up the track or moved violently out of the way. Rough riding gets you rough riding, and most of the time, the competitors around you suffer along with you.

Not a Good Way to Make Friends

Bullying your way to the front can sometimes make your day end sooner than you thought, but there is an upside to being a bully on the track. Drivers have made careers out of rough riding. In the early days of NASCAR, it was almost accepted as part of the show. Guys like Dale Earnhardt (our personal favorite), Jimmy Spenser, Cale Yarbough, and Junior Johnson made names for themselves early in their careers with exceptional, controversial driving styles. Driving like that earned them names such as "The Intimidator" and "Mr. Excitement." With names like these, you know something bad had to happen with the good. After a rough riding incident, you will see tempers flare. We have witnessed everything from arguments to all-out fights. Nothing brings a fight on faster than one team thinking it was unfairly passed. NASCAR goes to great lengths to keep this type of driving to a minimum. They penalize cars for continued rough riding by administering a stop and go penalty or giving a one lap penalty. NASCAR believes in good hard racing and fair play.

Rough riding has been around since the beginning of stock car racing, and we suspect it will always be part of racing. NASCAR has taken steps to lessen the amount of bullying, but like football, racing is a contact sport. Removing rough riding altogether would change the way fans see and enjoy auto racing.

Clean Racing

Let's not forget that clean racing is what is it all about. For all the bumping that goes on, there are 20 clean passes. Clean passing is made by positioning your car as to force a competitor to change his entry or exit of a corner. And doing this by strategic driving. Placing your car along side another going into the corner can make another car move up and give you space to race. This can be done without contact, and is, many times. During the course of the race, cars with a tire or engine advantage can easily do this. Great drivers will do it with equal equipment and make it look easy.

In this chapter, you learned about horsepower and torque and the effects these have on the speed of the car. We also described ways to pass someone during a race. The main thing to remember is that you can regulate your right foot, temper, and attitude. As much as you want to lean on another racer, keep in mind that you will get what you give. We haven't witnessed any other sport where immediate retaliation is not only administered, but it's expected.

But racing is not just a bunch of guys out there crashing into each other. Racers are some of the best athletes in the world doing what no one else can: Driving high-tech machines to the limit continuously for 500 laps. For every rough or contact pass that occurs, you will see 100 clean passes completed to precision in places where a car shouldn't have been able to fit and done at incredible speeds. Learning these maneuvers takes years of experience, steady nerves, and the confidence of professional drivers.

The Least You Need to Know

➤ Big horsepower can help you in passing.

➤ Torque is the great equalizer in getting off the corner.

➤ The bump-and-go move is the most common and easiest contact pass to make.

➤ Bumping an opponent on the right side of the car or while going into a turn will almost always result in a crash.

➤ Using brute force to get by an opponent will almost always get you return contact.

➤ Clean racing and passing should always be the way.

Chapter 21

Drafting—Two Cars Are Better Than One

In This Chapter

➤ What are the dynamics of drafting?

➤ Why doesn't drafting work all the time?

➤ Who is the best at bump drafting?

In NASCAR racing, sometimes simply having the fastest car is not enough to win the race; many other things factor into the winning equation. Sometimes the deciding factor is pit strategy or tire wear. Other times, it could be fuel mileage or avoiding the crash that took down all the leaders.

Still other times, the winning factor could be something called *drafting*. If you know something about racing or have watched the Daytona 500 on television, you probably have heard this term and know something about it. In this chapter, not only are we going to explain what drafting is, but we're also going to tell you how it works, why it does not work all of the time, and who, in our opinion, is the best at it.

The Dynamic of the Draft

Drafting is a very important aspect of racing. It can make a slower racecar faster than a better racecar. It can mean the difference between running up near the front to being sent to the back of the pack by a freight train.

The interesting thing about drafting is that no matter how good of a driver you are or how well your racecar is set up, you need another racecar in order to take advantage of it, which changes things somewhat from the norm on the racetrack. Usually, the racecars on the track are competing against each other, but in order to take advantage of drafting in racing, you need to work with another driver. Strange as it may sound, it is true.

What Drafting Is

So what is drafting? *Drafting* is the effect of the air as it passes over and around a racecar. In Chapter 5, "The Stock Car Itself," we told you that the air that passes over a racecar creates down force that helps the racecar stick to the racetrack. This is true, but the air also has another effect on the racecar.

Track Terms

Drafting is the effect of the air as it passes over and around two racecars that are traveling very close together.

The air creates down force on the racecar because the racecar itself is pushing the air in front of it over and around the racecar. Pushing the air takes away power from the racecar. In order to minimize the resistance from the air, race teams try to make their racecars as aerodynamic as possible. The less resistance there is on the front of the racecar, the faster it will go.

If one racecar is pushing on the air directly in front of another racecar, the second racecar is using less power to move air because the racecar in front of it has already moved the air. If the second racecar does not have to use force to move the air, it has more horsepower to propel the racecar itself. In other words, the racecar in front is working harder than the racecar behind it to go the same speed.

How Drafting Works

When two racecars travel around the racetrack very close to one another, almost bumper to bumper, a vacuum is created between the two racecars. This vacuum is the result of the air passing over and around both racecars at a very high rate of speed. As air passes over and around the racecars, it pulls out the air between the two racecars, creating a vacuum. This vacuum pulls the second racecar and allows it to travel using less power than it would be able to if it were all by itself on the racetrack.

The second racecar is not the only racecar benefiting from the effect of the draft. The racecar that is out in front is also benefiting from the draft. In addition to pulling the second racecar, the vacuum between the two racecars is also pushing the first racecar. This push is like adding a few more horsepower to the engine, and everybody wants that, right?

In order for drafting to work, two or more racecars need to be following each other very closely. How close are we talking about? To put it into perspective, let's make a comparison. When you are traveling down the highway at say 60 miles per hour, you are probably about 15 or 20 feet behind the car in front of you. When two racecars are going around the racetrack trying to draft off one another, they are no more than two or three feet apart, and sometimes they are even closer than that.

Before you get all excited about drafting, realize that it has a downside. (Doesn't everything?) Remember our discussion on down force and how it works on both the front and rear of the racecar? When the two racecars are drafting around the racetrack, the air thinks that the two racecars are one car. Because the racecars are so close together, the air travels over both racecars, never getting to the back of the first racecar or to the front of the second racecar. Without the air creating down force on the rear of the first racecar, it will have a loose condition in the turns. (In case you forgot, a loose condition is when the back of the racecar wants to slide around the front of the racecar, causing the car to spin.) This situation is called "taking the air off of someone's spoiler." This is not good, especially at speeds in excess of 190 miles per hour.

The second racecar, which is losing down force on the front of the racecar, will have a push condition in the turns. A push condition is when the racecar does not want to make the turn the driver wants to make. The reduced down force on the front of the racecar will cause the front end of the racecar to lift slightly off of the racetrack. The front end doesn't lift all the way off the racetrack; it just is not pressed into the racetrack as it would be if the down force were pushing on the front end. This reduction in down force on the front end can make the racecar less responsive to the driver. Imagine traveling at over 190 miles per hour, two feet from the racecar in front of you, and just as you start to go into the turn, the racecar decides it wants to go straight into the wall. This would probably cause you to stop and change your underwear at the very least.

Yellow Flag

Do not try to draft on the highway! Professional racecar drivers are expecting the racecar behind them to pull up very close, but the unsuspecting person on the highway in front of you will have no idea what you are trying to do. You will make this person very nervous and angry; he'll be concentrating on giving you obscene hand gestures instead of focusing on what's ahead of him. And drafting does not work at 55 miles per hour. Drafting takes place at high speeds—about 150 miles per hour and more.

Inside Track

Drafting changes the handling of the racecar. In some situations, the lead racecar becomes loose, and the trailing racecar picks up a push condition while drafting. Drafting on big tracks such as Daytona or Talladega need cars with no down force. It is better for you to have a car with good drafting abilities rather than down force.

What Happens When You Lose the Draft?

Now you know how drafting works and what the basic advantages and risks of it are. So what happens when you are drafting and for whatever reason lose the draft? When a racecar loses the draft, it falls out of the path of the air that is going over the racecars. The first thing that happens is that you immediately feel as though the racecar has slowed down, almost like the brakes were applied or someone tossed a boat anchor out the back of the racecar. This feeling is from the sudden reintroduction of air and down force on the racecar.

Track Terms

When you lose the draft, you almost immediately begin to slow down, at least it seems that way. What is actually happening is that all of the other racecars are about to **freight-train** you straight to the back of the pack.

The next thing you notice is that the racecars that are still in the draft are pulling away from you. If any racecars are behind you, they will pull out to pass you to keep up with the other racecars that are still drafting and now pulling even farther away from you. Chances are, not one of these racecars will give you the opportunity to get back in line and catch the draft again. They will be going by you so fast that they will look like a freight train passing you as you are standing still. Before you realize it, you are on your way to the back of the pack with a lot of track positions to make up. When this happens, it is called being *freight-trained,* and now you know why.

The key to staying in the draft is staying in line with the racecar in front of you. The only time you should pull out from behind a racecar in front of you is when you think you can pass that racecar. But if you pull out and the other racecars behind you do not follow you to keep the draft going behind you, you run the risk of being freight-trained.

Inside Track

When you lose the draft, the only thing you can do to get it back is to get in line behind another racecar as quickly as possible. The longer you are out there without a drafting partner, the greater your risk of losing track positions.

How Do You Get the Draft Back?

When a racecar loses the draft, the only thing the driver can do is try to get back in line as quickly as possible. The longer a racecar is out of the draft, the greater its chance of ending up in the back of the pack. If you are lucky, there may be an opening where you can get back into the draft without losing too many track positions. The only option you have is to find another racecar, team up by getting in line behind one another, and try to catch the pack that is out in front as quickly as you can. Remember that side-by-side racing hurts the draft, so stay in line and put your foot to the floor.

Why Drafting Doesn't Work All the Time

If drafting is an important aspect to stock car racing, do drivers use it all of the time? Whenever possible, drivers do take advantage of drafting in an effort to win a race. The problem is that drafting does not work all of the time. It only works on large tracks and tracks where high speeds can be maintained.

It does not work on small tracks or tracks configured in such a way that high speeds cannot be maintained. Examples of these tracks would be the Bristol Motor Speedway and Sears Point Raceway. The Bristol Motor Speedway, although it is a high-banked racetrack, is just not big enough for drivers to take advantage of the draft. The straightaways are not long enough for the racecars to get up enough speed to take advantage of the draft. The same is also true with racetracks like Sears Point Raceway in northern California. The Sears Point racetrack is configured as a road course, which means it has both left and right turns. This road course configuration does not provide enough room for the racecars to get up enough speed to take advantage of the draft.

Track Size

So how big does a racetrack need to be in order for a racecar driver to take advantage of the draft? To take advantage of the draft in a race, the track will generally need to be at least $1^{1}/_{2}$ miles in length. The straightaways also have to be very long in order for the racecars to pick up enough speed to create the draft. An exception to this is Darlington raceway in South Carolina. Its length of approximately $1^{1}/_{8}$ miles, and high banks allow high speeds and drafting abilities.

A perfect example of this kind of track is the Daytona International Speedway located in Daytona Beach, Florida. The Daytona International Speedway is $2^{1}/_{2}$ miles in length. The front straightaway is 1,900 feet long; the back straightaway is 3,800 feet long. The turns are banked at an angle of 31 degrees. The long straightaways and high banking of this track enable racecars to maintain a high rate of speed all the way around the racetrack. To give you an idea of how fast racecars can go on this track, NASCAR Winston Cup driver Bill Elliott set a qualifying record of just over 210 miles per hour back on February 9, 1987. He completed his lap in 42.78 seconds.

Inside Track

Tracks with high-banked turns and long straightaways are ideal for drafting. If you have never drafted in a race before, it would be a good idea to rent a racetrack with another team that has experience drafting and practice it with that team before the race. Don't try drafting for the first time during a race. Although NASCAR requires drafting experience before they will allow you to compete at these big facilities.

Because of the high speeds drivers were reaching, NASCAR required the use of a restrictor plate, which is designed to limit the horsepower a racecar can produce. In effect, restrictor plates slow down the racecars to about a maximum speed of about 200 miles per hour, but the use of the restrictor plates creates some very exciting racing. In a race where restrictor plates are used, the competition is even closer than normal. Due to the limited horsepower, close and side-by-side racing is very common.

Restictor Plates are required at the superspeedways. Currently they are used at Daytona and Talladega. Restrictor plates are also used on the NASCAR Featherlight Modified Tour cars at tracks 1 mile in length.

For many drivers, racing at these speeds in such tight quarters makes them feel uncomfortable. If something goes wrong on one racecar, that racecar usually takes at least one other racecar with it. It is not uncommon to see very large, multicar crashes at these racetracks. For this reason, many drivers are trying to have NASCAR remove the rule regarding restrictor plates, stating that the restrictor plates cause a more dangerous situation than the higher rate of speed. However, as long as these restrictor plate races continue to draw in the fans, NASCAR will not change that rule.

One way that drivers try to overcome the limitations of the restrictor plates is by drafting with one another. Two racecars drafting one another around the racetrack will go faster than any one racecar can by itself. Three racecars drafting are better than two are, and four racecars drafting are better than three racecars. But once you get more than five racecars together, the effect of the draft on all of the racecars is reduced. Four racecars are the ideal number for drafting.

Other racetracks were drafting comes in to play include the Michigan Speedway, which is 2 miles in length and is banked 18 degrees in the turns. The Talladega Superspeedway is $2^2/_3$ miles in length and is banked 33 degrees in the turns. The Indianapolis Motor Speedway, home of the Indianapolis 500, is $2^1/_2$ miles in length and is banked nine degrees in the turns. These racetracks are where you will see the highest speeds in NASCAR as well as some of the most exciting racing in the world.

Inside Track

Although drafting can occur at almost any speed, in stock car racing the racecars need to be traveling at speeds in excess of 150 miles per hour for the entire lap.

Speed

Racing of any kind is all about speed. The main issues in racing are how fast can you go and whether you can go faster than everyone else you are competing against. The pure thrill and excitement of the speed of racing is what draws people to the sport.

Drafting accelerates the speed at which a vehicle can travel. It allows a vehicle to go to the next level with the assistance of another vehicle. You have heard the saying that two heads are better than one; the same is true in racing and drafting.

In order for two racecars to draft one another, both racecars need to be able to sustain a high rate of speed. How fast are we talking about? Drafting can occur at almost any speed, but when you have two racecars, which are basically the same size and shape, drafting requires speeds in excess of 100 miles per hour. With NASCAR racing, the requirement is usually around the 150 miles per hour mark. These are speeds that you would never see in your everyday driving.

Why do we say that drafting can occur at any speed? The reason is that the size of the two vehicles drafting also affects when drafting can occur. When you drive on the highway behind an 18-wheel truck, the truck is obviously much bigger than the car you are driving. If you could get close behind the truck, you could draft behind it and still maintain the same speed without using the accelerator as much. The air being pushed out of the way by the truck would pass right around your vehicle and pull you along the road with the truck. Even though you would not be going over 100 miles per hour, you could draft because your car and the truck are so different in size. Because all NASCAR racecars are basically the same size, they have to rely on speed to create the draft effect.

Track Terms

Bump drafting is when one racecar bumps the back of another racecar in an attempt to make both racecars go faster. Because the car in front is breaking the air, the car behind can go faster behind it. By bumping and pushing the car in front, it helps both to go faster.

Bump Drafting

Drivers in many NASCAR racing series use a particular form of drafting called *bump drafting*. This dangerous technique should not be used by just anyone. It can have strong consequences if it is performed improperly or at the wrong time.

What Bump Drafting Is

Bump drafting has the same result as regular drafting, but the two racecars work with each other in a different and potentially dangerous way. With bump drafting, the second racecar bumps the back of the racecar in front to increase the speed of the two racecars. This bump is a boost to help accelerate the front car to a higher speed. However, like a shove in the back while you are running, that bump can cause the front car to spin out and even crash. The driver about to be bumped needs to be prepared for it, and the bumper needs to be prepared in case his sudden boost to the racecar in front of him causes the racecar to spin.

In addition to being a way to increase your speed with the assistance of another racecar, bump drafting can be a form of passing. By bumping the racecar in front of you,

you are disrupting the racecar, which can cause it to ride up the racetrack. In order to bring the racecar back under control, the driver will have to slow down. When this happens, it creates an opening for you to pass the driver.

How Bump Drafting Works

The way bump drafting works is pretty simple. Both racecars are traveling around the racetrack, and the racecar in front has to use some power to move the air over and around the racecar. Because the second racecar does not have to move the air, it has a little more power than the racecar in front. Even though the second racecar has more power than the racecar in front, it can go only as fast as the racecar it is drafting. If the second racecar pulls out alongside the first racecar, then the cars will no longer be drafting, both racecars will have to move the air around their respective racecars, and neither car will have the extra horsepower to pull away from the other car.

So the question is, how can the second racecar increase the power of the first racecar? The second racecar can help the first racecar by getting up against its rear bumper and pushing the racecar down the straightaways of the racetrack. By doing this, the second racecar is helping the first racecar increase his speed. The key to bump drafting is staying on the back bumper of the racecar in front of you. If you back off the bumper and then go up against it again repeatedly, you will cause the racecar to swerve each time you go back up against the bumper. The driver in front of you will not be very happy and will probably move around to make you lose the draft. Bad bump drafting is not a good way to make friends on the racetrack.

Who Is the Best at Bump Drafting?

Bump drafting is an art form in racing, so who then is the best at it? Because the NASCAR Winston Cup drivers are the ones who use this technique most often, they are the best at it. Of the NASCAR Winston Cup drivers, we feel that Dale Earnhardt is the best at the draft, as well as bump drafting.

Dale Earnhardt has been racing for several decades and has a reputation for intimidating other racecar drivers on the track with his style of driving. Dale is one tough competitor. He has won many races by using the draft to catch the leaders of the race, and he has used bump drafting on the last lap of a race to pass another racecar for the lead and victory.

Bump drafting first got it start in the IROC races back in the early 1980s. (IROC stands for the International Race of Champions.) Dale, who currently has won seven NASCAR Winston Cup championships, was a regular in the IROC races of the 1980s. In these races, drivers from several different series would compete in a race in the exact same type of racecar. The racecars were identical to the others in order to ensure that no one driver had an advantage over another driver. The purpose of this race was to determine who was the best racecar driver based on pure driving skill and not how good or bad a particular racecar was.

Because some of the IROC races were held on superspeedways, drafting was a key factor in determining the winner of the race. Bump drafting is used to pass during the race. If there are two lines of cars, several cars per line, the car behind the leader of one of these lines bumps and pushes the car in front of it to help it past the other line, giving both bumping partners an advantage.

Let us interrupt this story for a minute to tell you that although blocking is not illegal in racing, it is not looked upon in a very positive light. The only time blocking is sort of acceptable is when drivers are going for the win. Okay, let's get back to our story.

Inside Track

IROC stands for the International Race of Champions. Did you think it was just a model of the Chevrolet Camaro? Actually the Camaro was named after the series.

All of this bumping and blocking added to an already intense situation. Dale Earnhardt made the bump-and-go move famous. When Dale would bump another racecar and look to make a pass and the driver would come down to block him, Dale would fake a pass one way. Then after the driver committed to the block, Dale would go the other way and pass the driver for the lead. This move is kind of like a head fake in basketball or football and won Dale more races than we can think of. It also earned him the nickname "The Intimidator" because of the way he was able to intimidate the other racecar drivers in the series. Earnhardt still today continues to be the king of the draft.

In this chapter, we have talked about the dynamics of drafting and how it works to help racecars go faster. We also talked about why drafting doesn't work all the time, what happens when you lose the draft, and how to get the draft back. We also talked a bit about bump drafting and how it can help you win a race and make enemies on the racetrack.

The thing you need to remember about this chapter is that drafting is a technique used by professional racecar drivers. The key word is *professional* racecar drivers. Drafting can be very dangerous. At the speeds needed to draft on the racetrack, things happen very fast and can have disastrous results. NASCAR will not let just anybody behind the wheel of a 700-horsepower racecar and tell him to go draft at 200 miles per hour. Although racing is an awesome sport and the thrill of speed is addicting, racing should stay on the racetrack, where it is supposed to be and where it is safe for all.

The Least You Need to Know

➤ Drafting is the effect of the air on two or more racecars traveling at a high rate of speed and very close to one another.

➤ Drafting will sometimes change the handling of the racecars. The lead racecar will become loose while the trailing racecar will pick up a push condition.

➤ Drafting only works at large racetracks with high speeds. You won't see drafting at the $1/4$-mile oval raceway.

➤ Drafting does not work on small racetracks or road courses because the racecars need to sustain a high rate of speed to create the drafting effect.

➤ Bump drafting is when one racecar pushes on the back bumper of the lead racecar in an effort to make both of them go faster.

➤ Bump drafting is also a technique used in passing. Two cars can bump together to help pass another.

➤ If you have never drafted on racetrack before, rent a track with another team who has experience drafting and practice with that team. This practice experience is a requirement from NASCAR.

Chapter 22

Patience— You Can't Win on the First Lap

In this chapter, you learn about patience. Patience helps you decide when it's the right time to pass and when it's the right time to let someone go by. This might not sound like racing, but soon you will understand why racers sometimes need to make these decisions. You will learn when it's smart to pass and when to use your head instead of the bumper. Finally, we will talk about slowed mental and race paces, and how this will get you to the front.

When to Let Them Go

In Chapter 18, "Getting Past the First Lap," we said that you can't win on the first lap. This statement may seem obvious, especially when there could be as many as 499 laps left in the race, but some drivers need to be reminded of this fact. When the green flag drops, the first thing they do is run to the front. It doesn't matter if they start in the second row or the last. They feel the need to be out front. But even if you get to the front in one lap, you're still not the winner! You have to run the total of 500 laps in order to kiss the pretty girl at the end.

Running the race with patience may be the hardest thing for a racecar driver to do. Most drivers are very competitive. The need to be first becomes a little devil on the shoulder of the driver telling him to run to the front. This little demon even pulls out the cord of the radio so the spotter can't interfere. A spotter's job is to notify the driver of crashes, cars making moves on the driver, and holes the driver can fill. But sometimes no matter what the spotter says, the driver will swear he heard something else.

I am no different. I remember a big race that took place in Thompson, Connecticut, where I could see the leaders, and I wanted to be up there racing with them. It was a 300-lap race, so the attrition rate was going to be high. The car was handling better then ever. I had never run this well up to this point. With confidence and power to spare, I felt that I could win this race if I could get to the front. After only 35 laps of the race, my patience was already growing thin, and so were my tires.

Yellow Flag

Never make your move right off the green flag at the start of the race. The rules say you must first pass the start-finish line in double-file running order. Failure to do this will result in a black flag for you and a possible end to your chances of winning.

This car pulled out of line to pass, was caught low, and had to drop back into place. Lucky for him, there was space.

As many times as the spotter and crew chief told me about the saving the tires, all I could see was the cars in front of me and feel how I didn't want to be in that position. I leaned hard on the car, running the high groove and wearing the right front tire. On lap 50, I found myself slowing and losing the feel I once had. I ran the car as hard as I could to keep up only to run the right front tire flat and have to pit under a green flag. I lost two laps because of the pit stop and ended up running that way for the next 250 laps, ending up in twentieth place. A top 10 finish or maybe better was within my reach for that race, but my drive and desire for the win and disregard for the length of the race took that from me.

Why You Would Let Someone Pass

Maybe the worst thing a driver has to do is allow another car to pass him or her. Sometimes this is necessary in order to run at a pace that's appropriate for the setup and length of the race.

One of the rare regular users of this practice is Winston Cup driver Mark Martin. Mark Martin regularly allows faster cars to pass him early in the race, and as the laps go on, he reels them back in and goes on by. Martin typically has one the highest totals of practice laps for each race and knows almost exactly what will happen with the car and how fast it will go for the long term. They run lap after lap to watch the speed of the car and its long-term handling. His crew also knows how far and how long the competition can go at top speed, so being passed is a calculated risk. Some teams are better at calculating such a risk, and it often pays big dividends.

Reasons to let competitors by vary. One of the biggest reasons is tire wear or your tire pressure setup. Some teams set up for the long run by using lower tire pressure. This setup makes the car slightly less responsive in the opening laps or after pitting. But as the race goes on, the tires become more user-friendly, and the driver can gain more positions than he could if he had had better handling early on. It's a waiting game, and many drivers are willing to play that game in order to be in position to win. Some are not, and those are the drivers you need to let go by.

Impatient drivers who will take you out of the race by inadvertently causing an accident are also good candidates for a free pass early in the race. However, some drivers and owners don't see it this way and will waste their cars holding off such an opponent. But focusing solely on holding off opponents only reduces your chance for a good finish or win. I'm not saying a driver should pull over and let the field go by; drivers need to know who they can let by and the chances of those other racers burning up the tires, running out of gas, or just plain getting themselves in trouble. This knowledge comes from driving experience and good crew members with extensive backgrounds in racing.

Inside Track

Cars that are faster than you will get by you eventually. Allowing them to get by early and burn up their long-term speed will work in your favor later on in a long race. Most times, you will catch up and pass them into the turn when they have slowed down more than you have due to wearing out the car prematurely. At this point, you will still have a good car under you.

How Being Passed Can Help You

Being passed can help you. In the short term, you can almost never see the good side of letting another competitor go by. It always takes a number of laps to see the benefit of doing so. Everyone races at a different pace. A car passing you may be faster than you initially and slow to a pace that you pass 25 laps later.

You can see the proof of our point in sample average lap times over a 50-lap run. The second car may run as fast as 30 seconds per lap, but run as slow as 32 seconds per lap near the end of the race. The first car could be as fast as 30.3 seconds per lap and as slow as 31.5 seconds per lap. Even though the second car can go faster than the first car on a single lap or two, the average lap time is 31 seconds for the second car and 30.9 seconds for the first car. The second car will pass the first car in the beginning, but the first car will eventually catch and pass the first car and pull away.

On long-distance races where fuel mileage is an issue, you will witness a lot of what looks like unnecessary passing. Racecars with good mileage will let cars with worse mileage by because they know they will eventually catch up to those cars. In a five-stop race, some racers with great gas mileage only have to stop four times. That's a major advantage that is not easily made up by speed out on the track! Refueling requires an 18-second stop and extra seconds to slow into the stop and then accelerate back up to speed, so a driver can gain as much as a lap on the competition by not having to stop.

Don't Force a Situation; Let It Come to You

Racing is a dangerous sport, and sometimes the participants make it even more so. Being out on the track is usually exciting enough without the competition making it a hair-raising experience. Most racecar drivers want to win, and this need and desire to win often forces drivers into situations they would not ordinarily be subjected to.

Running in a pack will many times result in a big crash.

At 200 miles per hour in a pack of 40, one car will bring it to the inside and force a three-wide situation, which sometimes results in disastrous crashes involving 10 or more cars. Sometimes a few brave (or insane, depending on your perspective) drivers will break off and make the line four or even five cars wide, which makes racing impossible. In this circumstance, racing becomes a quest for survival.

Big-track, restrictor-plate racing may be the most exciting form of NASCAR competition, but this type of racing may also be breeding ground for impatient drivers. Many drivers speak out against restrictor-plate racing because it closes up the competition and makes for incredibly close racing with little room for error. Forcing a move in this situation can make for a short day if the drivers don't give respect and racing room.

In the first Busch Grand National Race of 1998 held at Daytona International Speedway, Dale Earnhardt Jr. was involved in an incident that serves as a fine example for this section. About mid-race, Earnhardt was already two laps down to the leaders because of early mechanical failure, but he was running in the lead pack of cars. On the inside and running fast, he pulled up beside Dick Trickle, who was on the lead lap and coming on strong. The cars got very close, and at this speed, the vacuum effect of the cars running in a pack like this forced the two to touch just slightly. This touch was enough to make Earnhardt turn to the right and toward the outside wall. Instead of Trickle backing out, which he couldn't to avoid being wrecked from behind by the pack of cars that followed, he turned left and pushed Earnhardt's car, forcing both in the grassy section at over 190 miles per hour.

Earnhardt's car went sideways, and with Trickle's car under him, the force of air picked up Earnhardt's car and flipped it 360 degrees in the air. It landed atop the Trickle car. Trickle hit the brakes, launching Earnhardt's car and flipping it violently several times before it came to a stop on all four wheels. A little patience and not forcing a situation would have saved both drivers wrecked cars and a poor finish.

Inside Track

Running four or five wide is like trying to run naked through a thorn bush. Something is going to get cut, and it's likely to be the goodies.

Inside Track

Restrictor plates are aluminum plates installed under the carburetor to reduce the size of the inlet from the carburetor to the manifold. These plates significantly reduce horsepower output and the terminal speed of the car. These NASACR required plates are installed to reduce the speed of the racecars. Speeds of 220 miles per hour or more would not be uncommon if they were eliminated.

Under the Hood

There aren't many races that go caution free. Most caution periods occur because two or more cars either crash or cause a reduction in speed and an unsafe condition, causing the rest of the field to slow. Most of these cautions are caused by impatience on a restrictor-plate track where having patience and giving a competitor a break is necessary. Officials often remind the drivers and teams of this fact before the race. They express it sternly in the drivers' meeting and place big penalties on drivers or teams who don't display extra sportsmanship. NASCAR is firm and fair about this issue.

You wouldn't think racecar drivers even have the capacity for driving patiently, but some of the greatest drivers can do this. Driving on a track is very similar to driving on a crowded freeway. Everyone wants to be in the fast lane, and no one wants to be passed or held up. Just as you would need to watch traffic and most likely cut off someone to get in the lane you would like to drive in, the racecar driver needs to do the same. He sits in line and waits for someone to make a mistake, lose just a little ground, or move slightly to allow him to get in line or provide enough room for him to force himself in line.

Under the Hood

Spotters are a major help to drivers passing within close tolerances. Spotters do the same thing your spouse does on the freeway; they tell you when to go, when to stay, when you can fit into a hole, and when they need to find a restroom. Well, they don't do that, but they are backseat drivers. Without them, many drivers would be lost out there, and cautions would take on a whole new meaning. Spotters are important, and the quality of spotting can be the difference between a good race and a bad race.

Staying Alert and Picking Your Spot

In some races, you must wait as many as 20 or more laps to gain a small advantage and a chance to pass. You must be patient, but you must also be ready at any time to capitalize on your opponent's mistakes. Getting in a groove and running a good line with consistent lap times is important, but don't let yourself be lulled into a rut. Running a pace slower than your car is capable of only puts you further behind and makes it harder to catch up.

While you run a comfortable pace, stay close to the car in front of you. Don't ride his bumper, but stay within striking distance. You need to know how fast your car will react and how fast you can get either on the inside or outside of the two cars directly in front of you. Knowing what your options are at all times will make your passing attempts more effective.

Slow Down to Go Faster

Slow down to go faster? Although it doesn't sound logical, it may be one of the most important pieces of advice you can get in racing. Instead of running the car past the edge, skidding the car through the turns, and fighting to keep control because you're going too fast, slow down and get a grip. Run the car into the turn a little bit slower, enough to keep the *corner speed* up, but not enough to break the tires loose going in.

This entry sets up the car for a better exit and a more controlled transition from the corner to the straightaway. You might feel as though you're going slower, but your lap times will increase dramatically and your car owner and crew chief will smile. The hardest time to heed this advise is when you're excited, aggravated, or being provoked.

Many times provoking another driver, even in the smallest way, can help you more than trying to pass him. All you need to do is continuously show him you're there. Run up on him and then look to the inside. Then look to the outside. You have no intentions of passing, but this maneuvering makes the other driver run harder into and off of the corner, which uses up his car. Meanwhile, you have slowed your pace and kept tires underneath you. By pushing your opponent with this subtle yet effective approach, you can get by him without using up your car.

Track Terms

Corner speed is more important than straightaway speed. If your corner speed is down, you will never get any straightaway speed at all. You need the fast run off the corner to propel you down that straightaway. Also, if you have low corner speed, passing others will become nearly impossible.

This outside pass cost some paint and body-work, but it did the job.

Don't be harsh on your car. Run the car as fast as it will go without tearing it up. If you have hit on the right setup for your car, you're going to have a good day. No driver can run the car 500 miles on the edge and have something left to race with at the end. You need to save some of your car's power if you want to win.

Ringing the Snack Bell

During the race, a driver needs plenty of beverages. Water or some kind of mineral-replenishing drink like Gatorade is more than a thirst quencher, it is like a jump start back into the race when a driver is depleted and dehydrated. Long races also deplete drivers' energy, and they need plenty of energy to hold onto that car in the closing laps. As a driver, you may want to consider having a sports bar available to you for caution periods. But be careful where you put it; not too many sports bars will survive the 140-degree heat of a racecar.

One of the biggest race days of the year happens in May when the Indianapolis 500 takes place in Indiana and the Coca-Cola 600 is run in North Carolina. Once in a while, a driver tries to compete in both races on this one day. Tony Stewart, the driver of the Joe Gibbs-owned Winston Cup car, drove all but four of the 500 miles in the Indianapolis 500. Then he was taken by helicopter to the airport and whisked away on a private jet headed to Charlotte. On the jet, he was given something to eat, sports bars, water, and Gatorade. After arriving at the track, he had only minutes to get himself together and get into the Winston Cup car.

Yellow Flag

Provoking another racecar driver is like poking a tiger with a stick. Poke the wrong way, and you're liable to lose an arm. Drivers are notorious for having short fuses. An official once told me that I was a nice, kind of a quiet driver, but I was like a bomb going off when I was provoked. I'm not sure whether that was a compliment.

The race went great for Stewart, who wound up running in second place and jockeying for the lead with only 20 laps to go. But he ran out of energy, slowed some, and ended up second. It was said that he hadn't been able to take in enough vitamins and minerals to sustain another long race and most likely just ran out of juice. This race would have been his first win. Stewart went on to win three races in 1999, making him the first Winston Cup rookie ever to do so. This example showed the relationship between proper nourishment and the ability to think and perform. With a depleted system, it becomes harder to drive a racecar, let alone drive competitively.

If you apply what your mother told you about patience to your driving, you will become a better driver. Drivers who force situations usually end up in the wall and on the business end of the tow truck. Know when to pass and when to be passed. Use your spotter and trust what he says; remember that a spotter gives you the extra set of eyes you most certainly do need. Use your head, and make sure you think before you act. Finally, be kind to your body; it needs to carry you all the way to the end of the race.

The Least You Need to Know

➤ Remember, you cannot win the race on the first lap.

➤ Let an opponent pass you if you know for sure that you can catch him in the long run.

➤ Running a racecar too hard early on in the race will hurt you at the end of the race when it matters most. The only lap to lead that counts is the last lap, not the first lap.

➤ Don't force your way past an opponent who wants to pass you or is blocking you. Let him make the mistake and not you.

➤ Keep your eyes open and choose openings with your head.

➤ Slow down; let your mind pace the race. If you let your emotions take over, you will lose the race before you start.

➤ Keep in shape and keep your body full of fuel, too, or it will let you down the same as your car can.

Chapter 23

Pit Stops—Ballet or Keystone Cops?

In This Chapter

➤ Counting crew members

➤ Checking under your hood

➤ Understanding which side is checked first

➤ Being in the wrong place at the wrong time

➤ Seeing the method behind the pit stop madness

A critical part of every NASCAR race is pit stops. Races are won and lost by how fast (and accurately) a pit stop is performed. In this chapter, we are going to discuss pit stops in general terms. There is no rule about what to do during a pit stop. The only unwritten rule is to get the pit stop completed correctly and as quickly as possible. The less time drivers spend on pit road, the better off they will be, and the better chance they will have of winning the race.

If you have watched a NASCAR race on television or have had the privilege to attend a race, you know that the entire event is very impressive. The excitement level is incredibly high. The speeds are something that you would never see on the streets or highways in your town, and the coordination between crew members is amazing. The first time you watch a pit stop performed it may look like a bunch of people running around a racecar at a frantic pace doing all sorts of things to the racecar. If you are old enough to remember, it may look like one of the old Keystone Cop movies. But it is nothing like that at all; it is more like a choreographed ballet.

By the end of this chapter, you'll know all the steps to the pit stop dance. We have broken this chapter down in sections that will help you to better understand what is being done, why it is being done, and why it is being done the way it is being done.

Pit Stop Safety

During a pit stop, the crew members are in the greatest danger of being hurt, by being hit by either another racecar or a flying piece of equipment. Because of this risk, NASCAR limits the number of crew members and limits the speed at which race-cars can travel down pit road.

Under the Hood

There is a limit to the speed at which racecars can travel down pit road, which is referred to as pit road speed. Pit road speed is limited to about 45 miles per hour for the safety of everyone on pit road. Smaller tracks have a slower pit road speed.

Back in the early 1980s, there was not a speed limit for traveling down pit road. Racecars could and would come into the pits as fast as possible and then lock up the brakes to stop the racecar in their pit stall. This created a very dangerous situation for the crew members and the officials working on pit road.

At one race, during a caution flag, several racecars came down pit road for service at the same time. NASCAR Winston Cup driver Ricky Rudd was one of those drivers. Ricky pulled into his pit stall for a four-tire change and a can of fuel. Even before Ricky was fully in his pit stall, his pit crew jumped into action to service the racecar. As Ricky pulled into the pit stall, the rear tire changer ran behind the racecar to get to the right side and immediately started to remove the lug nuts from the right rear tire with his air gun. Like most tire changers, his concentration was focused on removing the old tire and putting on the new tire as quickly as possible. His focus was so intense that he was unaware of all the other racecars that were either returning to the racetrack or coming into their pit stalls for service.

Pulling in and out of pit stalls is extremely hectic. Drivers are pulling into the pit stalls at the same time other racecars are trying to pull out of their pit stalls, and drivers are passing in front of one another. The situation is nerve-racking to say the least. As Ricky's right rear tire changer was removing the last lug nut from the tire, a racecar was coming down pit road for service at a high rate of speed. Another racecar pulled out in front of this racecar in an attempt to return to the race-track. In order to avoid crashing into the back of the other racecar, the driver of the first racecar locked up the brakes and turned the steering wheel to the left. With the steering wheel turned left and this rapid deceleration, the back of the racecar spun around and slammed into the right rear section of Ricky Rudd's racecar, instantly killing the right rear tire changer.

This tragic accident on pit road became the deciding factor to institute a speed limit on pit road. There are too many crew members and officials working on pit road to allow racecars to come into the pits at high speeds. In order to create as safe an environment as possible, NASCAR implemented the pit road speed rule, and no one objected. To this day, this rule is strictly enforced.

Yellow Flag

Pit road is the most dangerous place for crew members and race officials. Always be aware of your surroundings to keep yourself out of harm's way. Accidents do happen, but if you are aware of your surroundings you can minimize the chances of one happening to you.

How Many Crew Members Does It Take to Pit Stop?

You have probably seen that United Auto Workers and General Motors commercial with the little kids who are building a racecar. The catch phrase of the commercial is "Things come out better when we work together." It implies that if people work together on a project, the final product will be better than if one person worked on it alone. For the most part, this idea is true; however, there is a limit to the number of people who can work on a project at one time. If you had an unlimited number of people working on the same project at the same time, the people would start to bump into each other or get in one another's way. It would become a very unproductive project, even though you thought that more hands would make it better.

Performing a pit stop in a NASCAR race is no different. There is a limited number of crew members who can efficiently service the racecar in the least amount of time. For purposes of safety, NASCAR also limits the number of crew members allowed over the pit road wall to service the racecar.

In order to service a racecar during a pit stop as quickly as possible, you need to have the correct number of crew members going over the wall. In Chapter 8, "The Posse," we described each of the crew members and what their respective job or function is during a pit stop. To refresh our minds, let's briefly name each of the crew members who goes over the pit road wall to service the racecar:

➤ The jack man is responsible for jacking up the racecar and letting the driver know when it is okay to return to the racetrack.

➤ The front tire changer and the front tire carrier are responsible for servicing the front of the racecar.

➤ The rear tire changer and the rear tire carrier are responsible for the rear tires.

➤ The gas man and the catch can man, who also work on the rear of the racecar, are responsible for fueling the racecar.

Two on the front, four on the rear, and one on the jack makes seven pit crew members in total. This is the minimum number of pit crew members needed to service the racecar during a pit stop. At some racetracks, NASCAR allows one additional crew member to go over the wall to service the racecar, making eight crew members in total. The additional crew member may have the responsibility of cleaning the windshield for the driver.

Under the Hood

NASCAR limits the number of pit crew members allowed to go over the pit road wall to service the racecar. This limit keeps the number of crew members at risk of being hurt during a pit road incident to a minimum.

Who Goes First?

According to NASCAR rules, pit crew members are not permitted to go over the pit road wall until their racecar is one pit stall away from their pit stall. This rule limits the time crew members are allowed to be over the wall and minimizes the danger to them. When their racecar is coming down pit road, the pit crew members are lined up on the pit road wall waiting for their racecar. The order in which they line up on the wall is critical to how fast they can get to the racecar. Obviously, the front tire changer and carrier are lined up toward the front of the pit stall because they need to run around the front of the racecar. The rear tire changer, rear tire carrier, gas man, and catch can man are lined up at the back of the pit stall because they need to run around the rear of the racecar.

That leaves the jack man. Where does he line up? Because the jack man needs to go to the opposite side of the racecar in the middle, he could go either way around the racecar. The distance he must run is the same whether he goes around the front or the back of the racecar. Because the distance is the same and the quickest path from point A to point B is the one with the fewest obstacles (our version of physics), it is quicker for the jack man to go around the front of the racecar. The reason is that crew members are permitted to go onto pit road when their car is one pit stall away. The jack man will be the first over the wall onto pit road while he can make a straight line across to the right side and be there when the car comes to a stop. There are times when the jack man is actually hit by his own car. Running in front of a fast-moving car can be dangerous.

All this being said, the pit crew lines up on the wall in the following order from the front of the pit stall to the rear of the pit stall: jack man, front tire changer, front tire carrier, gas man, catch can man, rear tire carrier, and rear tire changer. The rear tire changer will be last on the wall so he is the first around the rear of the car to get to his position. The gas man and catch can man have only a few feet to go so they are last over the wall.

Inside Track

The order in which the pit crew lines up on the pit road wall affects how fast each member can get to the racecar. The crew member with the most work and the furthest distance lines up first—usually the jack man.

The Right Side

After the front tire changer and jack man have gone over the wall, the front tire carrier grabs the new tire by the opening in the rim and follows behind the jack man. After the front tire changer has removed the lug nuts from the wheel, he puts the air gun on the ground in front of him and grabs the old tire and removes it from the racecar, placing it between himself and the jack man. Meanwhile, the tire carrier puts the new tire on the wheel for the tire changer. After the tire changer has placed the old tire between himself and the jack man, he reaches for the air gun and immediately starts to tighten the lug nuts.

Under the Hood

New lug nuts are glued onto the rims of the new tires being placed on the racecar in order to eliminate the need for the tire changer to use the same lug nuts that were on the racecar.

After the front tire carrier has placed the new tire on the wheel for the front tire changer, he takes the old tire that is between the tire changer and the jack man back around the front of the racecar. The tire carrier lifts or rolls the old tire to a waiting crew member who is on the other side of the wall. As soon as the front tire changer has tightened all of the lug nuts on the right front tire, he runs around the front of the racecar to start working on the left front tire.

While all of this activity is going on in the front of the racecar, the same activity is going on in the back of the racecar. The rear tire changer is the first one to go around the back of the racecar and is followed by the rear tire carrier. Because the rear tire carrier does not have to wait for the jack man to pass, he usually gets to the rear tire changer before the lug nuts are removed and the old rear tire is ready to come off.

If an adjustment needs to be made to the chassis, the rear tire carrier will use this time to place a ratchet into the rear windshield in order to make the adjustment. By the time the rear tire carrier places the ratchet in the windshield, the rear tire changer will have removed all five lug nuts and the old rear tire. The tire carrier places the new tire on the wheel for the tire changer to give the tire changer about one second to reach for the air gun and begin tightening the new lug nuts on the wheel. After the tire carrier has placed the new tire on the wheel, he reaches up for the ratchet in the windshield, makes the chassis adjustment, and then removes the ratchet and runs back around the rear of the racecar.

After both tire changers have completed tightening the new lug nuts on the wheels, the jack man releases the jack, dropping the racecar back on the ground. The jack man then pulls the jack out from under the racecar, reaches down to pick it up, and runs around the front of the racecar to begin jacking up the left side of the racecar.

After the rear tire changer and tire carrier have gone around the back of the racecar to change the right rear tire, the catch can man and the gas man begin fueling the racecar. The catch can man places the catch can into the fuel overflow hose, and the gas man places the gas can nozzle into the quick fill opening on the left rear quarter panel of the racecar. As the fuel empties into the racecar, the catch can man also holds the gas can in place to allow the gas man to go back for the second gas can.

Under the Hood

A single gas can holds 11 gallons of fuel for a racecar. Each fuel cell or gas tank in a NASCAR racecar holds up to 22 gallons of fuel. In order to fill a racecar with fuel, two gas cans are required during a pit stop.

The Left Side

So far in our pit stop we have changed the right side tires and have put one can of gas into the racecar. All of this has been completed in about 10 seconds. Try doing that at your local gas station! Let's get back to the racecar and talk about changing the left side tires.

The front tire carrier waits against the pit road wall (where he had gone to drop off the old right front tire) for the front tire changer to come back around the front of the racecar. The reason he waits against the pit road and not the racecar is to give the tire changer an unobstructed path to the left front tire. This clear path enables the tire changer to start removing the lug nuts from the left front tire a lot quicker.

The front tire carrier stays against the pit road wall until the jack man has also come around the front of the racecar to give the jack man an unobstructed path to the left side of the racecar. After the jack man has moved to the left side of the car, the tire carrier grabs the new left front tire and places it on the wheel after the tire changer has removed the lug nuts and the wheel. After the new left front tire is on the wheel, the tire carrier reaches around the front of the racecar to clean off any rubber that may be stuck in the front grill of the racecar.

At the back of the racecar, a similar process is happening. By the time the rear tire changer is ready to return to the left side of the racecar, the gas man has already gone back for the second can of gas. The gas man waits at the pit road wall for the tire changer to come back around the racecar before he continues to fuel the racecar. As the gas man returns with the second gas can, the catch can man removes the first gas can from the quick fill, allowing the gas man to continue filling the racecar with the second gas can.

The rear tire carrier runs back around the gas man to get the new left rear tire. Meanwhile, the tire changer removes the lug nuts and the old tire from the wheel. The tire carrier places the new tire on the wheel while the tire changer reaches for the air gun and begins to tighten the lug nuts, which were glued to the new rim.

While this is going on, the jack man is looking at the tire changers and the catch can man for the signal that each one is finished with his respective job. When the tire changers have all of the lug nuts tight and the catch can man sees fuel coming out of the overflow tube, they raise their hands in the air to signal that they have completed their respective jobs. When the jack man sees everyone has finished, he drops the racecar back on the ground, which signals to the driver that he or she can return to the racetrack.

Not only are the racecars fast in NASCAR, the pit crews are also fast at what they do. The entire process we just described takes a NASCAR Winston Cup pit crew about 17 seconds to complete, and 15-second stops are becoming common among the top teams. Pit crews understand the importance of their jobs and how they can affect the teams' performance in a race. They take their jobs very seriously.

Hmmm, What Shall We Do?

The preceding section described what could be called a normal or standard pit stop; the crew changed four tires and fueled the racecar. This type of pit stop is common at any NASCAR race. However, not all pit stops are this straightforward. If a racecar is not handling properly or seems to have a problem with the engine, the crew chief will need to determine what additional service will be performed during a pit stop.

The following sections talk about the types of service that can be performed during a pit stop and what impact that service may have on the racecar and on the team's position on the racetrack. During some pit stops, crews may change two tires instead of four tires, fuel the racecar and not change any tires, or change two tires and adjust the chassis. These are just some of the possible changes a pit crew can make on the racecar.

Some changes take more time to perform than others do. However, the more time-consuming changes may make the racecar faster. This presents an interesting situation for the crew chief. Should his team spend more time on pit road to make the racecar faster, but lose more track position, or should his team make a quick change to improve track position but not have the best-performing racecar? Crew chiefs face this dilemma every race weekend. Sometimes they make the call that gives them a trip to victory lane, and sometimes they make the call that costs them the race.

Changing Tires

Tires are a critical part of the racecar. They allow the racecar to stick to the racetrack and enable the driver to pull away from another racecar. Tires can make or break a race team. (Refer to Chapter 12, "A Good Set of Rubbers," for a more detailed discussion on race tires.)

New tires work better than old tires. Old tires do not grip or hold the track as well as new tires. When a racecar's tires are starting to wear out, the racecar starts to slow down. Slowing down in a racecar is never a good thing. If you are running on old tires, you will not go as fast as a racecar on new tires, no matter how strong or powerful your engine is. New tires are just better. Trust us.

If new tires are always better, then pit-stop decisions during a race should be easy. If the racecar is slowing down, you should just come in and change four tires, right? It's not that simple. Any time you pull off of the racetrack, you lose or give up track position. The longer you are on pit road, the more track positions you are giving up. You may be thinking, "No big deal. After I get my new tires, I'll be faster than everyone else is and will get back the track positions I lost." If you have not lost too much track position and there are enough laps left in the race, you may be right. But you can't bank on it.

Under the Hood

Racecars on new tires are faster than racecars on old tires. Old tires do not grip the track surface the same way that new tires do. If you want the car to go as fast as possible, always use new tires.

Four Tires vs. No Tires

Suppose there are 15 laps left in a race on a one-mile track, and you are running in fourth place. The leaders are half a second in front of you, and the racecars in fifth, sixth, and seventh place are running one second behind you. The leader takes 32 seconds to complete a lap.

If you were to come into the pits on lap 15 to get four new tires, it would take your pit crew at least 17 seconds. That is half a lap. That means that you would be at least be half a lap down from the leaders. With only 14 laps left in the race, you will probably not have enough laps remaining in the race to make up that half a lap and still be able to catch the leader.

Because there are only a limited number of laps remaining in the race, you should stay out on the racetrack with the old tires and try to maintain fourth place. The answer would be different if there were more laps in the race. More laps in the race would give you more time to catch the leaders and make a run at the checkered flag.

Under the Hood

Circumstances on the racetrack and hands-on experience help a crew chief decide what to do during a pit stop. Sometimes he makes the right call; other times he doesn't. This decision can mean the difference between winning or losing the race.

Under the Hood

Changing four tires takes more time to do, but it gives you a better-handling racecar. Changing only two tires takes less time and may get you a better position on the race-track.

Two Tires vs. Four Tires

Suppose there are 50 laps left in a race, and your tires are wearing out. You need to come into pit road and change them. Several other racecars in front of you also come down pit road and are going to change four tires. You decide that instead of changing four tires you are only going to change two tires. Because changing only two tires takes less time than changing four tires, you can move up on the racetrack, simply because you spent less time on pit road than the other racecars.

When you came into the pits, you were in tenth position on the racetrack. After leaving pit road, you move up to the fifth position, simply because you changed only two tires when everyone else changed four tires. But do not get too excited just yet.

Changing two tires makes your racecar faster than if you had stayed out on the race-track on the old tires, but (there is always a but) you are not as fast as the racecars that changed four tires. Hopefully, you have enough of a lead on them to stay out in front of them until the end of the race, but do not be surprised if you see those race-cars in your rearview mirror catching up to you pretty fast. Just try to hold on for the last few laps and pray they do not pass you. Prayer is another racing tool that is often used in tense situations like this one.

Splash and Go, Go, Go

Racecars are like the cars that you drive every day to and from work or school—at least when it comes to the fuel they run on. Racecars need gas in order to race. No gas, no go. Gas mileage is just as important to race teams as it is to you, only for dif-ferent reasons. In Chapter 17, "Strategy and Victory Lane," we talked about why good gas mileage is important and how drivers can improve the mileage they get. In this section, we are going to talk about the advantages and disadvantages of fueling the racecar in certain situations.

When is it a good idea to fuel your racecar? We know that the racecar can't run without fuel, and you can't win a race when your car doesn't run. However, you want to avoid stopping for fuel only. If the racecar is running well and the tires are holding up, you do not want to come off the track just for a *splash-and-go.*

To avoid having to do a splash-and-go pit stop, it is usually a good idea to fuel the racecar every time you come into the pits for tire change. At most racetracks, a set of tires will wear out before you run out of fuel. If you fuel the racecar every time you change tires, you should be good to finish the race without stopping again for fuel.

Even if you are changing only two tires, the gas man can put at least one can of gas in the racecar in the same amount of time it takes the tire changers to change two tires. Fueling the racecar does not add time to a tire-change pit stop.

Another benefit to fueling the racecar is the weight the fuel adds to the racecar. Crews set up racecars based on four new tires and a full tank of gas. A gallon of racing fuel weighs just over 6 pounds, which means a full tank of 22 gallons of gas weighs 132 pounds. As the racecar uses up the fuel, the back of the racecar becomes lighter, which changes the handling of the racecar. Refueling the racecar adds weight back into the racecar, which makes the racecar handle more like it did at the beginning of the race, which may or may not be a good thing. The lighter weight and freed up rear of the car may make a good setup for the last few laps of the race.

> **Track Terms**
>
> A **splash-and-go** is when you come into the pits for a quick splash of fuel and then go right back out on the racetrack. This type of pit stop is usually done only late in a race and when you are positive you cannot finish the race on the fuel already in the fuel cell.

Instant Bodywork

Sometimes you are in the wrong place at the wrong time. On the racetrack, this usually means that your racecar is caught up in a wreck. When this happens, your pit crew needs to become repair specialists. The only thing you can do when your luck turns bad is to go to your pit stall as quickly as possible for your crew to assess the damage. If you have a little bit of luck, the damage may only be cosmetic. That means it is only body damage. To get you back into the race, your crew needs to become bodywork specialists.

Pit crews use a variety of tools to repair a racecar. The two most common tools are a heavy hammer and a roll of duct tape. Pit crews can do a large amount of quick repair work with these tools. The hammer is used to reshape the bent body panels, and the duct tape is used to patch or hold down any body panels that may have come loose.

Once a racecar is involved in a crash, the team's chances of winning the race are over. The goal becomes to simply finish the race. It is better to finish the race last and several laps down than not finish the race at all. The racecar may not look very good when the crew is done, but there are no championship points awarded to the best-looking racecar in the field.

Time Is of the Essence

At this point in the book, you know time is important in stock car racing. Whether it is lap times or the time you spend on pit road, the goal is to be as fast as possible.

Inside Track

A hammer and a roll of duct tape are the crew members' best tools for making quick repairs to a racecar.

In Chapter 13, "Shaking It Down," we talked about shaking down the racecar in a practice test session and the importance of testing your pit crew. The thing to remember is that if the crew is prepared for any situation, be it a normal pit stop or a crash-related pit stop, you should be able to get back on the racetrack. Things happen very fast in this sport. You can go from first to last or last to first in a single lap. If you are prepared for the worst, you should be okay. Remember to keep your cool. A person who thinks clearly and stays in control will be better off than a person who panics under pressure.

For the racing novice, a pit stop may look like a bunch of people running around the racecar like a chicken without its head. But now you know that there is a method behind this so-called madness called pit stops. The skills performed by the pit crews, the strategies unfolded by the crew chiefs, and the drivers' burning desire to return to the racetrack make watching the NASCAR pit stops just as exciting and thrilling as watching the race itself. After watching one of these events, how can anyone not say all of these participants are athletes? God, we love this sport!

The Least You Need to Know

➤ At least seven pit crew members are needed to service a racecar properly and efficiently during a pit stop.

➤ Limits for pit road speed and the number of crew members allowed over the wall to service a racecar are rules to protect the safety of everyone on pit road.

➤ Pit stops are orchestrated and practiced regularly by the pit crew members. The reason why things are done in a specific order is to minimize the amount of time a racecar spends on pit road.

➤ New lug nuts are glued onto the rims of the new tires being placed on the racecar to save time during tire changes.

➤ The jack man is responsible for signaling the driver that it is okay to return to the racetrack.

➤ A NASCAR Winston Cup pit crew can change four tires and fill a racecar with 22 gallons of fuel in less than 17 seconds.

➤ Changing four tires on a pit stop gives you a better-handling racecar, but it may cost you more track positions than if you changed only two tires.

➤ Anything can be fixed with a hammer and a roll of duct tape.

Chapter 24

WHAT?

You Talking to Me?

In This Chapter

➤ Communication: can't race without it

➤ Who calls the shots on a racing team?

➤ Racing lingo: get it or get lost

➤ Hand signals: be careful here

➤ Covert operation: listening in

➤ Was he waving that thing at me?

Communication is a very important factor in running a successful racing team. Members from the team need to communicate with one another about what services need to be performed on the racecar. Drivers need to communicate to one another while racing on the racetrack. Crew chiefs and NASCAR officials need to communicate to ensure the rules and regulations of the sport are being followed. So you can see that the communication, whether it be between team members, teams, or with the officials, is a very important part of the sport.

In this chapter, we are going to talk about who communicates with whom and why. We will also talk about how people in racing communicate with one another through two-way radios, hand signals, and flags.

Pit Crew Communication

Chapter 8, "The Posse," described the members of the pit crew and what functions each member performs. Part of being able to execute those functions is communicating with other members of the pit crew. The crew chief, who makes the call on what service is to be performed during a pit stop, needs to communicate that decision to the pit members.

If you have been on pit road during a NASCAR race, you know how loud it is. If you have not been on pit road before, know that pit road is so loud that you need to yell in a person's ear just so he can hear what you are saying. If the crew chief had to do that every time he or she wanted to talk with the pit crew, nothing would get done. Fortunately, the crew chief has other ways of communicating.

Inside Track

The order in which the pit crew lines up on the pit road wall affects how fast each member can get to the racecar. The crew member with the most work and the furthest distance lines up first—usually the jack man.

Inside Track

Radios with headsets enable crew members to communicate with one another and also provide protection for their ears.

On the Radio

In order to relay information to one another, teams use two-way radios and headsets. (Refer to Chapter 7, "Racing Stuff," for a picture of a two-way radio and headset.) These radios and headsets enable team members to remain in constant communication regardless of where they are at the racetrack. This capability is important because during a race weekend, team members may be scattered all over the racetrack. One team member can be on top of the grandstands, and another one can be back at the race trailer, and the two can communicate as if they were standing next to each other. In the days before two-way radios were used at the races, this type of communication was impossible.

The primary purpose of radios is to allow each team member to communicate with the others. If team members were not able to communicate or did not share information with one another, the team's chances of success would be drastically reduced. The secondary benefit of using radios and headsets is to protect your ears from the excessive noise. Prolonged exposure to excessively loud sounds will have an effect on your hearing. Stock car racing is so loud that it can make you deaf. (The only other type of racing that is louder is drag racing; funny car and top fuel dragsters are so loud that they make your chest pound and your ears ache.) John swears that I suffer from some hearing loss already, but that is another debate.

During a stock car race, the driver and crew chief must be able to communicate on how the racecar is performing. The driver tells the crew chief if the racecar has a push or loose condition. The two use the radios to discuss potential changes to the racecar while it is still out on the racetrack. After the decision is made, the crew chief uses the radio to tell the other crew members what changes to make.

Who Calls the Shots

Who decides what changes should be made to the racecar? Traditionally, the crew chief is responsible for deciding what changes should be made. However, in today's racing, this decision is not always made by the crew chief alone. Most drivers and, in some cases, the car owners also have a say in the decision process.

After racing for many years on the same racetracks, the drivers know just as much as the crew chief about what changes will improve the racecar. For example, Rusty Wallace, who drives the #2 Ford Taurus for Miller Lite beer, and his crew chief, Robin Pemberton, work very closely to determine the setup of the racecar. Not only does Rusty tell Robin how the racecar is performing, he also makes recommendations on what to change. Quite often, Rusty is in the garage area working with Robin on the decisions about the racecar. The car setup is truly a team effort.

Most other drivers are not as involved in the racecar setup as Rusty is. That is not to say that other racecar drivers are not involved at all. Although the crew chief has the final responsibility, he looks to other sources for information and input into the decision, and one of the most important sources is the driver.

Under the Hood

Did you know that you can buy a list of radio frequencies that NASCAR Winston Cup teams use? If you know the radio frequency your favorite race team uses, you can use a scanner to listen in on conversations between team members.

Racing Lingo

Another important factor in successful communication is using the proper terminology. Racing teams commonly use terms such as push, loose, stagger, and wedge (these terms are defined in Appendix C, "Glossary of Stock Car Terms," if you need a reminder). Outsiders or people who do not follow the sport closely may have no idea what these terms mean. However, these terms tell team members a lot of information about the racecar.

Hearing a phrase like, "We've got a 10-degree push in the right front tire," is common at the racetrack. This simple phrase describes what is happening with the racecar (it is pushing up the racetrack), what the problem is (a 10-degree increase in temperature across the tire), where the problem is (the right front tire), and what the possible cause is (too little camber in the wheel).

Terminology is an important part of stock car racing. Knowing the terminology enables you to keep up with what is going on; not understanding the terms means you will be confused for a while until you learn them. Reading this book will give you a good grounding in the most important terms. Another good way to learn the terminology is to watch television shows such as *NASCAR Garage* or *Inside NASCAR*. These shows provide an insider's view of the sport of stock car racing and can help you learn more about it.

Is He Telling Me to Pass or Flipping Me the Bird?

In addition to communicating with their crew members, drivers communicate with one another. Because drivers cannot communicate with each other via their two-way radios, they are forced to use other methods. These other methods include using hand signals, bumping one another, and having the spotter or crew chief talk to the other drivers' spotters or crew chiefs. Although hand signals are the most common method used, the bump method is also fairly common and very effective.

A Helping Hand

When you step on the brake pedal to slow down your car, your brake lights come on to let the cars behind you know that you are slowing down. When a racecar driver steps on the brake, there are no brake lights to come on to let the drivers behind him know that he is slowing down. In order to let the drivers behind him know that he is slowing down, a driver holds up his right hand. When drivers see the driver ahead of them making this signal, they know that the racecar in front of them is slowing down and that they should also be prepared to slow down. Usually, a driver only uses this hand signal when he or she is slowing down drastically or stopping.

Another common hand signal is the passing hand signal. Occasionally during a race, a driver will signal to another driver that it is okay to pass him or her. Usually the only time this happens is if a racecar has a problem and cannot keep up the speed of the other racecars around it. In this instance, a driver raises his or her right hand and waves it to the right side of the racecar. This signal tells the driver behind him or her that it is okay to pass on the outside of the racetrack. When a driver gives another driver this signal, the driver giving the signal moves down the racetrack in an attempt to get out of the way of the faster car. That is to say, the signaling driver should move down the racetrack and give the faster racecar the preferred line; unfortunately, not everyone does this.

In addition to these two commonly used hand signals, there are other hand signals drivers use to communicate to one another. Racing is a sport that can determine winners and losers by a fraction of a second. It is very competitive and very expensive. Drivers are putting a lot on the line when they climb into those racecars. Sometimes tempers get a little hot, and very rarely a driver may use an unofficial NASCAR hand gesture to communicate his or her displeasure with another driver. Because this book is intended for a general audience, we cannot show, demonstrate, or even discuss these unofficial gestures, but we think you understand our meaning here.

Inside Track

When drivers are just slightly pressing on the brake pedal, they do not hold up their right hands. The hand signal for slowing down is used only when a crash happens or when something in the racecar breaks and forces the racecar to slow down.

Doing the Bump

So far we have talked about how a driver can communicate with the drivers behind him. But what happens when a driver wants to communicate with the driver in front of him or her? This driver cannot rely on using hand gestures because he or she never knows whether the driver in front is looking in the mirror to see the gesture. Instead of using hand gestures, drivers use the *bump technique.*

The bump technique is when a racecar comes up and bumps the racecar in front of it in the rear bumper. When this happens, the driver in the back is trying to tell the driver up front, "Hey, I'm faster than you, so move over and let me go by." Not every driver uses this technique, but some do, and they use it very effectively. You may be thinking, "Bumping at over 150 miles per hour? Are they crazy?" It is not as bad as it sounds. Remember, it's only bumping; it's not running into the back of the racecar. The bump is just enough to let the driver know that a faster racecar is behind him or her. Most drivers do not have an issue with this technique, primarily because they have probably used it on someone else.

Inside Track

Bumping a racecar from behind is a common method drivers use to let another driver know they want to pass.

One of the things a driver wants to avoid doing is getting into a crash or tearing up the racecar. Both situations are very expensive and not a good way to keep a crew, car owner, or sponsor very happy. But racecars do make contact on a racetrack, and there is usually some damage to the bodies of the racecars. The next time you are at a race or watching one on television, look at the side of the racecars. You will see what looks like a black donut on the side of the racecar. That donut is not the latest advertising program from Dunkin' Donuts; it is a mark from the tire of another racecar. When two racecars are racing side by side and get a little too close, the tire of one racecar rubs up against the body of the other racecar. This situation is commonly called *rubbing*.

Besides bumping a racecar from behind, drivers may also bump one another on the sides. Bumping a racecar on the side is usually only done by accident when a driver moves up or down the racetrack. Side bumping usually happens in the turns as the drivers are looking for the best line around the track. If one driver starts to move up the racetrack while another driver is already there, the driver on the outside may bump the driver on the inside to let him know, "Hey, I'm on your outside, so don't come up here." The same is true on the bottom of the racetrack. If a driver on the outside wants to move down the racetrack, the inside driver will let the outside driver know that is not a good idea. Most of the time, side bumping occurs on the entrances and exits to the turns. Physics tells us that two objects cannot occupy the same physical space, but racecar drivers sometimes try to disprove this theory. Unfortunately, when they do, they usually crash.

Under the Hood

Teams look for as much information as possible about the racetrack, their racecars, and other racecars. Having access to as much information as possible allows teams to make informed decisions about their racecars. There is no such thing as too much information. The only bad thing is not having enough information. If you are ever in doubt about whether to relay some information, it is better to relay it and have someone say, "Thanks, I already knew that," than say nothing.

Pull It Over

In addition to two-way radios, teams also use *scanners* to monitor the communications from other teams and from the NASCAR officials. Scanners are one-way radio devices that allow a person to listen in on a range of radio frequencies. (Refer to Chapter 7 for a picture of a radio scanner.) They are referred to as one-way devices because they cannot be used to talk back to someone else. They are designed only for listening.

Both fans and race teams use scanners to monitor radio frequencies. Fans use them to listen in on the conversations of their favorite teams; race teams use them to listen to the NASCAR officials about conditions on the racetrack.

During a race, the NASCAR officials use both scanners and two-way radios to monitor communications during the race. The officials use the radios to communicate to one another. At every NASCAR race, there are many officials working to ensure that every race team follows the rules and regulations of the series. During the race, several officials watch the race from up in the scoring booth above the grandstands. By being in the scoring booth, race officials are able to see the entire racetrack. In addition to having officials in the scoring booth, race officials are also positioned along pit road to ensure that the pit crews follow the rules and regulations of the series. The officials on pit road communicate with the crew chief from each race team on all matters pertaining to their racecar.

Flags

During a stockcar race, the NASCAR officials communicate with both the pit crews and the drivers. NASCAR officials use their two-way radios to communicate one another and the pit crews. To communicate with the drivers on the racetrack, they use a series of colored flags. At all NASCAR races, one official located at the start/finish line has the responsibility of using the flags to signal to the racecars. This official, who is sometimes referred to as the flag man, is usually positioned on top of a stand that reaches over the racetrack.

Each colored flag has a different meaning and tells the drivers about what is happening on the track and with the race. The following sections talk about what each flag means and how each flag is used during a race.

Under the Hood

NASCAR can use as many as seven different flags during a race. However, most NASCAR races do not use all seven flags.

The Green Flag

When all of the racecars are on the racetrack and lined up in the correct starting order behind the pace car, the NASCAR officials use a green flag to signify the official start of the race. The green flag is waved at the start/finish line until each racecar has *taken the green.* "Taking the green" simply means that each racecar has passed the start/finish line and has officially begun the race. After each racecar has taken the green flag, that flag is put away until it is required again during the race. The green flag is also used to signal the restart of the race after a crash.

The Caution Flag

Officials use the caution flag to notify drivers of a problem on the racetrack. The caution flag is bright yellow and very distinct. The most common reason for the caution flag is a crash.

When one or more racecars crash or spin out on the racetrack, NASCAR officials immediately wave the caution flag. The purpose of the caution flag is to slow down the racecars on the track in order to create a safe condition for the rescue workers. Rescue and safety workers are posted at several locations around the racetrack to ensure the safety of the drivers in case of a crash. When a crash occurs, the safety workers go out on the racetrack to ensure the drivers are not hurt. If the drivers are unhurt, the safety workers will remove the racecars from the racetrack and bring them back to the garage area for the teams to work on.

In most NASCAR racing series, all drivers must reduce their speed and fall in line behind the cars in front of them once the caution flag is waved. In addition, passing is not allowed anywhere on the racetrack.

However, when a caution flag is waved in the NASCAR Winston Cup series, the racecars can race back to the start/finish line before they are required to reduce their speeds. This rule may give a driver the opportunity to gain a position or two on the racetrack. When a driver passes the start/finish line while a flag is being waved, the driver is considered to have taken that flag, and all of the rules of that flag apply. In the case of the caution flag that means the driver reduces his speed, holds his position on the racetrack, and doesn't pass. However, if a driver has just passed the start/finish line and then a crash occurs and the caution flag is waved, that driver has not taken the caution flag yet. He or she is allowed to maintain his or her speed and can pass any other racecar that has not taken the caution flag. This is referred to as "racing back to the flag." People in the racing industry have different opinions about whether drivers should be allowed to race back to the flag. The issue revolves mostly around competitiveness versus the safety factor.

The Passing Flag

Another flag that is commonly used during a NASCAR race is the passing flag. It is a blue flag with a white diagonal strip across it. The passing flag is waved only at certain drivers and does not apply to the entire field.

Under the Hood

There are two flags in NASCAR racing that apply only to certain racecars: the passing flag and the black flag. The passing flag is waved at a driver who is going too slow and needs to let the faster racecars pass. The black flag is waved at a driver who either violated a rule and needs to go to pit road or has something wrong with his or her racecar.

When the leaders of a NASCAR race begin to catch the slower racecars in the field, the passing flag is waved at the slower racecars. The passing flag tells drivers that there is a faster racecar behind them and that they need to move over and let the faster racecar pass them.

No driver in the world likes to have the passing flag waved at him and will do everything possible to keep the other racecars from passing him. So when the passing flag is waved at a particular driver, it is not unusual for that driver not to see the flag for a long time. When this happens, the NASCAR officials tell the driver's crew chief that if his driver does not let the faster racecars pass, he will be penalized. At this point, it is usually a good idea to let the faster racecars go by. If you are having problems keeping up with the rest of the field, you do not want to compound those problems by being penalized a lap.

The Black Flag

Black seems to be the color that represents bad things. For example, the cowboy in the old movies in the black hat is usually the bad guy. The same is true in racing: The *black flag* is the bad flag. No likes to see it or have it waved at them. The black flag is a solid black flag that is only waved at certain drivers and does not apply to the entire field.

The black flag is used under two circumstances. The first is when the NASCAR officials see a problem with a particular racecar. For example, if a racecar is smoking badly because of some problem within its engine, the NASCAR officials will wave the black flag at that driver. The black flag means

Track Terms

A **black flag** is used to let a driver know that he must report to pit road either for a problem with the racecar or for a penalty being assessed by NASCAR.

that the driver must report to pit road to have the racecar checked. Under these circumstances, the black flag is used to make sure safe racing conditions are maintained on the racetrack. It is a precaution that benefits everyone on the racetrack and everyone on pit road. Unfortunately, it also means that the flagged race team has a problem and is probably not going to win the race. No one likes it when that happens.

The other circumstance in which the black flag is used is when a driver has done something wrong on the racetrack. The NASCAR officials use the black flag to assess a penalty to the offending driver. The penalty is to report to pit road and be held there until NASCAR says it is okay to return to racing. Most penalties are what are called *stop-and-go penalties*. This means that a driver must report to his pit stall and stop the racecar, and then he can return to racing on the racetrack. Because there is a limit to the speed a driver can go while traveling on pit road, this penalty usually means that when the driver goes back out on the racetrack he or she will have lost valuable track position. Track position is hard enough to get, so you do not want to lose a lot of it by being assessed a stop-and-go penalty. Another type of penalty, which can be assessed from a black flag, is being held in the pit stall for an entire lap. This severe penalty is imposed only when an equally serious violation has occurred.

Yellow Flag

Speeding on pit road will result in a black flag and a stop-and-go penalty.

Inside Track

Some of the most exciting racing happens when the white flag is waved on the last lap of the race.

You may be wondering who determines the penalties for a particular violation. NASCAR has as the sole right to determine the penalty for all violations that occur during a racing event, including violations both on and off the racetrack. Although NASCAR retains this right, it has pretty much determined in advance what penalties will be assessed for certain violations. Some of the violations that will receive a black flag penalty are passing another racecar during a caution flag, speeding down pit road, or intentionally causing a crash.

Most of the drivers are aware of these penalties and are not surprised when they are assessed. However, drivers may argue whether they committed the offense. It is not uncommon to hear statements like, "I did not pass that racecar under caution; he just slowed and ended up behind me." Drivers, car owners, and the crew chief have the right to protest the penalty after the race, but during the race, they had better answer that black flag.

The White Flag

Another flag used in NASCAR racing is the white flag. The white flag signifies that there is only one lap left in the race. At this point in the race, many drivers change their mentality and driving style. The last lap means that this is their absolute last chance to gain a position or to make a run for the win. When the white flag is waved, all bets are off, and it is every driver for himself. It is almost like a Dr. Jekyll and Mr. Hyde scenario. Some drivers who have been fighting for track position all race long just give up when they see the white flag come out if they are not where they want to be. Drivers who were racing cleanly become extremely aggressive, take chances that they would not normally take, and risk everything they worked for all race long. It is pretty amazing when this happens.

In a race at the New Hampshire International Speedway, we saw two drivers who were racing each other cleanly all race long suddenly start pushing and bumping each other on the last lap. As they went into turn one, the driver on the outside cut in front of the driver on the inside to get the better line into the turn. The driver on the inside had to hit the brakes to avoid the racecar cutting him off. We thought there was going to be a crash. Fortunately, the driver on the bottom was able to slow down enough to let the other driver get the line, but he was not happy.

In turn two, the driver who was cut off decided to let the driver in front know that he was not happy with the move going into turn one. He came up behind the racecar and stuck the front bumper from his racecar under the back bumper of the racecar in front of him. This move was extremely dangerous because by doing this he lifted the rear wheels of the racecar in front of him off the ground. This meant that the racecar in front was being pushed and lifted by the racecar behind it. It is very difficult to control a racecar when its back end is in the air. The racecar in front started to turn, and when the other racecar slowed and dropped the back of the racecar, it swerved back and forth like a fish's tail during an upstream swim. The other racecar then passed the fishtailing racecar and headed down the back straightaway for turn three. We knew that that was not the end of it.

After he brought his fishtailing racecar under control, the driver caught the other racecar going into turn four. At this point, these guys were half a straightaway from the finish of the race. They were going to finish well in the race, probably somewhere in the top 10. Neither one had a chance to win, so you would think they would just focus on finishing the race in a respectable position and going home with their racecars intact. No, not these guys. The white flag had been thrown, and they were racing like their lives were hanging in the balance.

Off of turn four, the driver of the racecar that fishtailed decided to return the favor and then some. He hit the back of the racecar in front of him so hard that both racecars ended up hitting the outside wall off of turn four, going across the front straightaway, and hitting the inside wall, where both racecars came to a complete stop before the finish line. Because neither racecar could pass the finish line, both finished the race in the high 30s instead of in the top 10. These drivers were so stupid; we could not believe what we had just seen. Both drivers completely destroyed their racecars, gave up a large number of championship points, and lost a lot of prize money. And for what? All because the white flag came out, and they wanted to win at all costs. And oh boy, did it cost.

The Red Flag

The red flag is another flag no one likes to see. A red flag has the same meaning as a red light: Stop. When a red flag is waved, it means that for some reason, usually weather, NASCAR is stopping the race completely for a period of time.

When the red flag comes out, the pace car goes back out on the racetrack and slows down the field to a complete stop. During a red flag condition, the racecars are shut off, and the pit crews cannot work on the racecars. Even a racecar in the garage area that is being fixed in an attempt to go back on the racetrack cannot be worked on. Everything stops.

Another reason for a red flag is a serious and/or multicar crash. If NASCAR determines that the rescue and safety crews need more time than a caution flag would give to properly clean the racetrack and/or remove an injured driver from the racecar, the red flag will be waved. Stopping the race ensures that the greatest amount of safety is available to all who are involved in the incident. When a red flag is waved in this situation, a driver has probably been seriously hurt in the crash.

Inside Track

You cannot work on your racecar during a red flag condition on the racetrack. It is against the rules of NASCAR and can create an unfair advantage for a team.

The reason why everything must stop is so that one team does not get an unfair advantage over another team. If a racecar in the garage area is being fixed with the intention of returning it to the racetrack, it would be unfair to let that crew continue working, when the crew of a racecar still on the racetrack cannot work on its racecar. For this reason, everything must stop. No work is to be performed on any racecar during a red flag condition.

The Blue Flag with Yellow Stripe

This flag is to inform drivers they are about to be lapped by the leader and they must give way and make room for the leader. They can race him, but cleanly; any attempt to hold him up may result in a penalty or a little bumping from the leader.

The Checkered Flag

To signify the end of a race, officials use a black-and-white checkered flag. This is the most famous flag in all of racing. Every form of racing uses this flag to signify the end of the race. The high-speed Formula 1 racecars, the Indy Racing League, and its competitor series CART all use this flag as do motorcycle, truck, and boat racing. Regardless of the type of racing you compete in or are a fan of, everyone knows and wants to be the holder of the checkered flag at the end of the race.

The desire to hold this flag drives teams to make extreme sacrifices to race. It is the holy grail of the racing world. Everyone wants it, but only a few may possess it. It is the one flag that every driver strives for. It represents victory!

In this chapter, we have talked about the ways in which drivers, teams, and NASCAR officials communicate. After reading this chapter, you should have a better understanding of the methods of communication used during a NASCAR race. In the next chapter, we will talk in more detail about the rules and regulations of NASCAR.

The Least You Need to Know

➤ Communication is the key to a successful race team.

➤ Race teams use two-way radios with headsets and scanners to communicate with each other and to monitor the NASCAR officials and their competitors.

➤ Knowing the racing lingo will help you better understand what is going on during a NASCAR race.

➤ Drivers use hand signals to communicate with one another (sometimes to communicate their displeasure with one another). They also use bumping to communicate.

➤ NASCAR officials use two-way radios to communicate with each other and to monitor the racing.

➤ NASCAR officials use flags to communicate to the drivers on the racetrack. Seven flags are used in NASCAR racing, but not all flags are used in every race.

Chapter 25

The Don't-Even-Think-About-Its

In This Chapter

➤ Learning rules and regulations on and off the track

➤ Identifying the enforcers

➤ Understanding the penalties for breaking the rules

➤ Knowing when you can push the limits

Rules keep the competition fair, keep everyone honest, and protect the safety of all of the participants. If there were no rules about racing, things would quickly get out of hand. As it is, teams push the limits of the rules in order to find that little extra bit of speed they are looking for.

NASCAR's rules are broken down into three basic categories. First, there are rules that govern the general conduct of all NASCAR competitors. The second, and probably biggest, category of rules details the specifications every racecar must comply with in order to compete in a race. The third and final category contains the rules that govern the race itself. Over the next few pages, we will give you specifics about each of these categories and explain why these rules, regulations, and "Don't even think about its" are important to the sport of stock car racing. We will also talk about how these rules are enforced and what happens when a team breaks the rules.

General Conduct

The first category we mentioned involves the rules that govern the general conduct of every participant in the sport of stock car racing. Unlike the other two categories, these rules on general conduct apply, for the most part, to every series in NASCAR and not to just any one particular series. Each series within NASCAR has its own set of rules about the specifications of the racecar and what is and is not permitted on the racetrack during a race.

These rules are probably the least-enforced rules in all of NASCAR. They are more like basic guidelines than rules. The only time a participant is penalized for breaking one of these rules is in extreme cases. For the most part, people know how to conduct themselves in a professional sporting event. However, because stock car racing is a very intense and high-pressure sport and sometimes tempers do flare, there needs to be a set of rules that say, "No, no, no, that's not allowed, Billy. Now put down that jack handle and tell Bob you are sorry."

Several rules in the NASCAR rulebook talk about the penalties for fighting at a NASCAR event. There is one rule and penalty for fighting and another rule with a steeper penalty for fighting with a weapon. A weapon doesn't have to be a gun or a knife; many things around a racing garage could be used as a weapon in the event of a fight. A jack handle is a perfect example. NASCAR highly discourages fighting of any type and especially discourages fighting with a weapon. But like we said, we all know how hard it is to make it to the professional ranks of any sport, and no one in his right mind would jeopardize all of that hard work for something as stupid as fighting. It just does not make any sense whatsoever.

Yellow Flag

NASCAR highly discourages fighting of any type at an event. The penalties for this type of conduct are steep and swift. You are investing a lot of time and money to go racing, so don't do anything stupid that might get you thrown out of the sport.

Car Specs

In order to keep the competition on the racetrack close and as fair as possible, every racecar that competes in a NASCAR event must meet the specifications set for that series. NASCAR currently has several different series, each with its own set of rules about the specifications for the racecars. These specifications ensure that everyone is using the same basic type of equipment and that no one competitor has an unfair advantage over another competitor, at least from an equipment standpoint.

Under the Hood

Each of the racing series in NASCAR has specific rules about the type of equipment that can be used. These rules cover everything from the type of racecar to the size of the engine and the type of equipment used during a pit stop.

For this book, we are going to limit our discussion of rules about the racecar specifications to a more general level. In some cases, we will cite specific rules about a particular series, but it would be difficult to explain every rule for every series in NASCAR. Let's get started.

Weight

The lighter a racecar is, the faster it can travel. In order to keep things equal, NASCAR sets the rules regarding the minimum weight allowed for every racecar. Because having more weight in a racecar is a disadvantage rather than an advantage, there is no maximum amount of weight for a racecar. Race teams work very hard to get their racecars as close as possible to the minimum weight allowed for their series.

In addition to the total weight a racecar can be, NASCAR also determines how much weight can be on the right and left sides of the racecar. The more weight you have to one side, the easier the car turns to that side. If you have more weight on the left side of the racecar, it will turn better to the left. If you have more weight on the right side of the racecar, it will turn better to the right.

You may be wondering about the weight the driver adds to the racecar. Wouldn't a heavier driver have more of a disadvantage than a driver who does not weigh as much? The answer is yes; a heavier driver would have a disadvantage. NASCAR thought of

Inside Track

When building your racecar, try to get it as close as possible to the minimum weight allowed for the series you're racing in. The lighter your racecar is, the faster you will be able to go. The weight minimum should also be a good incentive to encourage the driver to stay as lean as possible. Remember, every piece of junk food the driver eats is another thousandth of a second added to his or her lap times.

that, too. In the NASCAR Winston Cup Series, the weight of the driver is included in the total weight of the racecar. When a racecar is weighed, the driver must be in the racecar as it goes over the scales. Including the weight of the driver in the racecar eliminates any advantage or disadvantage a team may have because of the weight of its driver. Not all series weight the car with the driver. In those series, the heavier driver will be at a disadvantage.

Down Force

Down force is a very important part of racing. As you may remember from earlier in the book, *down force* is the pressure placed on the racecar from the air as it passes over the racecar. The more down force that is applied to the racecar, the better it sticks to the racetrack. Racing teams are able to increase the amount of down force applied to a racecar by changing the shape of the racecar body.

For example, teams reshape the fenders of the racecar to make them flatter. The flatter the front fenders are, the more area the air has to press down on. The more area the air has to press down on in the front of the racecar, the more down force is created. By increasing the down force on the front of the racecar, teams make the back of the racecar lighter. When the back of the racecar becomes lighter, it does not grip the track very well, which makes the racecar loose in the turns.

Track Terms

Down force is pressure created by air as it passes over the racecar traveling around the racetrack. Down force comes into play more so on racetracks that are one mile or more in length. Put your hand out the window of a car in motion and you'll feel the wind blow your hand around. This air pressure has an effect on your car, too, even at slower speeds.

Racing teams can increase the down force on the rear of the racecars by increasing the size of the rear quarter panels. Making the rear quarter panels wider on the racecar and flattening out the top of the rear quarter panels increases the area in which the air can press down on the back of racecar. This increased area on the back of the racecar allows for increased down force, which helps the racecar grip the racetrack better in the turns.

So why don't race teams make the front fenders and the rear quarter panels as wide and as flat as possible? The answer is that they do. Teams make these body parts as flat and as wide as NASCAR allows. During pre-race inspections, NASCAR officials check the size and shape of the front fenders and the rear quarter panels to make sure they don't exceed NASCAR specifications. If a racecar's fenders are too wide or too flat, the team will be required to fix them before it is able to qualify for the race. The same is true for the rear quarter panels. However, most teams know how wide and how flat they can make the front fenders and rear quarter panels before they get to the racetrack, so it is pretty rare to see a NASCAR Winston Cup team making changes to a racecar body at the racetrack.

Although down force helps a racecar stick to or grip the racetrack, it requires a lot of speed before down force kicks in. Down force comes into play more so at tracks that are one mile or longer. On smaller tracks, the racecars do not pick up enough speed for the down force to help the racecar grip the track. Because of this, racing teams build racecars specifically designed for the larger racetracks. These racecars have the wider and flatter front fenders and rear quarter panels.

To give you an idea of what we are talking about in regards to the width and shape of the front fenders, take a look at your car. The front fenders are curved from the hood of the car down to the side and end in a position vertical to the ground over the tire. The entire fender is a nice, smooth curve. The front fenders on a NASCAR Winston Cup racecar are shaped a little differently. When you look at a front fender on a racecar, look at the center of the fender, which is directly over the center of the tire. The fender at this location is almost completely horizontal to the ground. It looks more like an extension of the hood than a curved fender. This area is where teams create more down force on the front of the racecar.

The shape of the rear quarter panels is also a little different. In order to create as much down force as possible, teams start to flatten out the rear quarter panels from the end of where the doors would be on the racecar. What they do is gradually shape the top half of the rear quarter panels flat until they reach the rear bumper of the racecar. This creates a ramp effect up over the rear quarter panels. The closer they get to the rear of the racecar, the more the rear quarter panels become flat. Usually if you look at the side of the racecar by the rear windshield, you should see what looks like a small shelf. This shelf is the area where the greatest amount of down force is created on the rear of the racecar. NASCAR officials are constantly "policing" this area, because teams will widen this area for each race unless the officials watch over them. The car must fit the templates used by NASCAR, and creative rulebending is kept to a minimum.

Engines

Engines are a critical part of stock car racing. The rules regarding the engines are pretty specific and clear about what you can and cannot have in them. Racing engines for the NASCAR Winston Cup series are limited to a *small block V8*.

One of the rules regarding engines states that the engine you use in your racecar must be from the same manufacturer as the body style of your racecar. What this means is that if the body style of your racecar is a Ford Taurus, you must use a Ford

Track Terms

A **small block V8** is an engine classified by the manufacturers in the 1960s and 1970s whose cubic inches do not total more than 358 inches and no less than 350. These engines are the original Chevrolet 350 engines, Ford 351 engines, and Chrysler 340 engines.

engine in your racecar. If the body style of your racecar is a Pontiac Grand Prix or a Chevrolet Monte Carlo, you must use a General Motors engine. (General Motors manufactures both Pontiac and Chevrolet.) You can't run a General Motors engine in a Ford racecar or vice versa. The same goes for Dodge, Plymouth, and Chrysler teams.

In addition to rules about the type of engine, there are some basic rules about the engine compression. The bigger the compression, the more horsepower an engine can produce. NASCAR limits the engine compression for all racecars in an effort to give each race team an equal chance of winning the race. Of course, engine compression is not the only thing that can increase the amount of horsepower that an engine can create. Professional racing engine builders have many other ways to build horsepower into an engine.

At every NASCAR race, officials check the amount of compression in a racecar before it goes out onto the racetrack. If an engine is found to have more than the maximum allowed compression, the team must change the engine or lower the compression before the racecar is allowed to go onto the racetrack. This rule is to ensure that no one race team has an unfair advantage.

There are many other rules and regulations on the specifications of a NASCAR racecar; these are just a few of the main ones. If you are interested in learning more about the rules of NASCAR, you can contact NASCAR directly for more information by calling 904-253-0611.

Yellow Flag

NASCAR limits the amount of compression a race engine can have. If, during inspection, your race engine is found to exceed this maximum amount of compression, you will be required to change the compression before competing in the race. If this violation is determined in a post-race inspection, you can be disqualified from the race.

On-Track Conduct

We talked briefly about the racecars; let's now talk about some of the rules that regulate the action on the racetrack during a race. These rules, like most of the rules in NASCAR, are geared toward creating a level playing field for all competitors and to ensure the greatest amount of safety for all competitors and their crew members.

Some of the rules regarding on-track conduct cover things such as starting procedures, passing, and rules of behavior when there's a caution on the racetrack. What most people do not realize is that pit road is also governed by the rules related to on-track conduct; the drivers are not the only ones who must follow these rules. Although the majority of these rules do pertain to the drivers, many rules pertain directly to the crew in the pits.

The following discussion is limited to a select number of rules that pertain to on-track conduct. If you would like more information on these rules, you can contact NASCAR directly for a copy of the rulebook that pertains to the series you are interested in.

The Pace Car

At all NASCAR events, the pace car controls the speed at which the racecars can run while it's on the racetrack. The pace car has two purposes during a race. The first is to let the drivers know how fast they can travel when on pit road. The way the pace car does this is by leading the racecars around the racetrack for a few laps at the speed they can go while on pit road. Because stock cars do not have speedometers, they must determine how fast they are going by looking at the tachometer and seeing how many RPMs they are turning while in a specific gear. While the pace car is leading the field around the racetrack, the drivers make a mental note of what gear they are in and how many RPMs they are turning while traveling at the pit road speed. This way, when they need to come down pit road, they know that if they are in that same gear and turning the same number of RPMs as they enter pit road, they will not be penalized for speeding.

The other purpose of the pace car is to slow down the field during a caution on the racetrack. When the caution flag is waved during a race, it means that a hazardous condition exists on the racetrack and the field needs to slow down to the pit road speed. After the caution flag has been waved and the field starts to slow down, the pace car goes out onto the racetrack to gather up the field. Once the pace car is out in front of the leaders, it slows down to the pit road speed. Racecars may come into the pits for service only after the pace car has passed the entrance of pit road. Racecars entering pit road before the pace car has passed the entrance to pit road or while pit road is closed are penalized.

The pace car remains on the track and in front of the field until the hazard on the racetrack has been cleared. After the hazard is removed, the pace car continues to lead the field around the track for one more lap. During this final lap of caution, the lights on top of the pace car are turned off to signal to the drivers that there is one lap to go before returning to racing. As the pace car comes off of turn four on the final caution lap, it makes a left turn and proceeds down pit road.

Inside Track

The pace car sets the starting pace for the field at the beginning of the race. It also lets the drivers know what the pit road speed is by leading them around the track for a few laps at this speed.

Yellow Flag

At the start of the race, racecars are not allowed to pass another racecar on the inside until they have passed the start/finish line. If you do pass another racecar before the start/finish line, you will be subject to a stop-and-go penalty. You may pass to the outside, although most racers will block you by running close to the wall.

Starting Procedures and Restarts

According to the NASCAR rulebook, at the beginning of a race, racecars are not allowed to pass one another until they have reached the start/finish line. If one driver passes another driver before reaching the start/finish line, that driver will be penalized. This violation is often referred to as jumping the start of the race.

Restarts of a race are very exciting. As the green flag is waved, drivers either try to pass to the outside, which is allowed, or run up along the inside, not passing until they go past the start/finish line, where passing is permitted on both sides.

Although we have described only a few of the rules involved in NASCAR racing, we have tried to give you more of an insight into the rationale behind the rules. The *1999 NASCAR Rulebook* is over 60 pages in length and covers all the rules of racing.

The Enforcers

Rules are useless unless there is someone to enforce them. In NASCAR, the officials are both rule enforcers and judges rolled up into one person or function. Think of them as both the cop who arrests you and the judge who sentences you to your punishment.

Don't get us wrong, we are not saying that the officials are not nice people. They are very nice people and are fair and straightforward about the rules of NASCAR. We have a lot of respect for the officials and the job they do every weekend to make sure the races are competitive and exciting for all of the NASCAR fans who come out to the racetracks. Many of these officials have regular day jobs, just like many of the crew members who work on the race teams.

Officials have a very difficult job that we would not want to have. Sure, officials get to go to every NASCAR event and have some of the best seats in the house, but they also have to deal with a lot of hassles every weekend. Just think of the number of whining prima donnas in racing who are convinced that someone else is getting away with something while they are being picked on by the officials. It takes a lot of self-control for the officials not to tell these racers where they can take their complaints.

Inside Track

NASCAR officials ensure that everyone obeys the rules of the sport. Without the officials running and coordinating the event, NASCAR would not be as successful as it is today.

A group of officials attend the races to ensure that the rules and regulations of NASCAR are being followed. Because there are a number of areas on the racecars that need to be inspected before any racecar can take to the track, the officials are assigned to specific jobs when at the racetrack. There is a division director, chief technical director, and a technical engine inspector. In addition, a number of officials are assigned to inspect certain areas of the racecar, including the carburetor, chassis, suspension, body and templates, and general safety. The following sections detail each one of these jobs.

Division Director

The division director is the boss for a certain NASCAR series. Working closely with NASCAR in Daytona Beach, Florida, the division director controls the activities at the racetrack and works with racetrack officials, who, by the way, are not part of the NASCAR organization, on race day. The division director also assigns tasks and responsibilities to the other officials at the racetrack.

Our division director says that he tries to rotate his officials through a number of different tasks and responsibilities at the racetrack. The reason for this is to give each of the officials a chance to learn more about the other areas in racing that they may not be as experienced in. We guess this is his way of broadening their horizons in order to make them better officials. The other benefit of doing this is that it ensures that every competitor is getting the same treatment in regards to the rules for a specific area. In other words, no one official is playing favorites to a particular team for a particular set of rules. Again, this is good because it keeps everything on the up-and-up.

Chief Technical Director

The chief technical director ensures that all of the technical rules and specifications of a particular series are being adhered to by the competitors in that series. Each of the officials assigned to inspect a technical area of the racecars is the responsibility of the chief technical director.

The chief technical director probably has the most difficult job of all the NASCAR officials at the racetrack. The reason we say this is because race teams are always looking for new ways to make their racecars faster than everybody else's on the racetrack. As technology advances, it becomes harder and harder to enforce the rules and to determine what is within the rules and what is outside the rules. Crew chiefs are smarter than ever and always looking for that small advantage to get them to victory lane. It takes a very smart technical director with a keen eye to keep everyone honest. The technical directors in the NASCAR series are second to none. They are the best at what they do, and we take our hats off to them.

Technical Engine Inspector

The technical engine inspector ensures that all of the engines in the racecars are within the guidelines specified in the NASCAR rulebook. This challenging task requires a keen eye for spotting anything unusual that might be lurking under the hood.

The technical engine inspector has a routine set of procedures that he or she must follow and perform for every racecar. Although using the same set of procedures

Yellow Flag

If the technical engine inspector finds something on the race engine that is outside the rules set by NASCAR, that something must be removed before the car can compete in the race.

ensures that every racecar is checked and inspected the same way, it also opens up the door for the possibility of the introduction of some interesting engine practices. Some creative ways to cheat have been to pump up the compression in all but two cylinders in the engine and make the exhaust so only those two cylinders can be tested. Another creative rule-bending practice is to drill holes in the intake manifold in restricted motors. This allows more air to be used by the engine, and you just richen the fuel delivery to compensate for this and gain extra horsepower. To prevent this from happening, teams may be subject to random inspection. If an engine is found with something that is not allowed by the rules (we don't like to use the word illegal), that something must be removed before the racecar can go out on the racetrack.

Carburetor Inspector

The carburetor is the heart of the engine. It controls the amount of fuel that is delivered to the engine. Many things can be done to a carburetor to cause it to make more horsepower. The carburetor inspector ensures that each carburetor meets the strict, and we do mean strict, specifications in the NASCAR rulebook regarding carburetors. After completing the inspection, the carburetor inspector applies a metal seal to one of the bolts that mounts the carburetor to the engine. If that seal is found to be broken because the carburetor was changed after inspection, that team can be subject to fines and penalties.

Chassis Inspector

The chassis inspector ensures that the chassis or skeleton of the racecar meets with the specifications defined by NASCAR. The rules regarding the construction and type of steel tubing that can be used in the construction of the chassis are very specific. The rules state where specific pieces of tubing need to be located and describe the thickness of the tubing itself. The reason these rules are so specific is to ensure the greatest amount of safety for the driver of the racecar. It is possible to use thinner tubing in the chassis, but after years of racing, NASCAR has determined what thickness of steel tubing offers the greatest protection. For the most part, teams do not try to cut corners when it comes to the chassis of their racecars. They will produce a safe, stiff chassis and make it as light as possible.

You may be wondering how an official can determine the thickness of a steel tube if the tube is sealed all the way around. The chassis inspector has a sonic checking device that is able to determine the thickness of the tubing. If a piece of tubing is found to be too thin, the team must replace the tubing before the racecar is allowed to go out on the racetrack.

Suspension Inspector

The suspension inspector checks that the suspension components of the racecar meet the guidelines specified in the rulebook. The suspension is a very important part of the racecar; it determines how the racecar will perform on the racetrack. A race team can do quite a number of things to the suspension in order to make the racecar handle better on the racetrack. Creative lightweight alloys are the most widely mis-used items. A lightweight part will rotate easier and turn faster than its heavyweight counterpart. An example of this would be rolling a bowling ball across the floor and kicking it to change its direction. It takes quite a kick and some force to change its direction. Try the same thing with a beach ball, and you'll find you can reverse its direction with little effort. It is up to the suspension inspector to ensure that any modifications to the suspension are within the rules defined by NASCAR.

Body/Templates Inspector

Checking the body of a racecar to ensure that it meets the guidelines specified in the NASCAR rulebook requires multiple officials or inspectors. Because the body of the racecar directly affects the amount of down force applied to the racecar, it is very important to ensure that every racecar is within the guidelines of the rulebook. Because it is very hard to make every single type of racecar the exact same shape, NASCAR uses a series of templates that have a tolerance built into them. As long as the body of the racecar is within these tolerances on the templates, the racecar is permitted to compete in the race. The tolerances given allow for a wide variety of shapes and creative license.

The primary template that is used to check the body of the racecar is one that goes from the nose of the racecar, up the hood, over the roof, and down the trunk of the racecar (known as the over-the-top template). This template ensures that the racecar's overall length as well as specific areas down the middle of the racecar are within the tolerances set by NASCAR. Because there is more than one type of racecar body available to the race teams, NASCAR has a template for each of the available body styles. The available styles are the Chevrolet Monte Carlo, Ford Taurus, Pontiac Grand Prix, and, starting with the 2001 season, the Dodge Intrepid.

Inside Track

NASCAR uses templates to ensure that every racecar body meets the specifications set forth in the rulebook for that series. There is a set of templates for each individual style of car approved for competition by NASCAR.

Although the over-the-top template is the primary template, it is not the only template used by the body inspectors. There are templates that check the width of the hood, the length and width of the windshield, the height of the sides of the racecar, and the width and length of the trunk. The front bumper is checked to make sure it hasn't been narrowed or reshaped, as are the door and front fender. There is even a template that checks the height, width, and angle of the rear spoiler. Basically, you name it, and there is a template for it.

Safety Inspector

The safety inspector checks to ensure that all of the required safety features are installed in the racecar. These features include the racing harness or seat belts that strap the driver into the racecar, the window net on the driver's side of the racecar, the fire extinguisher system, the main electrical cut-off switch to the racecar, and the individual switches for all of the components in the racecar, such as the gauges and electrical fan.

As you can see from this section, many things need to be inspected at a NASCAR event even before the teams are allowed out on the racetrack. The NASCAR officials are responsible for making sure that all of the rules and regulations set forth by NASCAR are followed, not just for the competition, but also to ensure the safety of all involved in the sport.

Yellow Flag

Penalties for violating a NASCAR rule can be loss of points, monetary fines, and/or suspension and disqualification. The heaviest fine for a team during a race is the stop-and-go or loss of a lap penalty. The loss of track position is very hard to overcome and *is* a very expensive price to pay.

Penalties for Breaking the Rules

We have talked about the rules, but we haven't talked about what happens when a team or a driver breaks one of these rules. This section talks about the fines and penalties imposed by NASCAR for violating one of the rules of the sport.

The penalties assessed by NASCAR for violating a rule or disobeying an instruction from an official can be in the form of loss of points, monetary fines, disqualification, probation, or suspension from competition. NASCAR is very serious about the rules of this sport, so unless you are willing to accept the fines, don't do the crime. (Why does that sound familiar?)

General Conduct Penalties

NASCAR may assess these fines for the violation of the general conduct rules:

➤ Any member performing an act determined to be detrimental to the sport or NASCAR is subject to a fine of at least $100 and/or suspension or loss of championship points.

➤ Any member who permits someone else to use his or her license is subject to a fine of at least $100 and/or suspension or loss of championship points.

➤ Any member who assaults a NASCAR official is subject to a fine of at least $500 and/or suspension or loss of championship points.

➤ Any member found drinking alcohol or being under the influence of illegal drugs during a NASCAR event is subject to a fine of at least $500 and/or suspension or loss of championship points.

➤ Any member involved in a fight is subject to a fine of at least $1,000 and/or suspension or loss of championship points.

➤ Any member who assaults someone with a weapon is subject to a fine of at least $1,000 and/or suspension or loss of championship points.

➤ Any drivers and/or crew chiefs not in attendance at the mandatory pre-race drivers' meeting are subject to a fine of at least $100 and/or relinquish their starting positions and must start in the back of the field.

➤ Any car owner who allows a nonlicensed person to drive a racecar is subject to a fine and/or suspension.

On-Track Penalties

The more common penalties that are imposed on a race team or a driver are minor violations that occur during a race. These are the most frequent types of penalties you will see during a race.

Here are some of the on-track fines that NASCAR may assess:

➤ Any driver who does not answer a flag waved by the flag man is subject to a lap or time penalty. Lap or time penalties are commonly referred to as stop-and-go penalties.

➤ Any driver who intentionally attempts to cause a caution on the racetrack is subject to a stop-and-go penalty.

➤ Pushing a racecar past the end of pit road is subject to a stop-and-go penalty.

➤ Any driver exceeding the pit road speed limit is subject to a stop-and-go penalty.

➤ A racecar that runs over any piece of pit road equipment while leaving the pits is subject to a stop-and-go penalty.

➤ If service performed in the pit is not completed when the racecar returns to the racetrack, the team is subject to a stop-and-go penalty.

Inspection Penalties

There are a number of things that can be done with the racing equipment that the NASCAR rulebook would deem illegal. NASCAR may assess these equipment fines:

➤ Any concealed pressure device or activating device found in the racecar is subject to a fine of at least $1,000 and/or disqualification or loss of championship points.

➤ Any device that allows for the lowering of the racecar during a race is subject to a fine of at least $1,000 and/or disqualification or loss of championship points.

➤ Any modification that allows for more than 11 gallons of fuel in one gas can is subject to a fine of $100 per gas can and/or suspension.

➤ Any engine used in competition that is outside of the specified sizes is subject to a fine of at least $2,500 and/or disqualification or loss of championship points.

➤ Any racecar found to be using any monitoring devices is subject to a fine of at least $2,000 and/or disqualification or loss of championship points.

➤ Any racecar found to be using any device that aids in the traction of the racecar is subject to a fine of at least $2,000 and/or disqualification or loss of championship points.

➤ Any racecar found to have tires with a chemical treatment is subject to a fine of at least $1,000 and/or disqualification or loss of championship points.

If a piece of equipment or a racecar itself is removed from the racetrack after competing in a race without the prior approval of a NASCAR official, fines and loss of championship points may be imposed. Also, along those same lines, if a crew member refuses to tear down a racecar for a post-race inspection, a fine of at least $500 and/or disqualification and loss of championship points would be imposed.

This is not an all-inclusive list of the rules and penalties for violations found by NASCAR, but it does give you a good idea of the types of things that can get you in trouble with NASCAR.

Pushing the Limits

Even with as strict as many of these rules are, there is still some room for race teams to push the limits of the rules in an attempt to gain that one or two extra horsepower or to cut $1/10$ second off of their lap time. Although $1/10$ second or one extra horsepower does not sound like it would make a big difference, it does. The competition in NASCAR racing is so close that sometimes $1/10$ second difference in a lap time could mean the difference between starting on the pole to starting in the back of the field. Imagine 43 racecars separated by $^1/_{10}$ second. That is extremely close competition, and in order to run up front, a race team cannot afford to give anything away, not even one horsepower.

Tolerances

By definition, *tolerance* is the amount of variation allowed from the standard. There are many areas on a racecar where the NASCAR rulebook allows for a tolerance. These tolerances enable race teams to pick up that one extra horsepower or even shave $^1/_{10}$ second off of their lap times.

One of the areas where race teams have a tolerance is the body of the racecar. Earlier in the chapter we talked about the templates the officials use, and we said that a tolerance is built into these templates. As long as the racecar does not exceed these tolerances, it can compete in the race.

The NASCAR officials are not the only ones who have these templates. Any race team can buy these exact same templates, and most teams do. By having their own sets of templates, race teams can build the bodies of their racecars right up to the edge of these tolerances back in their racing shops. This gives them a definite advantage over teams who cannot afford to buy their own templates or who do not build their own car bodies.

Inside Track

Building a racecar to the maximum tolerance allowed by the rules can offer a slight advantage over a racecar that is not built to the maximum tolerance. In NASCAR racing, every little bit helps, and nothing should be overlooked. The competition is just too tough.

Innovative Parts

Another area where race teams are able to push the limits of the rules is with innovative parts and equipment. Although the NASCAR rules are very specific about what can and what cannot be used on a racecar, every year new technology comes out that can be used on a racecar. Many of the crew chiefs look to use the new technology to improve their performances at the racetrack. Because of this, NASCAR is constantly updating and revising the rulebook to cover the new technology. However, until NASCAR makes an official ruling about a new technology that is not covered in the rulebook, race teams will try to use it. If something is not specifically mentioned in the rulebook, teams will use it until told otherwise. But new or prototype pieces must have written approval for use in competition. To obtain this approval, the piece must be submitted to NASCAR for approval prior to its use. That doesn't stop teams from trying to bend each rule to sidestep doing so, though.

Under the Hood

The development of new technology and the innovative ways in which teams use that new technology force NASCAR to create new rules. All rulings by NASCAR are final and not negotiable.

In this chapter, we have discussed the rules and regulations of NASCAR racing. The purpose of the rules is to provide an equal opportunity for all competitors and to provide for the greatest amount of safety for all participants in the sport. Just as with many professional sports today, a certain amount of risk and danger is involved in auto racing. Everyone who participates in the sport is aware of these risks and does everything possible to avoid the risk of injury. NASCAR does an exceptional job of providing for the safe competition of all involved. If you were to ask anyone involved in NASCAR about whether they were worried about safety, they all would say the same thing. They understand the risks they are taking, and they still would not do anything else in the world.

The Least You Need to Know

➤ The rules are set to ensure that no one team has an unfair advantage over another team.

➤ NASCAR rules apply to the racecars and to all members of the race team.

➤ NASCAR officials enforce the rules and assess penalties as set forth in the rulebook.

➤ At every NASCAR event, a number of officials are assigned to the pre–race inspection process.

➤ Penalties for violating a NASCAR rule can be monetary fines, loss of points, suspension, and even disqualification.

➤ Although the rules are strict and specific, there are areas where teams can push the limits of the rules without breaking them.

➤ New technology and innovative parts force the creation of new rules to keep the competition fair to all who participate in the sport.

Chapter 26

The Sweet Smell of Victory Lane

In This Chapter

➤ Getting to the winner's circle

➤ Hard work and then some

➤ Fame and fortune await

➤ The hidden benefits of victory lane

At the beginning of a typical racing season in NASCAR, you start out the season all pumped up and excited and anxious to get things rolling. The outcome of the first race sets the tone for the entire season. Along the way, some positive and not-so-positive things happen, but you forge ahead regardless of what is happening. No matter how many laps down you go, you continue to fight to get back on the lead lap. Your pit crew continues to give you the best performance possible. You get one lap back and then another lap back. Before you realize it, you are back on the lead lap. Now all you have to do is to pass the 40-plus racecars in front of you before the end of the race, and you will be on your way to victory lane.

Doesn't sound so easy, does it? It isn't. But when you do make it to victory lane, it is even better than you could have imagined. Everything suddenly smells better. The air feels cleaner, and the aches and pains you picked up on the way there suddenly do not hurt anymore. You are in victory lane, and life is good.

How to Get to Victory Lane

The question that everyone wants an answer to is: How do I get to victory lane? There is no one quick answer to this question. Getting to victory lane in NASCAR takes a lot of hard work, dedication, and resources. It takes the right setup on the racecar; a good, experienced driver; quick, flawless pit stops; and the skill and good luck to avoid accidents.

Inside Track

There is no one secret to winning a race. It takes a combination of hard work, dedication, skill, experience, and financial resources to succeed in NASCAR.

Financial Resources

It takes more than just a desire to win to make it to victory lane. As with most things in life, you need strong financial resources behind your racing team. Without good funding to get the equipment you need, you will never be a contender. Everybody wants to win, but not everybody has the financial resources to make it happen.

In order to run a competitive NASCAR Winston Cup team, you need a multi-million-dollar-a-year deal. Although at first that amount of money may seem like a lot, it really isn't. It goes very fast, especially when you start to factor in time and money for testing and development; the cost of the equipment, racecars, and team salaries; and the cost of transportation to attend 34 races held all across the country. In Chapter 9, "Paying the Bills," we talked in detail about the major expenses involved in running a NASCAR Winston Cup team. All of these expenses are a must if you want to get to victory lane on a regular basis.

Inside Track

Strong financial resources are an important part of NASCAR racing. They enable you to have the best equipment and the best staff to work on the team. They also enable you to practice and test your equipment and team before you get to the races. The real key to success is a team's dedication, hard work, and relentless pursuit of victory.

While multi-million-dollar deals are needed to run the Winston Cup Series, there are other NASCAR series you can run that do not require such a large financial investment. Money does play an important role in many of the NASCAR series, but it is not the only thing that will get you to victory lane, as many teams who have found their way to victory lane prove. Not even the biggest financial investment can replace or overcome the dedication, skill, and experience needed to win in NASCAR.

Hard Work

Once you have financial backing from sponsors, you need to have team members who are willing to work harder than they probably ever have before in their lives. Hard work and dedication are the most important factors in getting to victory lane. Every member on your race team has to work harder than the members of every other race team who are also trying to get to victory lane, and that is no easy task.

You do not need to be an expert on racecar setups and pit strategy to get to victory lane. No team falls into victory lane by mistake. The best team wins the race. This doesn't always mean the fastest car wins. It's a total team effort. The best plan can fall apart during a race. The team that reaches victory lane is the team that can overcome any obstacle that may be in the way, be it a slow pit stop, a mistake by the driver, or a bad call by the spotter. The winning team does not let any of these things get in its way. The team members focus on the job at hand, work hard to get the job done without error, and then prepare for the next challenge. If you allow yourself or any of your crew members to dwell on a mistake or a bad call, it will affect your next task, and you will fall back even further from your goal. Teams need to stay focused on their goals and not let anything get in the way of meeting those goals.

Inside Track

In addition to having the best equipment and strong financial resources, you need team members who will make the necessary sacrifices to be successful. Hard work and dedication are just as important as having a fast racecar.

Team Effort

In addition to working hard and staying focused on their goals, all crew members need to work together as a team. No one person can get the team to victory lane; even the driver needs the help of his pit crew and the help of every person back in the racing shop to win the race.

Every member of a team has a specific job, and he or she knows what the job involves. If each person makes his best effort on his responsibility, which includes working and communicating with the other team members, the whole team will succeed.

Of course some positions on a race team are more important than others or have a greater amount of responsibility than others, but none of the people

Inside Track

Just like a baseball, basketball, football, or any other sports team, all of the members of the racing team need to work together in order to reach an overall common goal. If the team does not work together, it will never make it to victory lane.

in those positions can do it alone. If one person could do it alone, why then are there so many members on a NASCAR Winston Cup team (or any other [NASCAR] team, for that matter)? The reason is simple. With the competition as close and intense as it is today, you need to have a team of people all working together on a common goal to be successful. The common desire of every individual allows the team to overcome any obstacle and to reach common goals. Teamwork and desire are the fuel for the trip to victory lane.

Lots of Luck

If we told you that financial resources, hard work, and a team effort were the only things you need to get to victory lane, we would be fooling you. Another big contributor to the formula for getting to victory lane is pure luck. Sometimes the luck is with you, and sometimes it is not; it is just that simple. One race you may be fortunate enough to drive through that big crash in turn four, and the next race the big crash includes you and sends you home early.

Luck is the one factor that teams have no control over. You can do some things to minimize your bad luck and maximize your good luck, but racing still is a game of chance and circumstance to a certain extent. Sometimes you win; sometimes you lose. The only thing you can do is take nothing for granted, double-check all of your equipment, and try to keep yourself out of trouble. But realize that sometimes you just end up in the wrong place at the wrong time.

Ernie Irvan knows about luck. In the mid-1980s Ernie Irvan began driving for Robert Yates, owner of the Dale Jarret Ford Taurus and 1999 Winston Cup champion. At the Michigan Speedway, Ernie was involved in a horrific crash that almost took his life. After examining him, doctors gave Ernie only a 10 percent chance at survival and said he would never race again. Less than two years later, Ernie not only survived and recovered from his injuries, but he also climbed back in a racecar and was able to race again. Later that same year, on his return to the Michigan Speedway, Ernie won the race, putting behind him any bad luck that some thought followed him after the crash.

This past year, while practicing his NASCAR Busch Series racecar at the Michigan Speedway, Ernie once again was involved in a crash that forced him to be flown to a nearby hospital with head injuries. Fortunately, Ernie recovered from his injuries and decided to retire as a driver from the NASCAR Winston Cup Series.

The point to this story is that although Ernie had some of the best equipment, dedicated team members,

Inside Track

Luck is one thing a race team cannot control. Sometimes it is on your side, and other times it turns its back on you. That's just the way it is in racing. Circumstance plays a major role in the outcome of almost everything.

and an excellent team owner in Robert Yates, luck was not with Ernie on the race-track. He was unlucky enough to be involved in two terrifying and life-threatening crashes, yet he was lucky enough to cheat death and to return home to his wife and family. Sometimes luck is on your side, and other times it is not. The key is knowing when your luck is about to run out.

Accolades of Winning

Everyone probably has some idea of what the benefits are of winning a race. The prize money is an obvious benefit, but there are other benefits as well. These other benefits include exposure for your sponsors, which they like very much. After all, everyone likes to be a part of a winning team. Winning also brings exposure to the team. People start to learn more about the driver and the other team members, such as the crew chief and team owner. The more famous a team becomes, the higher the demand is for that team. It is amazing how quickly opportunities arise for those who consistently win races.

Prize Money and Bonuses

The most obvious benefit of winning is the prize money. In most cases, the prize money is a rather large sum. The NASCAR Winston Cup Series pays out on average well over one million dollars in prize money at every race. This money, depending on contractual agreements, goes to the team owner. But in many cases, the team owner gives an incentive bonus to each of the team members for winning a race. This way, each member of the team can share in the financial success of the team. The more races a team wins, the more money each member of the crew can make.

During a recent NASCAR Winston Cup race, Joe Gibbs, owner of the #18 InterState Batteries Pontiac Grand Prix driven by Bobby Labonte and the #20 Pontiac Grand Prix driven by Tony Stewart, talked about the performance bonus program he has with both pit crews. In an effort to give both pit crews an incentive to keep the pit stops as short as possible, Joe structured the bonus to be based on the amount of time each pit stop required. For any pit stop completed in 17 seconds, no bonus would be paid. For any pit stop in 16 seconds, a bonus would be paid to the crew. For a pit stop of 15 seconds, a bigger bonus would be paid. However, a pit stop of 18 seconds or longer means the crew would pay Joe a bonus.

Although this bonus system may seem unconventional, it all but guarantees that both of Joe's

Inside Track

Sharing the prize money with the entire team is a great way to keep everyone motivated to win. It also reinforces the sense of teamwork. Everyone on the team should share in both its successes and its failures.

racecars are out of the pits in under 17 seconds. No employee likes to pay their boss, so the crew makes sure that the pit stops are done in record time. Now that Joe has shared his system with the world, we would expect more team owners to do the same with their teams.

In addition to the race bonus, team owners offer a championship bonus to the entire team. The last two NASCAR Winston Cup champions were paid over two million dollars for winning the championship in addition to the prize money they won at each race. There is big money to be won in this sport, and the amount is all based on performance. The better you are, the more you can win.

Inside Track

Performance bonuses are a great way to ensure that everyone on the team is giving 100 percent to the team.

Exposure for the Sponsor

Earlier in this chapter and in Chapter 3, "The Silent Team Member," we talked about sponsors and the role they play in NASCAR. Sponsors are the lifeblood of the racing world. Without sponsors backing the teams, the sport of stock car racing would not have become as big as it is today.

What do corporate sponsors want in exchange for the big dollars they give to race teams? They want exposure, which is why their company names are plastered all over the racecars, uniforms, equipment, and trailers. Sponsors believe that advertising in NASCAR, be it the Winston Cup, Busch, Busch North, or any other series, will help expose their company to the general public that they would otherwise not be able to reach. They also know that racing fans are incredibly loyal to the sponsors of their favorite driver, so sponsoring a NASCAR racing team helps them sell more products. The more products they sell, the more money they make.

So what does this have to do with the benefits of a team winning a race? Think about it. A winning team is interviewed on national television and written up in newspapers and magazines all over the country. Merchandise sales for drivers increase with each race they win. All of this is increased exposure for the sponsor.

Sponsors love it when their driver wins a race. It means that until the next race, everyone will be talking about the racecar they sponsor. Race fans often identify a racecar by the name of the sponsor

Inside Track

The winner of a race always receives the most media attention of all the race teams that compete in the race. Sponsors like the media coverage race teams bring them because it helps them sell more products.

plastered on the side of the racecar. Even if they forget the name of a particular driver, they will refer to the team by the sponsor name. All this attention gets the sponsor's name in front of millions of people every week.

The more exposure a team can bring to a corporate sponsor, the better the chances that the sponsor will remain in the sport. So the next time you win a race, be sure to mention your sponsors while in victory lane. After all, they helped you get there.

Exposure for the Team

Winning races makes everyone famous. The driver gets the most exposure, but the rest of the team also gets exposure. After the driver, the person who receives the most exposure is the crew chief. In Chapter 8, "The Posse," we talked about the different members of the crew and what each of their responsibilities are. The crew chief, who makes decisions about the setup of the racecar, suddenly becomes the center of attention from the media and the other crew chiefs. Suddenly everyone believes that the winning crew chief has found the secret behind getting to victory lane. Even though everyone in the sport knows that there is no one secret to winning, everyone still continues to go after the crew chief to find out what he knows. The more a team wins, the more popular its crew chief becomes.

A perfect example of this is Ray Evernham, former crew chief for Jeff Gordon. Back in 1994, when Jeff and Ray first came to the Winston Cup Series, Ray was not well known. He was just another very hard-working crew chief making his way up the racing ladder. By the 1999 NASCAR season, Jeff and Ray had won three NASCAR Winston Cup championships, and Ray was being referred to as the greatest crew chief in many years. During the summer of the 1999 season, Ray announced that he was leaving Jeff Gordon and Hendrick Motorsports to become a team owner and help bring Dodge back into the sport of stock car racing after 20 years. This opportunity was a result of the repeated success and exposure Ray received while winning races during his five years with Jeff.

Inside Track

A successful race team brings more attention to everyone on the race team. People believe that the winning team is or has the necessary combination to win races. This belief increases the winning team members' value to other race teams.

Fame and Fortune

The other benefits of winning races are the fame and fortune that come along with it. Anyone who is involved in the sport of stock car racing does it for the love of the sport. Team members sacrifice many things in order to be competitive in the sport, and everyone wants to be number one or at least be the best at what they do. People in any sport or business have a natural desire to succeed. They enjoy the limelight that success brings and dwell in it for as long as it lasts. Public admiration and rewards bring a sense of satisfaction and fulfillment that we all crave. Do not underestimate how fame and fortune can motivate people.

Hidden Benefits of Victory Lane

By know you know that race teams live and die by the sponsors they have. Keeping the sponsors happy is just as important to a race team as winning a race. Of course, the more races a team wins, the happier the sponsor is. But you don't have to win to produce great returns for a sponsor. Represent your sponsor well, run the best race you can every time, and you'll go a long way with your sponsor. In the following section, we talk about how running well and winning races keeps the sponsors happy and how winning helps in the search for new sponsors.

Attract More Sponsors

Everyone wants to be part of a winning team. Whether the person is an actual member of the team or just a fan, everyone wants to say they are involved with a winner. Corporations are no exception to this rule.

Any team that is successful in racing is always looking to repeat that performance. When a team is able to prove that victory is not just a one-time occurrence, the value of that team increases. When a team has a proven track record of success, its search for new or additional sponsors becomes a lot easier. Because corporations write very large checks to sponsor a race team, they want to make sure that the investment they are making in that team will return the benefits they are expecting. And NASCAR teams have proven to the world that sponsorship in NASCAR at every level works. No matter what series sponsors chose, the advertising does it's job.

Inside Track

Winning races makes attracting new sponsors to the team a lot easier. Showing a sponsor that you can win races makes it much easier for them to sign on with you.

When a new team that does not have a track record of winning tries to sign a sponsor, the sponsor may be a little reluctant due to the fact that the team has yet to prove itself capable of delivering the level of exposure the sponsor is looking for. This is not to say that a new team cannot deliver the level of advertising exposure for the sponsor, but having a proven track record of advertising exposure makes new sponsors more likely to sign on the dotted line. One of the hidden benefits to winning races is that it shows potential sponsors that the team is capable of winning races and can deliver on the promises of additional exposure made to the sponsor. The more consistent a team is at demonstrating strong performances, the better the chances are that a team will be able to secure a new sponsor. You do not have to win races in order to get sponsors.

Another benefit to winning races is that the search for potential sponsors becomes a little easier. In Chapter 3, we talked about the search for a sponsor and how to close the deal. When a race team has a history of success, the sponsors come to the team looking to get involved. It is very nice when corporate sponsors come to you looking to give you a check to go racing, instead of you going after them.

Increase Exposure for Existing Sponsors

When a corporate sponsor has signed on with a race team and that race team is able to deliver on the promise of increased exposure, the sponsor is usually very happy and is likely to continue to work with that team. If the team is very successful, the sponsor will most likely want to use the team more in its advertising campaigns. It will want to brag that the race team is a success due to the fact that the team uses its products.

For example, after Jeff Gordon, who drives #24 Dupont Chevrolet Monte Carlo, won his first NASCAR Winston Cup Championship, Quaker State motor oil, who was supplying Jeff with both financial and product sponsorship, starting running television commercials with Jeff. In the television commercials, Jeff talked about the abuse that his engines endure during a 500-mile race and the fact that since he started using Quaker State motor oil, he had seen an improvement in the performance of his engines. He went so far as to say that the use of Quaker State motor oil in his engines allowed him to win the NASCAR Winston Cup championship.

This is a prime example of how existing sponsors increase their advertising efforts using the race team after a major win in order to help sell more products. Corporations who sponsor race teams use racing as a proving ground to the general public as to the quality of their products. The more successful a race team, the easier it is for the general pubic to believe that the products are worth buying.

As you can see from this chapter and from just watching the sport of stock car racing, there are a number of benefits to being a successful race team. Best of all is the feeling of satisfaction that all of the hard work and investment have paid off in a number of ways.

Inside Track

A successful race team brings more attention to the primary sponsor on the racecar. Increasingly, corporations use the race team in promotional advertisements, which benefits both the sponsor and the race team.

The Least You Need to Know

➤ No one thing will get a team to victory lane. Winning requires a combination of efforts from everyone on the race team.

➤ In addition to the best equipment, practice and experience will help get a team to victory lane.

➤ Everyone on the race team needs to give 100 percent effort to the team in order to get the team to victory lane.

➤ Luck sometimes determines where a team finishes in the race, and when luck happens, good or bad, you can't do anything about it.

➤ Winning brings teams more than just the prize money; it also helps to bring in more sponsors.

➤ A performance bonus is a good way to keep a team motivated to do the best job possible.

Track Directory

Alabama

Fairgrounds Raceway
Birmingham, Alabama
205-674-6193

Chatom International Raceway
Chatom, Alabama
334-847-3575

Chilton County Speedway
Clanton, Alabama
205-668-0569

Flomaton Speedway
Flomaton, Alabama
334-296-7223

Green Valley Speedway
Gadsden, Alabama
205-492-6242

J&J Speedway
Grand Bay, Alabama
334-666-7241

East Hanceville Speedway
Hanceville, Alabama
205-352-6765

Hollis Crossroads Speedway
Hollis Crossroads, Alabama

Huntsville Speedway
Huntsville, Alabama
256-882-9191
www.huntsvillespeedway.com/

Mobile International Raceway
Irvington, Alabama
334-957-2026

Central Alabama Motor Speedway
Jasper, Alabama
205-221-0500

L.A. Raceway
Loxley, Alabama
334-947-7223

Marbury Dirt Track
Marbury, Alabama
205-755-0465

Montgomery Motor Speedway
Montgomery, Alabama
334-262-7223

Montgomery Motorsports Park
Montgomery, Alabama
334-260-9660

Moulton Speedway
Moulton, Alabama
334-974-6382

Onycha Raceway
Opp, Alabama
334-4939573

South Alabama Motor Speedway
Opp, Alabama
334-565-3539

Penton Raceway
Penton, Alabama
205-864-0666

East Alabama Motor Speedway
Phenix City, Alabama
334-297-2594

Thunder Mountain Speedway
Rainsville, Alabama
205-623-7223

Heart O' Dixie Speedway
Sayre, Alabama
205-648-2041

Talladega Grand Prix Raceway
Talladega, Alabama
205-362-9985

Talladega Short Track
Talladega, Alabama
205-831-1413

Talladega Superspeedway
Talladega, Alabama
256-362-2261

North Alabama Speedway
Tuscumbia, Alabama
205-381-0881

Lakeside Speedway
Wilsonville, Alabama
205-669-6508

Super Six Speedway
Winfield, Alabama
205-487-3836

Holiday Raceway
Woodstock, Alabama
205-938-2123

Alaska

Fairbanks Racing Lions
Fairbanks, Alaska
907-452-8913

Robert Mitchell Memorial Raceway
Fairbanks, Alaska
907-452-3500

Twin City Raceway
Kenai, Alaska
907-262-9520

Kodiak Island Raceway
Kodiak, Alaska
907-487-4395

Alaska Raceway Park
Palmer, Alaska
907-273-9842

North Star Speedway
Palmer, Alaska
907-746-OVAL
www.alaska.net/~speedshp/race/

Capitol Speedway
Willow, Alaska
907-495-6420

Arizona

Mohave Valley Raceway
Bullhead City, Arizona
520-346-3000

Central Arizona Raceway
Casa Grande, Arizona
602-723-0007

Firebird International Raceway
Chandler, Arizona
602-268-0200

Canyon Raceway
Phoenix, Arizona
602-258-7223

Manzanita Speedway
Phoenix, Arizona
602-276-7575

Phoenix International Speedway
Phoenix, Arizona
602-252-3833

Tri-City Speedway
Safford, Arizona
520-485-3043

Thunder Raceway
Show Low, Arizona
520-537-1111

Tucson Raceway Park
Tucson, Arizona
520-762-9200

Phoenix Raceway Park
Wittman, Arizona
602-256-0333

Yuma Speedway
Yuma, Arizona
520-726-9483

Arkansas

Batesville Speedway
Batesville, Arkansas
501-251-1777

Beebe Speedway
Beebe, Arkansas
501-882-5513

Mount Clair Road Speedway
Cove, Arkansas
501-387-6371

Thunder Valley Speedway
Fayetteville, Arkansas
501-582-1319

Thunder Mountain Super Speedway
Glenwood, Arkansas
501-356-3861

Harrisburg Speedway
Harrisburg, Arkansas
501-578-9447

I-30 Speedway
Little Rock, Arkansas
501-945-5380

Bear Creek Speedway
Marshall, Arkansas
501-448-5926

Lake Ouachita Speedway
Mount Ida, Arkansas
501-867-3428

Orchard Park Speedway
Murfreesboro, Arkansas
501-845-5177

Crowley's Ridge Raceway
Paragould, Arkansas
501-236-3141

Northwest Arkansas Speedway
Pea Ridge, Arkansas
501-451-1900

Plumersville Speedway
Plumersville, Arkansas
501-354-8560

Pocahontas Speedway
Pocahontas, Arkansas
501-892-9240

Prescott Raceway
Prescott, Arkansas
501-887-3984

Midway Racing Center
Sheridan, Arkansas
501-942-2054

Meadowland Speedway
Texarkana, Arkansas
501-772-4065

Stateline Speedway
Texarkana, Arkansas
501-779-1406

Crawford County Speedway
Van Buren, Arkansas
501-474-1942

Riverside Speedway
West Memphis, Arkansas
501-735-8071

California

Sun Rise Valley Raceway
Adelanto, California
619-246-7262

Shasta Speedway
Anderson, California
916-221-8008

Antioch Speedway
Antioch, California
510-754-0222

Fast Friday Speedway
Auburn, California
916-878-7223

313

Bakersfield Raceway
Bakersfield, California
805-399-2210

Bakersfield Speedway
Bakersfield, California
805-393-3373

Mesa Marin Raceway
Bakersfield, California
805-366-5711

Blythe Speedway
Blythe, California
619-922-7223

Calistoga Speedway
Calistoga, California
707-942-5111

Carlsbad Raceway
Carlsbad, California
619-480-8369

Cedarville Speedway
Cedarville, California
916-279-2913

Silver Dollar Speedway
Chico, California
916-891-6535

Del Mar Speedway
Del Mar, California
714-533-4444

Cajon Speedway
El Cajon, California
619-488-8900

Imperial Raceway
El Centro, California
619-352-4071

Redwood Acres Raceway
Eureka, California
707-442-3232

Prairie City Raceway Park
Folsom, California
916-985-6009

California Speedway
Fontana, California
909-429-5000

Ernie Purssell Memorial Speedway
Grass Valley, California
916-273-2692

Kings Speedway
Hanford, California
209-584-3318

Holtville Aerodrome International
Raceway
Holtville, California
619-356-4641

Irwindale Speedway
Irwindale, California
626-358-1100
irwindalespeedway.com/

Lakeport Speedway
Lakeport, California
707-274-2844

Raceway Park
Los Angeles, California
310-521-8462

Madera Speedway
Madera, California
559-673-7223

Twin Cities Speedway
Marysville, California
916-742-9222

Merced Fairgrounds Speedway
Merced, California
www.mercedspeedway.com/

Laguna Seca Raceway
Monterey, California
408-648-5100

Los Angeles County Raceway
Palmdale, California
805-533-2224

Independent Motorsports Park
Pearsonville, California
619-384-2673

Petaluma Fairgrounds Speedway
Petaluma, California
707-778-3100

314

Pomona Raceway
Pomona, California
909-593-7010

Rocky Hill Speedway
Porterville, California
209-781-8502

Quincy Speedway
Quincy, California
916-832-4272

Barona Speedway
Ramona, California
909-582-2292

Sun County Fairgrounds
Red Bluff, California
916-527-9199

Redding Raceway
Redding, California
702-267-4668

Willow Springs Motorsports Park
Rosamond, California
805-256-2471

All American Speedway
Roseville, California
916-786-2025

Placerville Speedway
Roseville, California
916-783-7223
www.johnpadjenmotorsports.com/

Sacramento Raceway Park
Sacramento, California
916-366-2653

Glen Helen Speedway
San Bernardino, California
909-880-3354

Orange Show Speedway
San Bernardino, California
909-885-5757

San Jose Speedway
San Jose, California
408-294-7223
www.sjspeedway.com/

Fairgrounds Raceway Santa Maria
Santa Maria, California
805-937-8584

Santa Maria Speedway
Santa Maria, California
805-466-4462

Sears Point Raceway
Sonoma, California
800-870-7223
www.searspoint.com/

Delta Speedway
Stockton, California
209-983-0271

Stockton 99 Speedway
Stockton, California
209-466-9999
www.stockton99speedway.com/

High Desert Speedway
Susanville, California
916-257-5474

Altamont Raceway Park
Tracy, California
925-606-0274
www.altamontraceway.com

Thunderbowl Raceway
Tulare, California
209-688-0909

Ukiah Speedway
Ukiah, California
707-462-9495
www.ukiahspeedway.com/

Solano County Fairgrounds
Vallejo, California
707-577-6019

Ventura Raceway
Ventura, California
805-985-5433

Plaza Park Raceway
Visalia, California
209-651-5114

Watsonville Speedway
Watsonville, California
831-462-6101
watsonville.com/speedway/

Thunderhill Park
Willows, California
916-934-5588

Goldrush Speedway
Yreka, California
541-857-1292
www.goldrushspeedway.com/

Northern California Speedway
Yreka, California
916-842-2714

Colorado

Pikes Peak International Raceway
Colorado Springs, Colorado
719-382-7223

Fairgrounds Raceway
Cortez, Colorado
970-565-3671

Bandimere Speedway
Denver, Colorado
303-697-6001

Rocky Mountain Speedway
Denver, Colorado
303-371-1600

Second Creek Raceway
Denver, Colorado
303-371-6661

Colorado National Speedway
Erie, Colorado
303-665-4173

I-76 Speedway
Fort Morgan, Colorado
303-867-2101

Two Rivers Raceway
Grand Junction, Colorado
970-434-9625

Hayden Speedway
Hayden, Colorado
970-824-2195

La Junta Raceway
La Junta, Colorado

Lamar Speedway
Lamar, Colorado
719-336-3205

May Valley Speedway
Lamar, Colorado
719-336-9407

Mountain View Motor Sport Park
Mead, Colorado
303-535-4907

Thunder Mountain Speedway
Olathe, Colorado
970-323-6494

Beacon Hill Speedway
Pueblo, Colorado
719-542-6105

Pueblo Motorsports Park
Pueblo, Colorado
719-545-0878

Blue Ridge Speedway
Wellington, Colorado
800-545-4994

Connecticut

Lime Rock Park
Lime Rock, Connecticut
860-435-5000

Stafford Motor Speedway
Stafford Springs, Connecticut
860-684-2783

New Thompson Speedway
Thompson, Connecticut
860-923-2280

Waterford Speedbowl
Waterford, Connecticut
203-442-1585

Delaware

Delaware International Speedway
Delmar, Delaware
302-846-3968

Dover Downs International Speedway
Dover, Delaware
302-674-4600

Seacoast Speedway
Georgetown, Delaware
302-856-6632

Delaware State Fairgrounds
Harrington, Delaware
302-856-7437

Airport Speedway
New Castle, Delaware
302-328-8302

Delaware Memorial Sports Park
Seaford, Delaware
302-629-6535

Florida

North Okaloosa County Raceway
Baker, Florida
904-537-4980

Volusia County Speedway
Barberville, Florida
904-985-4402

Desoto Speedway
Bradenton, Florida
813-748-3171

Bronson Motor Speedway
Bronson, Florida
904-486-4911

Sugarland Raceway Park
Clewiston, Florida
813-902-0633

Daytona International Speedway
Daytona Beach, Florida
904-254-2700

Gainesville Raceway
Gainesville, Florida
904-377-0046

Hialeah Speedway
Hialeah, Florida
305-821-6644

Homestead Motorsports Complex
Homestead, Florida
305-379-7223

Miami-Homestead Speedway
Homestead, Florida
305-230-5200

Citrus County Speedway
Inverness, Florida
904-726-9339

Jax Raceways
Jacksonville, Florida
904-757-5425

Columbia Motorsports Park
Lake City, Florida
904-755-9302

Lake City Speedway
Lake City, Florida
904-754-8800

USA International Speedway
Lakeland, Florida
800-984-7223

Southern Raceway
Milton, Florida
904-626-8224

Florida Sports Park
Naples, Florida
813-774-2701

New Smyrna Speedway
New Smyrna Beach, Florida
904-427-4129
www.newsmyrnaspeedway.com/

Ocala Speedway
Ocala, Florida
904-622-9400

Orange County Raceway
Orlando, Florida
407-568-2271

Orlando Speed World
Orlando, Florida
407-568-1367

Walt Disney World Speedway
Orlando, Florida
407-824-4321

Thunder Valley Speedway
Palatka, Florida
904-649-9906

Moroso Motorsports Park
Palm Beach Gardens, Florida
407-622-1400

Five Flags Speedway
Pensacola, Florida
904-944-0480

Sunshine Speedway
Pinellas Park, Florida
813-573-4598

Charlotte County Speedway
Punta Gorda, Florida
813-575-2422

St. Augustine Speedway
St. Augustine, Florida
904-825-2886

Sebring International Raceway
Sebring, Florida
813-655-1442

East Bay Raceway
Tampa, Florida
813-677-2632

Gulf County Speedway
Wewahitchka, Florida
904-832-2613

Auburndale Speedway
Winter Haven, Florida
813-965-7223

Panama Raceway Park
Youngstown, Florida
904-722-7223

Georgia

Augusta Motor Speedway
Augusta, Georgia
706-855-6727

Sugar Creek Raceway
Blue Ridge, Georgia
706-632-5550

Road Atlanta Raceway
Braselton, Georgia
770-967-6143

North Georgia Speedway
Chatsworth, Georgia
706-695-3313

New Cochran Speedway
Cochran, Georgia
912-929-3328

Cordele Motor Speedway
Cordele, Georgia
912-273-5102

Seven Flags Speedway
Douglasville, Georgia
770-949-7223

441 Speedway
Dublin, Georgia
912-984-4455

Lanier National Speedway
Gainesville, Georgia
770-967-8600

Atlanta Motor Speedway
Hampton, Georgia
770-946-3921
www.atlantamotorspeedway.com/

Hartwell Motor Speedway
Hartwell, Georgia
706-743-3532

Peach State Speedway
Jefferson, Georgia
706-367-9004

New Lavonia Speedway
Lavonia, Georgia
706-356-2220

Silver Dollar Raceway
Reynolds, Georgia
912-847-4414

Chattanooga Raceway Park
Ringgold, Georgia
706-891-0902

Rome Speedway
Rome, Georgia
770-926-5315

Oglethorpe Speedway Park
Savannah, Georgia
912-964-7223

Roebling Road Raceway
Savannah, Georgia
912-748-4205

Senoia Raceway
Senoia, Georgia
404-461-4647

Speedway Park
Swainsboro, Georgia
912-237-2444

Swainsboro Raceway
Swainsboro, Georgia
912-594-1874

Thunderbowl Speedway
Valdosta, Georgia
912-794-3400

Waycross Motor Speedway
Waycross, Georgia
912-283-0900

Golden Isles Speedway
Waynesville, Georgia
912-778-5821

Winder-Barrow Speedway
Winder, Georgia
770-867-6327

Dixie Speedway
Woodstock, Georgia
404-926-5315

Hawaii

Hawaii Raceway Park
Ewa Beach (Oahu)
808-841-6288

Kauai Raceway Park
Mana (Kauai)
808-332-8038

Idaho

Firebird Raceway
Boise, Idaho
208-344-0411

Treasure Valley Speedway
Boise, Idaho
208-376-5050

Noise Park Raceway
Idaho Falls, Idaho
208-523-2416

Meridian Speedway
Meridian, Idaho
208-888-2813

Pocatello Speedway
Pocatello, Idaho
208-233-4350

Empire Raceway
Post Falls, Idaho
208-773-8942

Stateline Stadium and Speedway
Post Falls, Idaho
208-773-5019

Lemhi County Motorsports
Salmon, Idaho
208-756-4500

Magic Valley Speedway
Twin Falls, Idaho
208-734-3700

Illinois

Mercer County Speedway
Aledo, Illinois
309-582-2350

Godfrey Motor Speedway
Alton, Illinois
618-466-6905

Belle-Claire Speedway
Belleville, Illinois
618-233-0052

Raceway Park
Blue Island, Illinois
708-385-4035

Fayette County Speedway
Brownstown, Illinois
618-427-5285

Spoon River Speedway
Canton, Illinois
309-668-2622

Charleston Speedway
Charleston, Illinois
217-345-2929

Vermilion County Speedway
Danville, Illinois
217-443-6588

DuQuoin State Fairgrounds
DuQuoin, Illinois
618-542-9373

East Moline Speedway
East Moline, Illinois
309-796-2444

Gateway International Raceway
East St. Louis, Illinois
618-482-5501

Fairbury American Legion Speedway
Fairbury, Illinois
815-692-2253

Farmer City Raceway
Farmer City, Illinois
217-928-9110

Freeport Raceway Park
Freeport, Illinois
815-233-0390

Tri-City Speedway
Granite City, Illinois
618-931-7836
314-947-7287

South Central Motorplex
Greenville, Illinois
618-664-1412

Mason County Raceway
Havana, Illinois
309-543-6124

Highland Speedway
Highland, Illinois
618-654-6656

Jacksonville Raceway
Jacksonville, Illinois
217-243-5896

Kankakee Speedway
Kankakee, Illinois
815-933-2090

74 Raceway
Knoxville, Illinois
309-289-9501

LaSalle Speedway
LaSalle, Illinois
815-223-6900

Rockford Speedway
Loves Park, Illinois
815-633-1500

Macomb Speedway
Macomb, Illinois
309-836-9511

Macon Speedway
Macon, Illinois
217-764-3770
217-764-3224

Gateway International Raceway
Madison, Illinois
618-482-5501

Southern Illinois Speedway
Marion, Illinois
618-982-2611

Coles County Speedway
Mattoon, Illinois
217-536-5917

Grundy County Speedway
Morris, Illinois
815-942-5043

K and L Raceway
Mount Vernon, Illinois
618-244-5782

P.M.C. Race Park
Peoria, Illinois
309-697-4981

Peoria Speedway
Peoria, Illinois
309-673-3342

Riverside Speedway
Pittsfield, Illinois
217-723-9306

Bureau County Speedway
Princeton, Illinois
815-872-0538

Quincy Raceway
Quincy, Illinois
217-224-3843

Blackhawk Farms Raceway
Rockton, Illinois
815-389-3323

Illinois State Fairgrounds
Springfield, Illinois
217-524-0869

Sycamore Speedway
Sycamore, Illinois
815-895-5454

Wayne County Speedway
Wayne City, Illinois
618-242-1443

Santa Fe Speedway
Willow Springs, Illinois
708-839-1050

Indiana

Anderson Speedway
Anderson, Indiana
317-642-0206

Angola Motor Speedway
Angola, Indiana
219-495-7223

Avilla Motor Speedway
Avilla, Indiana
219-897-3332

Bloomington Speedway
Bloomington, Indiana
812-824-7400

Benton County Speedway
Boswell, Indiana
317-295-0218

County Line Raceway
Brazil, Indiana
317-672-4670

Brownstown Speedway
Brownstown, Indiana
812-358-5332

Camden Raceway
Camden, Indiana
219-686-2889

Greater Evansville Raceway
Chandler, Indiana
812-925-3685

Charlestown Speedway
Charlestown, Indiana
812-256-6339

Indianapolis Raceway Park
Clermont, Indiana
317-291-4090

Southlake Speedway
Crown Point, Indiana
219-662-4007

Bear Field Speedway
Fort Wayne, Indiana
219-747-7223

Elkhart County 4-H Fairgrounds
Goshen, Indiana
419-476-8048

Decatur County Fairgrounds
Greensburg, Indiana
812-689-4899

Tri-State Speedway
Haubstadt, Indiana
812-768-5995

Indianapolis Motor Speedway
Indianapolis, Indiana
317-481-8500
www.brickyard.com/

Indiana State Fairgrounds
Indianapolis, Indiana
317-927-7500

Indianapolis Speedrome
Indianapolis, Indiana
317-353-8206

Sportsdrome Speedway
Jeffersonville, Indiana
812-282-7551

Evan's Kokomo Speedway
Kokomo, Indiana
317-459-3877

Lawrenceburg Speedway
Lawrenceburg, Indiana
812-537-3599

Union County Speedway
Liberty, Indiana
317-458-6479

U.S. 24 Speedway
Logansport, Indiana
219-753-6922

Martin County Speedway
Loogootee, Indiana
812-295-3370

Jefferson County Fairgrounds
Madison, Indiana
812-689-4899

Morgan County Fairgrounds
Martinsville, Indiana
812-689-4899

Shady Hill Speedway
Medaryville, Indiana
219-843-8892

Montpelier Lions Raceway
Montpelier, Indiana
317-728-2327

U.S. 41 International Speedway
Morocco, Indiana
219-285-2200

Putnam Park Road Course
Mount Meridian, Indiana
317-526-2290

Lion's Delaware County Fair
Muncie, Indiana
317-288-1854

Mount Lawn Speedway
New Castle, Indiana
317-521-9802

New Paris Speedway
New Paris, Indiana
219-831-3050

Twin Cities Raceway Park
North Vernon, Indiana
812-346-4034

Ripley County Speedway
Osgood, Indiana
812-689-4724

Paragon Speedway
Paragon, Indiana
317-537-2366

Miami County Speedway
Peru, Indiana
317-985-2181

Capitol Speedway
Plymouth, Indiana
219-935-4414

Lincoln Park Speedway
Putnamville, Indiana
317-653-3485

Rush County Fairgrounds
Rushville, Indiana
812-689-4899

Salem Speedway
Salem, Indiana
812-923-9851

Thunder Valley Raceway
Salem, Indiana
812-883-8808

Illiana Motor Speedway
Schereville, Indiana
219-322-5311

Shelby County Fairgrounds
Shelbyville, Indiana
812-689-4899

South Bend Motor Speedway
South Bend, Indiana
219-287-1704

Sullivan Speedway
Sullivan, Indiana
812-268-5610

Terre Haute Action Track
Terre Haute, Indiana
812-232-9627

Winchester Speedway
Winchester, Indiana
317-584-9701

Iowa

Kossuth County Raceway
Algona, Iowa
515-295-3666

Butler County Speedway
Allison, Iowa
319-267-2200

Buena Vista Raceway
Alta, Iowa
712-284-1095

Audubon County Speedway
Audubon, Iowa
712-563-2250

Bloomfield Speedway
Bloomfield, Iowa
515-664-3712

Hawkeye Raceway
Blue Grass, Iowa
319-381-2416

Boone Speedway
Boone, Iowa
515-987-1220

Hancock County Speedway
Britt, Iowa
515-843-4513

34 Raceway
Burlington, Iowa
319-754-8704

Cedar Falls Raceway
Cedar Falls, Iowa
319-987-2138

Hawkeye Downs Speedway
Cedar Rapids, Iowa
319-366-3278

Louisa County Speedway
Columbus Junction, Iowa
319-728-2527

Adams County Speedway
Corning, Iowa
712-785-3271

Cresco Speedway
Cresco, Iowa
319-547-3400

Davenport Speedway
Davenport, Iowa
319-326-5338

Nordic Speedway
Decorah, Iowa
319-382-8514

Crawford County Speedway
Denison, Iowa
712-263-8221

Des Moines Ruan Grand Prix
Des Moines, Iowa
515-243-5515

Iowa State Fair Speedway
Des Moines, Iowa
515-262-3111

Lee County Speedway
Donnellson, Iowa
319-835-5523

Dubuque Fairgrounds Speedway
Dubuque, Iowa
319-588-1406

Eddyville Raceway Park
Eddyville, Iowa
515-969-5596

Eldon Raceway
Eldon, Iowa
515-652-3310

Greenbelt Speedway
Eldora, Iowa
515-858-5572

Jefferson County Fairgrounds
Fairfield, Iowa
515-937-5312

Farley Speedway
Farley, Iowa
319-857-4647

Shelby County Speedway
Harlan, Iowa
712-755-7223

Independence Motor Speedway
Independence, Iowa
319-334-4685

Greene County Speedway
Jefferson, Iowa
515-386-8540

Knoxville Raceway
Knoxville, Iowa
515-842-2572

Jackson County Speedway
Maquoketa, Iowa
319-652-2428

Marshalltown Speedway
Marshalltown, Iowa
515-752-9676

I-35 Speedway
Mason City, Iowa
515-424-6515

Great Jones County Fairgrounds
Monticello, Iowa
319-465-3275

Southern Iowa Speedway
Oskaloosa, Iowa
515-673-7004

Rapid Speedway
Rock Rapids, Iowa
712-472-3742

Calhoun County Speedway
Rockwell City, Iowa
515-576-5608

Clay County Fairgrounds
Spencer, Iowa
605-582-3819

Stuart Speedway
Stuart, Iowa
515-523-1319

Tipton Speedway
Tipton, Iowa
319-886-2328

Benton County Speedway
Vinton, Iowa
319-472-4603

Wapello Speedway
Wapello, Iowa
319-523-8152

Hamilton County Speedway
Webster City, Iowa
515-832-5382

West Liberty Raceway
West Liberty, Iowa
319-627-2414

Fayette County Raceway
West Union, Iowa
319-422-5768

Kansas

Belleville High Banks
Belleville, Kansas
913-527-2488

Mitchell County Fairgrounds
Beloit, Kansas
913-427-3130

Caney Valley Speedway
Caney, Kansas
316-876-2769

Clay County Fairgrounds
Clay Center, Kansas
913-427-3130

Stateline Speedway
Coffeyville, Kansas
316-251-3200

Thomas County Speedway
Colby, Kansas
913-462-7827

Cloud County Fairgrounds
Concordia, Kansas
913-427-3130

Wallbanger Speedway
Garden City, Kansas
316-275-2566

Sherman County
Goodland, Kansas
913-899-3809

Great Bend Motorplex
Great Bend, Kansas
316-793-5626

Dirtona Raceway
Hugoton, Kansas
316-544-7891

Humboldt Speedway
Humboldt, Kansas
316-473-3694

Hutchinson Raceway Park
Hutchinson, Kansas
316-662-2213

Kansas State Fairgrounds
Hutchinson, Kansas
316-669-3600

Plaza Speedway
Junction City, Kansas
913-238-7223

Lakeside Speedway
Kansas City, Kansas
913-299-2040

Fairgrounds Speedway
Liberal, Kansas
316-744-1322

Midwest Raceway
Manhattan, Kansas
913-776-7223

Thunder Hill Speedway
Mayetta, Kansas
913-364-3491

Oberlin Speedway
Oberlin, Kansas
913-475-3581

Osage County Fairgrounds
Osage City, Kansas
913-427-3130

Linn County Speedway
Pleasanton, Kansas
816-241-7523

Salina Raceway
Salina, Kansas
913-825-0044

Heartland Park Topeka
Topeka, Kansas
913-862-4781

Topeka Raceway Park
Topeka, Kansas
913-379-0410

Wakeeney Speedway
WaKeeney, Kansas
913-743-2084

81 Speedway
Wichita, Kansas
316-755-1781

Wichita International Raceway
Wichita, Kansas
316-729-4448

Yates Center Raceway
Yates Center, Kansas
316-431-2470

Kentucky

River Cities Raceway Park
Ashland, Kentucky
606-928-3116

Bluegrass Speedway
Bardstown, Kentucky
502-349-1260

Beech Bend Raceway Park
Bowling Green, Kentucky
502-476-8283

Clay City Speedway
Clay City, Kentucky
606-663-2153

Mountain Parkway Motorplex
Clay City, Kentucky
606-663-2344

Corbin Speedway
Corbin, Kentucky
606-523-5800

Barren County Speedway
Glasgow, Kentucky
502-678-5418

Fleming County Raceway
Goddard, Kentucky
606-849-4064

U.S. 60 Raceway
Hardinsburg, Kentucky
502-756-6744

Perry County Speedway
Hazard, Kentucky
606-886-7223

Ponderosa Speedway
Junction City, Kentucky
606-854-6808

Louisville Motor Speedway
Louisville, Kentucky
502-966-2277

Madisonville Motor Speedway
Madisonville, Kentucky
502-322-8498

Central Park Raceway
McHenry, Kentucky
502-274-9455

Pennyrile Raceway Park
Mortons Gap, Kentucky
502-258-5905

Carter County Showtime Speedway
Olive Hill, Kentucky
606-286-8502

Windy Hollow Speedway
Owensboro, Kentucky
502-785-4300

Windy Hollow Raceway Park
Owensboro, Kentucky
502-785-4300

Purchase Raceway Park
Paducah, Kentucky
502-527-2730

201 Speedway
Paintsville, Kentucky
606-265-3201

Thunder Ridge
Prestonsburg, Kentucky
606-886-7223

Richmond Raceway
Richmond, Kentucky
606-623-9408

Salyersville Speedway
Salyersville, Kentucky
606-349-3511

Cumberland Speedway
Somerset Lake, Kentucky
606-561-9223

Mud Lick Valley Raceway
Tollesboro, Kentucky
606-796-3111

Florence Speedway
Union, Kentucky
606-485-7591

Ohio Valley Raceway
West Point, Kentucky
502-922-4152

Mountain Motor Speedway
Whitesburg, Kentucky
606-633-7230

Kentucky Motor Speedway
Whitesville, Kentucky
502-233-5777

Louisiana

Baton Rouge Raceway
Baton Rouge, Louisiana
504-774-4524

I-20 Motor Speedway
Calhoun, Louisiana
318-982-7680

Super Bee Speedway
Chatham, Louisiana
318-322-0145

Louisiana Raceway
Eunice, Louisiana
318-546-6031

Forest Hill Speedway
Forest Hill, Louisiana
318-748-7733

Webster Speedway
Haughton, Louisiana
318-371-0077

B & D Speedway
Lacombe, Louisiana
504-882-5254

Leesville Motorsports Park
Leesville, Louisiana
318-473-8308

Spillway Speedway
Loranger, Louisiana
504-878-2908

Bayou Speedway
Minden, Louisiana
318-371-0903

Boothill Speedway
Shreveport, Louisiana
318-938-5373

Maine

Speedway 95
Bangor, Maine
207-945-9595

Spud Speedway
Caribou, Maine
207-325-4795

Oxford Plains Speedway
Oxford, Maine
207-539-8865

Beech Ridge Motor Speedway
Scarborough, Maine
207-885-0111

Unity Raceway
Unity, Maine
207-948-2525

Beech Ridge Motor Speedway
West Scarborough, Maine
207-883-6030

Winterport Dragway
Winterport, Maine
207-667-6134

Wiscasset Raceway
Wiscasset, Maine
207-882-4271

Maryland

Maryland International Raceway
Budds Creek, Maryland
301-884-9833

Potomac Speedway
Budds Creek, Maryland
301-884-4200

Capitol Raceway
Crofton, Maryland
410-721-9879

Cumberland Raceway
Cumberland, Maryland
301-729-5050

Hagerstown Speedway
Hagerstown, Maryland
301-582-0640

75-80 Dragway
Monrovia, Maryland
301-865-5102

Massachusetts

Riverside Park Speedway
Agawam, Massachusetts
413-786-9300

Seekonk Speedway
Seekonk, Massachusetts
508-336-8488

Whip City Speedway
Westfield, Massachusetts
413-785-1357

Michigan

Tri-City Motor Speedway
Auburn, Michigan
517-662-7223

Dixie Motor Speedway
Birch Run, Michigan
810-468-5654

Michigan International Speedway
Brooklyn, Michigan
800-354-1010

Waterford Hills Road Race Course
Clarkston, Michigan
810-623-0070

Crystal Raceway
Crystal, Michigan
517-235-4511

Cherry Speedway
Fife Lake, Michigan
616-933-7223

Flat Rock Speedway
Flat Rock, Michigan
313-782-2480

Auto City Speedway
Flint, Michigan
810-686-9500

Galesburg Speedway
Galesburg, Michigan
616-665-4600

Grattan Raceway Park
Grattan, Michigan
616-691-7221

Adventure Mountain
Greenland, Michigan
906-883-3536

Hartford Speedway
Hartford, Michigan
616-621-3376

Kalamazoo Speedway
Kalamazoo, Michigan
616-349-3978

Kinross Speedway Park
Kinross, Michigan
906-363-7180

Merritt Speedway
Lake City, Michigan
616-328-4351

Valley Motor Sports
Lake Linden, Michigan
906-337-1589

I-96 Speedway
Lake Odessa, Michigan
616-642-6500

Spartan Speedway
Lansing, Michigan
517-676-5404

Thunder Valley Raceway
Marquette, Michigan
906-249-3354

Mottville Speedway
Mottville, Michigan
616-483-9503

Mount Pleasant Speedway
Mt. Pleasant, Michigan
517-773-2387

Mid Michigan Raceway Park
Muir, Michigan
517-521-3985

Thunderbird Raceway
Muskegon, Michigan
616-766-3300

Norway Speedway
Norway, Michigan
906-563-9877

Onaway Speedway
Onaway, Michigan
517-733-6038

Manistee County Fairgrounds
Onekama, Michigan
616-864-2398

Silver Bullet Speedway
Owendale, Michigan
517-678-4447

Owosso Speedway
Owosso, Michigan
517-834-2249

Butler Motor Speedway
Quincy, Michigan
517-542-3627

Michigan Motorsports Park
Reed City, Michigan
616-832-5525

Winston Motor Speedway
Rothbury, Michigan
616-893-3023

Michigan Ideal Speedway
Springport, Michigan
517-857-3333

Standish Asphalt Raceway
Standish, Michigan
517-846-4949

Mid-Michigan Motorplex
Stanton, Michigan
517-762-5190

Whittemore Speedway
Whittemore, Michigan
517-756-2280

Minnesota

Norman County Fair Raceway
Ada, Minnesota
218-784-7984

Aitkin Raceway
Aitkin, Minnesota
218-927-2791

Viking Speedway
Alexandria, Minnesota
612-762-1559

Arlington Raceway
Arlington, Minnesota
612-964-5947

Chateau Speedway
Austin, Minnesota
507-433-4578

Bemidji Raceway
Bemidji, Minnesota
218-751-8197

Island Speedway
Bird Island, Minnesota
612-523-2011

Brainerd International Raceway
Brainerd, Minnesota
612-475-1500

North Central Motor Speedway
Brainerd, Minnesota
218-828-1545

Proctor Speedway
Duluth, Minnesota
218-624-0606

Elko Speedway
Elko, Minnesota
612-461-7223

Fairmont International Raceway
Fairmont, Minnesota
507-235-6996

I-94 International Speedway
Fergus Falls, Minnesota
218-739-5205

Weetown Outlaw Speedway
Fergus Falls, Minnesota
218-864-5088

Greenbush Race Park
Greenbush, Minnesota
218-782-2144

Grove Creek Motor Sports Park
Grove City, Minnesota
612-857-2152

Hibbing Raceway
Hibbing, Minnesota
218-262-4941

Jackson Speedway
Jackson, Minnesota
507-847-2084

Dodge County Speedway
Kasson, Minnesota
507-634-4281

Madison Speedway
Madison, Minnesota
612-598-7615

Fiesta City Speedway
Montevideo, Minnesota
612-286-2168

Buffalo River Speedway
Moorhead, Minnesota
218-498-2281

Steele County Fairgrounds
Owatonna, Minnesota
507-451-5305

Princeton Speedway
Princeton, Minnesota
612-389-3135

Redwood Speedway
Redwood Falls, Minnesota
507-641-3867

Olmsted County Fairgrounds
Rochester, Minnesota
612-565-4145

Winona County Speedway
St. Charles, Minnesota
507-932-3445

Minnesota State Fair Speedway
St. Paul, Minnesota
612-642-2200

I-94 Speedway
Sauk Centre, Minnesota
612-352-5263

Golden Spike Speedway
Sauk Rapids, Minnesota
612-251-8125

Raceway Park
Shakopee, Minnesota
612-445-2257

Murray County Raceway
Slayton, Minnesota
507-836-8152

Back Forty Speedway
Staples, Minnesota
218-894-2074

Kandi Raceway
Willmar, Minnesota
612-235-5881

Worthington Speedway
Worthington, Minnesota
515-683-3984

Mississippi

N.E. Mississippi Motorsports
Aberdeen, Mississippi
601-369-6888

Pine Ridge Speedway
Baldwyn, Mississippi
601-365-8070

Byhalia Raceway
Byhalia, Mississippi
601-838-4350

Columbus Speedway
Columbus, Mississippi
601-327-8590

Mississippi Motorplex
Columbus, Mississippi
601-328-1088

North Mississippi Motor Park
Corinth, Mississippi
601-287-2296

Greenville Speedway
Greenville, Mississippi
601-332-3926

Sun Coast Speedway
Gulfport, Mississippi
601-864-7638

Hattiesburg Speedway
Hattiesburg, Mississippi
601-765-6900

Jax Trax
Jackson, Mississippi
601-373-0076

Atalla Speedway
Kosciusko, Mississippi
601-289-2661

Pike County Speedway
Magnolia, Mississippi
601-684-9230

Simpson County Speedway
Mendenhall, Mississippi
601-936-4668

Whynot Speedway
Meridian, Mississippi
601-644-9668

Chickasaw Speedway
Okolona, Mississippi
601-447-3922

Missouri

Adrian Speedway
Adrian, Missouri
816-297-4400

Missouri International Racepark
Benton, Missouri
314-545-4242

Bethany Speedway
Bethany, Missouri
816-425-2305

Double X Speedway
California, Missouri
314-796-3451

US 36 Raceway
Cameron, Missouri
816-675-2279

Saint Francois County Raceway
Farmington, Missouri
314-756-9248

Jamesport Speedway
Jamesport, Missouri
816-684-6250

Capital Speedway
Jefferson City, Missouri
314-896-5500

Joplin 66 Speedway
Joplin, Missouri
417-782-0660

North Fork Speedway
Joplin, Missouri
417-642-5254

Kansas City International Raceway
Kansas City, Missouri
816-358-6700

Lebanon I-44 Speedway
Lebanon, Missouri
417-532-2060

Moberly Speedway
Moberly, Missouri
816-228-0415

Monett Speedway
Monett, Missouri
417-235-5112

Nevada Speedway
Nevada, Missouri
417-667-9993

I-70 Speedway
Odessa, Missouri
913-299-2040

I-55 Raceways
Pevely, Missouri
314-479-3219

Ozark International Raceway
Rogersville, Missouri
417-738-2222

Saint Charles Speedway
St. Peters, Missouri
314-447-5330

Savannah Speedway
Savannah, Missouri
816-324-4135

State Fair Raceway
Sedalia, Missouri
314-796-3451

Airport Speedway
Springfield, Missouri
417-767-2591

Interstate Raceway
Sweet Springs, Missouri
816-335-4522

Central Missouri Speedway
Warrensburg, Missouri
816-747-2166

Mid-America Raceways
Wentzville, Missouri
314-673-2434

Southern Missouri Raceway
West Plains, Missouri
417-256-1244

West Plains Motor Speedway
West Plains, Missouri
417-257-2112

Montana

Lost Creek Raceway
Anaconda, Montana
406-563-5161

Magic City Speedway
Billings, Montana
406-245-8647

Hub of the Valley Speedway
Bozeman, Montana
406-586-2898

Electric City Speedway
Great Falls, Montana
406-727-4884

Capital City Speedway
Helena, Montana
406-227-5862

Raceway Park
Kalispell, Montana
406-257-7223

Lewistown Raceway
Lewistown, Montana
406-538-2670

Mission Valley Speedway
Polson, Montana
406-675-2975

Tuscor Speedway
Trout Creek, Montana
406-827-4251

Nebraska

Boone County Raceway
Albion, Nebraska
402-395-6880

Alliance Speedway
Alliance, Nebraska
308-436-7709

Beatrice Speedway
Beatrice, Nebraska
402-228-2264

US 30 Speedway
Columbus, Nebraska
402-563-1561

Mid-Continent Racetrack
Doniphan, Nebraska
402-744-4391

Oregon Trail Speedway
Gering, Nebraska
308-436-3650

I-80 Speedway
Greenwood, Nebraska
402-944-2233

Cedar County Raceway
Hartington, Nebraska
402-254-3521

Kam Raceway
Hastings, Nebraska
402-463-8015

Kearney Raceway Park
Kearney, Nebraska
308-832-0302

Dawson County Speedway
Lexington, Nebraska
308-324-5000

Eagle Raceway
Lincoln, Nebraska
402-781-2929

State Fair Park Raceway
Lincoln, Nebraska
402-473-4110

Rivera Raceway
Norfolk, Nebraska
402-371-3936

Lincoln County Raceway
North Platte, Nebraska
308-532-0381

Sunset Speedway
Omaha, Nebraska
402-493-5271

Speed Bowl Speedway
Red Cloud, Nebraska
402-746-4182

Nebraska Motorplex
Scribner, Nebraska
402-238-2900

Stuart Community Track
Stuart, Nebraska
402-924-3365

Cornhusker Raceway Park
Waverly, Nebraska
402-786-5588

Nevada

Battle Mountain Raceway
Battle Mountain, Nevada
702-635-5321

Outlaw Speedway
Carson City, Nevada
702-267-2801

Silver State Raceway
Carson City, Nevada
702-885-2079

Thunderbowl Speedway
Carson City, Nevada
702-883-8876

Summit Raceway
Elko, Nevada
702-738-8810

Rattlesnake Speedway
Fallon, Nevada
702-423-7483

Top Gun Raceway
Fallon, Nevada
702-423-3104

Hawthorne CenTennesseeial Speedway
Hawthorne, Nevada
702-945-5715

Las Vegas Motor Speedway
Las Vegas, Nevada
702-644-4444

Las Vegas Speedway Park
N. Las Vegas, Nevada
702-643-3333

Pahrump Valley Speedway
Pahrump, Nevada
702-727-7172

Tonopah Speedway
Tonopah, Nevada
702-482-5082

New Hampshire

Canaan U.S.A. Speedway
Canaan, New Hampshire
603-523-9112

Claremont Speedway
Claremont, New Hampshire
603-543-3160

Star Speedway
Epping, New Hampshire
603-679-5306

Riverside Speedway
Groveton, New Hampshire
603-636-2005

Hudson Speedway
Hudson, New Hampshire
603-882-7293

Lee USA Speedway
Lee, New Hampshire
978-462-0008

New Hampshire International Speedway
Loudon, New Hampshire
603-783-4744
www.NHIS.com

White Mountain Motorsports Park
N. Woodstock, New Hampshire
603-745-6727

Sugar Hill Speedway
Weare, New Hampshire
603-529-2479

Nor-Way Pines Racway
Wentworth, New Hampshire
603-353-4589

Hi-Groove Speedway
Winchester, New Hampshire
603-239-6245

Mondanock Speedway
Winchester, New Hampshire
603-239-4067

New Jersey

Wall Stadium
Belmar, New Jersey
908-681-6400

Bridgeport Speedway
Bridgeport, New Jersey
609-467-4407

Flemington Speedway
Flemington, New Jersey
908-782-2413

New Egypt Speedway
New Egypt, New Jersey
908-656-1399

New Mexico

Duke City Raceway
Albuquerque, New Mexico
505-873-7223

Aztec Speedway
Aztec, New Mexico
505-326-2408

Carlsbad Speedway
Carlsbad, New Mexico
505-885-4802

Gallup Speedway Park
Gallup, New Mexico
505-979-0409

Uranium Capital Speedway
Grants, New Mexico
505-287-3508

Southern New Mexico Speedway
Las Cruces, New Mexico
505-524-7913

Pecos Valley Raceway
Roswell, New Mexico
505-622-4731

New York

Accord Speedway
Accord, New York
518-756-3633

Afton Raceway Park
Afton, New York
607-639-2414

Genesee Speedway
Batavia, New York
716-344-2424

Kelly Memorial Raceway Park
Batavia, New York
315-676-4401

Brewerton International Speedway
Brewerton, New York
315-668-6906

Bridgehampton Race Circuit
Bridgehampton, New York
516-725-0888

Brookfield Speedway
Brookfield, New York
518-792-4368

Lancaster Speedway
Buffalo, New York
716-759-6818

Canandaigua Speedway
Canandaigua, New York
716-694-0961

Thunder Mountain Speedway
Center Lisle, New York
607-849-3810

Skyline Raceway
Cortland, New York
607-849-6600

Freedom Raceway
Delavan, New York
716-492-1564

Black Rock Speedway
Dundee, New York
607-243-8686

Rolling Wheels Raceway
Elbridge, New York
315-689-7809

Fonda Speedway
Fonda, New York
518-853-4235

Fulton Speedway
Fulton, New York
315-593-6531

Paradise Speedway
Geneva, New York
315-789-7293

Erie County Fairgrounds
Hamburg, New York
716-649-3900

Frogtown International Speedway
Hogansburg, New York
518-358-9017

Holland International Speedway
Holland, New York
716-537-2272

Stateline Speedway
Jamestown, New York
716-664-2326

Five Mile Point Speedway
Kirkwood, New York
607-775-5555

CAN-AM International Speedway
La Fargeville, New York
315-658-4431

Limerock Speedway
Le Roy, New York
716-538-2597

New York International Raceway Park
Leicester, New York
716-382-3030

Malone International Raceway
Malone, New York
518-483-8256

Albany-Saratoga Speedway
Malta, New York
518-587-0220

Orange County Fair Speedway
Middleton, New York
914-342-2573

Niagara Falls Convention Center
Niagara Falls, New York
716-832-4419

Oswego Speedway
Oswego, New York
315-342-0646

Tioga Speedway
Owego, New York
607-687-7025

Perry Speedway
Perry, New York
716-237-3235

Airbourne International Raceway
Plattsburgh, New York
518-561-3208

New Hope Farm Arena
Port Jervis, New York
201-948-3800

Mid-Hudson Speedway
Poughkeepsie, New York
203-355-9639

Ransomville Speedway
Ransomville, New York
716-759-6818

Riverhead Raceway
Riverhead, New York
516-842-7223

New York State Fairgrounds
Syracuse, New York
716-334-5959

New Utica-Rome Speedway
Vernon, New York
315-829-4557

Watkins Glen International
Watkins Glen, New York
607-535-2486

Cayuga County Fair Speedway
Weedsport, New York
716-334-5959

Lebanon Valley Speedway
West Lebanon, New York
518-794-9606

Sullivan County Speedway
White Lake, New York
914-583-4427

Williamson International Speedway
Williamson, New York
315-589-3018

North Carolina

Ace Speedway
Altamahaw, North Carolina
336-584-6354

Caraway Speedway
Asheboro, North Carolina
336-629-5803

Asheville Motor Speedway
Asheville, North Carolina
828-236-2969

Fairgrounds Raceway
Boone, North Carolina
704-264-5731

Tri-County Raceway
Brasstown, North Carolina
707-837-3815

Champion Raceway
Brinkleyville, North Carolina
919-586-6600

Charlotte Motor Speedway
Charlotte, North Carolina
704-455-3200

Metrolina
Charlotte, North Carolina
704-596-0020

Concord Motor Speedway
Concord, North Carolina
704-782-5863

Orange County Speedway
Durham, North Carolina
919-364-1222

Dixieland Speedway
Elizabeth City, North Carolina
919-335-7412

Friendship Speedway
Elkin, North Carolina
910-835-4962

Fayetteville Motor Speedway
Fayetteville, North Carolina
910-486-5020

Northside Speedway
Fayetteville, North Carolina
910-822-8053

Carolina Speedway
Gastonia, North Carolina
704-867-7205

Harrells Raceway
Harrells, North Carolina
910-532-2363

Harris Speedway
Harris, North Carolina
704-245-6799

Hickory Motor Speedway
Hickory, North Carolina
704-464-3655

Tri-County Motor Speedway
Hudson, North Carolina
910-672-9000

Southern National Speedway
Kenly, North Carolina
919-284-1114

Thunder Valley Speedway
Lawndale, North Carolina
704-732-2685

Lincoln County Speedway
Lincolnton, North Carolina
704-732-0907

311 Motor Speedway
Madison, North Carolina
910-427-0816

New Bern Motorsports
New Bern, North Carolina
919-637-7701

North Wilkesboro Speedway
North Wilkesboro, North Carolina
910-724-7932

Wayne County Speedway
Pikeville, North Carolina
919-242-6680

Wake County Speedway
Raleigh, North Carolina
919-779-2171

Hammer Down Speedway
Red Springs, North Carolina
910-276-6192

Thunder Valley Raceway Park
Red Springs, North Carolina
910-843-2934

East Carolina Motor Speedway
Robersonville, North Carolina
919-795-3968

North Carolina Motor Speedway
Rockingham, North Carolina
910-582-2861

Brewer's Speedway
Rocky Mount, North Carolina
919-446-2631

County Line Raceway
Rocky Mount, North Carolina
919-237-4757

Roxboro Motorsports
Roxboro, North Carolina
910-364-3724

East Lincoln Motor Speedway
Stanley, North Carolina
704-875-0563

Carteret County Speedway
Swansboro, North Carolina
919-393-6250

New Taylorsville Speedway
Taylorsville, North Carolina
704-635-0777

337

Smoky Mountain Speedway
Whittier, North Carolina
704-369-2566

Bowman Gray Stadium
Winston-Salem, North Carolina
910-724-7932

North Dakota

Turtle Mountain Speedway
Belcourt, North Dakota
701-477-3544

Missouri Valley Speedway
Bismarck, North Dakota
701-255-4207

North Dakota Motorsports Park
Bismarck, North Dakota
701-223-5413

Thunder Mountain Speedway
Bottineau, North Dakota
701-263-4801

Southwest Speedway
Dickinson, North Dakota
701-225-6853

Grand Forks Speedway
Grand Forks, North Dakota
701-772-3421

Hamilton Speedway
Hamilton, North Dakota
701-265-4185

Jamestown Speedway
Jamestown, North Dakota
701-252-7316

Blue Ribbon Speedway
Langdon, North Dakota
701-256-5011

Sheyeene River Speedway
Libson, North Dakota
701-683-5301

Dacotah Speedway
Mandan, North Dakota
701-663-6843

Nodak Speedway
Minot, North Dakota
701-838-6464

Geographical Center Speedway
Rugby, North Dakota
701-776-5266

McKean County Speedway
Underwood, North Dakota
701-442-3544

Red River Valley Speedway
West Fargo, North Dakota
701-282-2200

TNT Speedway
Williston, North Dakota
701-572-7142

Tri-County Speedway
Wishek, North Dakota
701-754-2317

Ohio

Attica Raceway Park
Attica, Ohio
419-426-8911

Barberton Speedway
Barberton, Ohio
216-628-2653

Bryan Raceway
Bryan, Ohio
419-636-6886

Bear Creek Speedway
Canton, Ohio
216-484-3901

K-C Raceway
Chillicothe, Ohio
614-663-4141

Edgewater Sports Park
Cincinnati, Ohio
513-353-4888

Columbus Motor Speedway
Columbus, Ohio
614-491-1047

Ace High Speedway
Conneaut, Ohio
216-594-2222

Expo Speedway
Cortland, Ohio
216-889-3451

Midway Speedway
Crooksville, Ohio
614-342-2602

Shady Bowl Speedway
DeGraff, Ohio
513-585-9456

Millstream Speedway
Findlay, Ohio
419-423-4386

35 Raceway
Frankfort, Ohio
614-998-2278

Fremont Speedway
Fremont, Ohio
419-332-6937

Sharon Speedway
Hartford, Ohio
216-772-5481

Marion County International Raceway
La Rue, Ohio
614-499-3666

Lakeville Speedway
Lakeville, Ohio
419-827-2160

Allen County Fairgrounds
Lima, Ohio
419-476-8048

Limaland Speedway
Lima, Ohio
419-534-3104

Mansfield Motorsports Speedway
Mansfield, Ohio
419-525-7223

McCutchenville Speedway U.S.A.
McCutchenville, Ohio
419-981-6348

Midvale Speedway
Midvale, Ohio
216-339-3977

Norwalk Raceway Park
Norwalk, Ohio
419-668-5555

Dunaway's 93 Speedway
Oak Hill, Ohio
614-682-7559

Buckeye Raceway
Orrville, Ohio
216-682-7435

Painesville Speedway
Painesville, Ohio
216-354-3505

Portsmouth Raceway Park
Portsmouth, Ohio
614-354-3278

Southern Ohio Raceway
Portsmouth, Ohio
614-776-4520

Eldora Speedway
Rossburg, Ohio
513-338-3815

Brown County Speedway
Russellville, Ohio
513-522-5983

Brush Run Park
St. Clairsville, Ohio
614-695-5095

Sandusky Speedway
Sandusky, Ohio
419-625-4084

Friendship Park Raceway
Smithfield, Ohio
614-733-8058

Lorain Speedway
South Amherst, Ohio
216-986-2703

Nelson Ledges Road Course
Southington, Ohio
216-548-8551

Skyline Speedway
Stewart, Ohio
614-662-4111

Toledo Speedway
Toledo, Ohio
419-729-1634

Vinton Raceway Park
Vinton, Ohio
614-446-7406

Oakshade Raceways
Wauseon, Ohio
419-337-6850

Wilkesville Raceway
Wilkesville, Ohio
614-669-5200

Kil-Kare Speedway
Xenia, Ohio
513-426-2764

Muskingum County Speedway
Zanesville, Ohio
614-754-9199

R & R Speedway
Zanesville, Ohio
614-454-0747

Oklahoma

Oklahoma Sports Park
Ada, Oklahoma
405-332-5383

Altus Speedway
Altus, Oklahoma
405-482-2754

Sooner International Raceway
Altus, Oklahoma
405-482-2754

Arbuckle Speedway
Ardmore, Oklahoma
405-653-9001

Ardmore Raceway
Ardmore, Oklahoma
405-653-2711

Devil's Backbone Speedway
Ardmore, Oklahoma
405-226-4280

Beaver Co. Fairgrounds Speedway
Beaver, Oklahoma
316-721-3331

Hub City Speedway
Clinton, Oklahoma
405-323-7880

Elk City Speedway
Elk City, Oklahoma
405-225-6050

Enid Speedway
Enid, Oklahoma
405-233-2014

Dutton's Speedway
Fort Cobb, Oklahoma
405-654-2095

Hallett Motor Racing Circuit
Hallett, Oklahoma
918-356-4384

Faxon Speedway
Lawton, Oklahoma
405-355-9181

Lawton Speedway
Lawton, Oklahoma
405-355-6417

Meeker Speedway
Meeker, Oklahoma
918-866-2424

Muskogee Speedway
Muskogee, Oklahoma
918-687-1051

Thunder Valley Raceway Park
Norman, Oklahoma
405-872-3420

State Fair Speedway
Oklahoma City, Oklahoma
405-948-6752

Tri-State Speedway
Pocola, Oklahoma
918-436-2691

Salina Speedway
Salina, Oklahoma
918-825-4990

Mid-America Speedway
South Coffeyville, Oklahoma
918-255-6203

66 Raceway Park
Tulsa, Oklahoma
918-247-6675

Port City Raceway
Tulsa, Oklahoma
918-438-7856

Tulsa Expo Raceway
Tulsa, Oklahoma
918-322-9424

Tulsa International Raceway
Tulsa, Oklahoma
918-438-1294

Tulsa Speedway
Tulsa, Oklahoma
918-425-7552

West Siloam Springs Speedway
West Siloam Springs, Oklahoma
918-422-5488

Oregon

Sunset Speedway
Banks, Oregon
503-526-0842

Coos Bay International Speedway
Coos Bay, Oregon
503-269-2474

Riverside Speedway
Cottage Grove, Oregon
503-942-7561

Eugene Speedway
Eugene, Oregon
503-686-6488

Race City USA
Hermiston, Oregon
503-567-8320

LaGrande Speedway
LaGrande, Oregon
503-963-6981

Willamette Speedway
Lebanon, Oregon
503-258-8503

Madras Speedway
Madras, Oregon
503-475-6036

Southern Oregon Speedway
Medford, Oregon
503-772-6264

Portland International Raceway
Portland, Oregon
503-285-6635

Portland Speedway
Portland, Oregon
503-285-2883

Douglas County Speedway
Roseburg, Oregon
503-770-5767

River City Speedway
St. Helens, Oregon
503-397-2393

Clatsop Speedway
Seaside, Oregon
503-325-6481

Pennsylvania

Granview Speedway
Bechtelsville, Pennsylvania
610-754-7688

Bedford Speedway
Bedford, Pennsylvania
301-623-2787

Bradford Speedway
Bradford, Pennsylvania
814-465-3542

West End Fairgrounds
Brodheadsville, Pennsylvania
717-646-4273

Numidia Raceway
Catawissa, Pennsylvania
717-799-0480

Clearfield Mountain Speedway
Clearfield, Pennsylvania
814-768-7225

Hidden Valley Speedway
Clearfield, Pennsylvania
814-768-7223

McKean County Fair Raceway
East Smethport, Pennsylvania
814-887-2600

Ebensburg Speedway
Ebensburg, Pennsylvania
814-472-7125

Erie Speedway
Erie, Pennsylvania
814-825-5661

Penn National Speedway
Grantville, Pennsylvania
1-800-553-4531

Trail-Way Speedway
Hanover, Pennsylvania
717-359-4310

Hesston Speedway
Huntington, Pennsylvania
814-658-2823

Pittsburgh's Pa Motor Speedway
Imperial, Pennsylvania
412-695-0393

Jennerstown Speedway
Jennerstown, Pennsylvania
814-629-6677

Linda's Speedway
Jonestown, Pennsylvania
717-865-5330

Challenger Raceway
Kent, Pennsylvania
712-726-5494

Blanket Hill Speedway
Kittanning, Pennsylvania
412-337-3999

Sportsman's Speedway
Knox, Pennsylvania
814-797-2568

MOC-A-TEK Speedway
Lakeville, Pennsylvania
717-226-3372

Latrobe Speedway
Latrobe, Pennsylvania
412-737-5300

Mahoning Valley Speedway
Lehighton, Pennsylvania
610-377-5536

Liberty Race Track
Liberty, Pennsylvania
717-324-5600

Clinton County Speedway
Lock Haven, Pennsylvania
717-649-5405

Pocono International Raceway
Long Pond, Pennsylvania
717-646-2300

Marion Center Speedway
Marion Center, Pennsylvania
412-397-2620

Silver Spring Speedway
Mechanicsburg, Pennsylvania
717-766-7215

Williams Grove Speedway
Mechanicsburg, Pennsylvania
717-697-5000

Michaels Mercer Speedway
Mercer, Pennsylvania
412-662-2555

Somerset County Speedway
Meyersdale, Pennsylvania
814-634-0916

Greenwood Valley Action Track
Millville, Pennsylvania
717-458-5142

Big Diamond Raceway
Minersville, Pennsylvania
717-544-6434

Dunn-Hill Raceway
Monroeton, Pennsylvania
717-265-7223

Nazareth Speedway
Nazareth, Pennsylvania
610-759-8000

Keystone Raceway Park
New Alexandria, Pennsylvania
412-668-7600

Hickory Speedway
New Castle, Pennsylvania
412-652-8814

Lincoln Speedway
New Oxford, Pennsylvania
717-790-9242

Susquehanna Speedway
Newberrytown, Pennsylvania
717-938-9170

Port Royal Speedway
Port Royal, Pennsylvania
717-527-2303

Evergreen Raceway
St. Johns, Pennsylvania
717-788-5924

Lernerville Speedway
Sarver, Pennsylvania
412-353-1350

Clyde Martin Memorial Speedway
Schaefferstown, Pennsylvania
717-295-2960

Selinsgrove Speedway
Selinsgrove, Pennsylvania
717-374-8822

Hill Valley Speedway
Shirleysburg, Pennsylvania
814-447-5528

Motordrome Speedway
Smithton, Pennsylvania
412-872-7555

Pocono Rough Riders Arena
Snydersville, Pennsylvania
908-475-8537

Path Valley Speedway
Spring Run, Pennsylvania
717-349-7650

Motorsport Speedway
Sugar Grove, Pennsylvania
814-489-0213

Penn Can Speedway
Susquehanna, Pennsylvania
717-853-3434

Windber Speedway
Windber, Pennsylvania
814-467-8533

South Carolina

Anderson Motor Speedway
Anderson, South Carolina
803-226-5481

I-20 Speedway
Batesburg, South Carolina
803-657-7854

Chester Motor Speedway
Chester, South Carolina
803-789-7223

Columbia Speedway
Columbia, South Carolina
803-796-4491

Darlington Raceway
Darlington, South Carolina
843-395-8499
www.darlingtonraceway.com/

Cherokee Speedway
Gaffney, South Carolina
704-732-2685

Greenville-Pickens Speedway
Greenville, South Carolina
803-269-0852

Lake View Speedway
Lake View, South Carolina
803-759-9537

Lancaster Motor Speedway
Lancaster, South Carolina
803-285-1877

Laurens Speedway
Laurens, South Carolina
803-984-2427

Thunder Valley Speedway
Leesville, South Carolina
803-532-4194

Myrtle Beach Speedway
Myrtle Beach, South Carolina
803-236-0500

Summerville Speedway
Summerville, South Carolina
803-873-3438

Gamecock Speedway
Sumter, South Carolina
803-481-3499

Florence Motor Speedway
Timmonsville, South Carolina
803-346-7711

Riverside Speedway
Travelers Rest, South Carolina
803-836-8328

Westminster Speedway
Westminster, South Carolina
803-647-0101

South Dakota

Brown County Speedway
Aberdeen, South Dakota
605-229-1020

Red Devil Speedway
Hartford, South Dakota
605-528-6380

State Fair Speedway
Huron, South Dakota
605-352-8450

Interstate Speedway
Jefferson, South Dakota
605-966-5408

Park Jefferson Speedway
Jefferson, South Dakota
605-966-5517

Lake Andes Speedway
Lake Andes, South Dakota
605-487-7288

Lake County Speedway
Madison, South Dakota
605-582-3919

Roll-N-Wheel Raceway
Mitchell, South Dakota
605-996-9851

Black Hills Speedway
Rapid City, South Dakota
605-393-2122

Central State Fairgrounds
Rapid City, South Dakota
605-393-9550

Huset's Speedway
Sioux Falls, South Dakota
605-582-3536

Tomahawk Speedway
Wagner, South Dakota
605-384-3123

Casino Speedway
Watertown, South Dakota
605-882-2855

Winner Speedway
Winner, South Dakota
605-842-2655

Tennessee

Clayhill Motorsports
Atwood, Tennessee
901-669-3344

Big Foot Speedway
Baxter, Tennessee
615-738-5329

Bristol Motor Speedway
Bristol, Tennessee
423-764-6555
www.bristolmotorspeedway.com/

Volunteer Speedway
Bulls Gap, Tennessee
615-235-5020

Riverview Speedway
Carthage, Tennessee
615-847-2826

Clarksville Speedway
Clarksville, Tennessee
615-645-6523

Cleveland Speedway
Cleveland, Tennessee
615-479-8574

Crossville Raceway
Crossville, Tennessee
615-456-0222

N.W. Tennessee Motorsports
Dresden, Tennessee
901-648-9567

Dyersburg Speedway
Dyersburg, Tennessee
901-285-9940

Highland Rim Speedway
Greenbrier, Tennessee
615-643-8725

Northeast Tennessee Raceway
Greeneville, Tennessee
615-234-0772

Stateline Speedway
Guys, Tennessee
601-287-2901

Hohenwald Motor Sports
Hohenwald, Tennessee
615-796-2179

Big South Fork Raceway
Huntsville, Tennessee
615-663-2222

Kingsport Motor Speedway
Kingsport, Tennessee
615-246-6489

Atomic Speedway
Kingston, Tennessee
615-986-3589

411 Motor Speedway
Knoxville, Tennessee
615-573-5031

Macon County Raceway
Lafayette, Tennessee
615-847-2826

Garner Town Speedway
Luray, Tennessee
901-968-0019

Laurel Mountain Speedway
Madisonville, Tennessee
615-442-4346

Smokey Mountain Speedway
Marysville, Tennessee
615-856-3478

Memphis Motorsports Park
Memphis, Tennessee
901-358-7223

Milan Raceway
Milan, Tennessee
901-686-8866

Music City Raceway
Nashville, Tennessee
615-876-3406

Nashville Speedway USA
Nashville, Tennessee
615-726-1818

Newport Raceway
Newport, Tennessee
615-623-6039

Thunderhill Raceway
Summertown, Tennessee
615-964-2120

Tazewell Speedway
Tazewell, Tennessee
615-562-1316

Wartburg Speedway
Wartburg, Tennessee
615-346-6750

Duck River Motor Speedway
Wheel, Tennessee
615-684-8200

Winchester Speedway
Winchester, Tennessee
615-967-0066

345

Texas

Abilene Motor Speedway
Abilene, Texas
915-691-1881

Texas Motor Speedway
Alvin, Texas
713-393-1177

Dirt Track Speedway
Amarillo, Texas
806-381-2322

Route 66 Motor Speedway
Amarillo, Texas
806-335-3478

Longhorn Speedway
Austin, Texas
512-243-1122

Houston Raceway Park
Baytown, Texas
713-383-2666

Speedway 90
Beaumont, Texas
409-752-5860

Texas All Star Speedway
Bellmead, Texas
817-867-1500

Grayson County Speedway
Bells, Texas
903-892-3157

Boyd Raceway
Boyd, Texas
817-433-5587

Texas World Speedway
College Station, Texas
409-690-2500

Rocky Point Speedway
Copperas Cove, Texas
817-547-6834

Corpus Christi Speedway
Corpus Christi, Texas
512-289-8847

South Texas Speedway
Corpus Christi, Texas
512-814-4100

Thunderbird Speedway
Crandall, Texas
214-287-5574

Devil's Bowl Speedway
Dallas, Texas
214-222-2421

International Racetrack
Edinburg, Texas
210-318-0355

Texana Raceway
Edna, Texas
512-782-2700

El Paso Speedway Park
El Paso, Texas
915-857-3478

85 Speedway
Ennis, Texas
214-875-8500

Texas Motorplex
Ennis, Texas
214-875-2641

Fastrack Raceway
Forney, Texas
214-557-3730

Cowtown Speedway
Fort Worth, Texas
817-433-5587

Texas Raceway
Fort Worth, Texas
817-483-8410

Central Texas Raceway Park
Georgetown, Texas
512-388-2086

Shady Oaks Speedway
Goliad, Texas
210-658-8945

DFW Speedway
Grand Prairie, Texas
214-264-5800

Super Bowl Speedway
Greenville, Texas
903-883-2504

Oak Hill Raceway
Henderson, Texas
903-836-2660

Battleground Speedway
Houston, Texas
713-946-7223

Houston Speedway
Houston, Texas
713-458-1972

Lone Star Speedway
Kilgore, Texas
903-984-3699

Cen-Tex Speedway
Killeen, Texas
817-628-2888

Hallsville Raceway
Longview, Texas
903-668-2858

Hub City Speedway
Lubbock, Texas
806-748-0750

Idalou Motorsports
Lubbock, Texas
806-842-3842

West Texas Speedway
Lubbock, Texas
806-863-2188

Rio Grande Speedway
McAllen, Texas
210-843-2789

Navasota Raceway
Navasota, Texas
409-825-8725

Odem International Speedway
Odem, Texas
512-364-2826

Penwell Raceway
Odessa, Texas
915-366-9335

Twin Cities Speedway
Odessa, Texas
915-563-3983

North Texas Motor Speedway
Royse City, Texas
214-636-4400

Thunder Mountain Motorplex
Rusk, Texas
903-586-2376

San Angelo Speedway
San Angelo, Texas
915-655-1178

San Antonio Speedway
San Antonio, Texas
210-628-1522

Texas Dirt Speedway
San Antonio, Texas
210-628-4009

Silsbee Speedway
Silsbee, Texas
409-385-2264

Stephenville 281 Speedway
Stephenville, Texas
817-965-3092

Rosebowl Speedway
Tyler, Texas
903-877-2061

Heart O'Texas Speedway
Waco, Texas
817-829-2294

Red River Speedway
Wichita Falls, Texas
405-639-2354

Lake Cypress Speedway
Winnsboro, Texas
903-365-7300

Utah

Red Rock Speedway
Moab, Utah
801-259-6802

347

Carbon County Speedway
Price, Utah
801-637-5493

St. George Raceway Park
Saint George, Utah
801-635-2447

Booneville Raceway Park
Salt Lake City, Utah
801-250-2600

Rocky Mountain Raceways
Salt Lake City, Utah
801-252-9557

Suntana Raceway
Springville, Utah
801-298-2980

Vermont

Thunder Road International
Speedbowl
Barre, Vermont
802-479-2151

Bear Ridge Speedway
Bradford, Vermont
802-222-4052

Devil's Bowl Speedway
Fair Haven, Vermont
802-265-3112

Virginia

Amelia Motor Raceway
Amelia, Virginia
804-561-4739

Franklin County Speedway
Callaway, Virginia
703-483-0713

Southampton Speedway
Capron, Virginia
804-658-7223

Danville Speedway
Danville, Virginia
804-822-5013

New River Valley Speedway
Dublin, Virginia
703-639-1700

Elk Creek
Elk Creek, Virginia
703-674-4161

Langley Speedway
Hampton, Virginia
757-865-1100

Old Dominion Speedway
Manassas, Virginia
703-361-7223

Martinsville Speedway
Martinsville, Virginia
703-956-3151
www.martinsvillespeedway.com/

Natural Bridge Speedway
Natural Bridge, Virginia
703-291-2856

Virginia Motorsports Park
Petersburg, Virginia
804-862-3174

Richmond International Raceway
Richmond, Virginia
804-345-7223

Southside Speedway
Richmond, Virginia
804-744-1275

Virginia Raceway
Saluda, Virginia
804-758-3906

South Boston Speedway
South Boston, Virginia
804-572-4947

Suffolk International Raceway
Suffolk, Virginia
807-726-2242

Eastside Speedway
Waynesboro, Virginia
703-943-9336

Winchester Speedway
Winchester, Virginia
703-667-8143

Wythe Raceway
Wytheville, Virginia
703-686-4261

Washington

Skagit Speedway
Alger, Washington
206-724-3567

Deming Speedway
Bellingham, Washington
206-592-5025

Hannegan Speedway
Bellingham, Washington
360-734-8295

Bremerton Raceway
Bremerton, Washington
360-674-2280, Washington

Norman A. Welch Memorial Speedway
Connell, Washington
509-547-4340

Wenatchee Valley Raceway
East Wenatchee, Washington
509-884-8592

Elma National Raceway
Elma, Washington
206-482-3068

Ephrata State Central Speedway
Ephrata, Washington
509-754-0732

Seattle International Raceway
Kent, Washington
206-631-1550

Mansfield International Raceway
Mansfield, Washington
509-683-1257

Evergreen Speedway
Monroe, Washington
206-776-2802

Northport International Raceway
Northport, Washington
509-684-6524

Port Angeles Speedway
Port Angeles, Washington
360-452-4666

Eagle Track Raceway
Republic, Washington
509-775-3508

Spokane Raceway Park
Spokane, Washington
509-244-3663

Spanaway Speedway
Tacoma, Washington
206-537-7551

South Sound Speedway
Tenino, Washington
360-273-6420

Tri-City Raceway
West Richland, Washington
509-582-5694

Renegade Raceway
Yakima, Washington
509-877-4621

Yakima Speedway
Yakima, Washington
509-248-0647

West Virginia

Beckley Motor Speedway
Beckley, West Virginia
304-253-3606

Summit Point Raceway
Charles Town, West Virginia
304-725-8444

Interstate 79 Speedway
Clarksburg, West Virginia
304-592-0916

Elkins Motor Speedway
Elkins, West Virginia
412-441-8975

Ona Speedway
Huntington, West Virginia
304-743-4523

Tyler County Speedway
Middlebourne, West Virginia
304-758-2660

Ohio Valley Speedway
Parkersburg, West Virginia
304-863-8417

West Virginia Motor Speedway
Parkersburg, West Virginia
304-489-1889

Pennsboro Speedway
Pennsboro, West Virginia
304-659-2976

Princeton Speedway
Princeton, West Virginia
304-425-9429

Mountaineer Raceway Park
Ripley, West Virginia
304-372-3903

Wisconsin

Langlade County Speedway
Antigo, Wisconsin
715-627-7879

ABC Raceway
Ashland, Wisconsin
715-682-4990

Beaver Dam Raceway
Beaver Dam, Wisconsin
414-887-1600

Dodge County Fairgrounds
Beaver Dam, Wisconsin
414-885-3586

St. Croix Speedway
Centuria, Wisconsin
715-646-2611

Calumet County Raceway
Chilton, Wisconsin
414-849-2071

Central Wisconsin Speedway
Colby, Wisconsin
715-223-6550

Columbus 151 Speedway
Columbus, Wisconsin
414-623-4393

K G Raceway
Eagle River, Wisconsin
715-479-8313

Rock Falls Raceway
Eau Claire, Wisconsin
715-875-4233

Road America
Elkhart Lake, Wisconsin
800-365-7223

Tri-Oval Speedway
Fountain City, Wisconsin
608-687-8480

Jefferson Speedway
Jefferson, Wisconsin
414-648-2705

Wisconsin International Raceway
Kaukauna, Wisconsin
414-766-5577

Lake Geneva Raceway
Lake Geneva, Wisconsin
414-248-8566

Luxemburg Tri-Star Speedway
Luxemburg, Wisconsin
414-845-2300

Manitowoc County Expo Speedway
Manitowoc, Wisconsin
414-683-4378

Marshfield Super Speedway
Marshfield, Wisconsin
715-384-8325

Red Cedar Speedway
Menomonie, Wisconsin
715-235-6318

Hales Corners Speedway
Milwaukee, Wisconsin
414-778-4700

Madison International Speedway
Oregon, Wisconsin
608-835-8305

Golden Sands Speedway
Plover, Wisconsin
715-423-4660

Sheboygan County Fair Park
Plymouth, Wisconsin
414-892-2927

Rice Lake Speedway
Rice Lake, Wisconsin
715-234-8591

Seymour Tri-Oval Raceway
Seymour, Wisconsin
414-833-7726

Shawano Speedway
Shawano, Wisconsin
715-526-6570

Slinger Super Speedway
Slinger, Wisconsin
414-644-5921

Cedar Lake Speedway
Somerset, Wisconsin
715-248-7119

Thunder Hill Speedway
Sturgeon Bay, Wisconsin
414-845-5379

Angell Park Speedway
Sun Prairie, Wisconsin
608-837-5252

Superior Speedway
Superior, Wisconsin
715-394-7848

TNT Speedway
Three Lakes, Wisconsin
715-272-1049

Tomah/Sparta Speedway
Tomah, Wisconsin
608-372-5786

Tomahawk Speedway
Tomahawk, Wisconsin
715-453-5144

State Park Speedway
Wausau, Wisconsin
715-842-4777

Milwaukee Mile
West Allis, Wisconsin
414-453-5761

Lacrosse Fairgrounds Speedway
West Salem, Wisconsin
608-786-1525

Wilmot Speedway
Wilmot, Wisconsin
414-862-2446

Wisconsin Dells Motor Speedway
Wisconsin Dells, Wisconsin
608-254-7822

Wyoming

Casper Speedway
Casper, Wyoming
307-235-5555

Big Country Speedway
Cheyenne, Wyoming
307-632-2107

Douglas International Raceway
Douglas, Wyoming
307-358-2347

Gillette Thunder Speedway
Gillette, Wyoming
307-686-2195

Sweetwater Speedway
Rock Springs, Wyoming
307-352-6791

Sheridan Speedway
Sheridan, Wyoming
307-672-3340

Resources

Official NASCAR Web Sites

➤ **76fuel.com.** Official fuel of NASCAR

➤ **Budmoore.com.** Owner of a NASCAR Winston Cup team

➤ **Budnascar.com.** Official beer of NASCAR

➤ **Daytona500.com.** News and history about the great American race

➤ **Featherlitemfg.com.** Official trailer of NASCAR

➤ **Goodyear.com.** Official tire of NASCAR

➤ **MRNradio.com.** Official radio station of NASCAR

➤ **Napaonline.com.** NASCAR sponsor

NASCAR Television Shows

The cable networks ESPN, ESPN2, TNN, and TBS all broadcast races and report on NASCAR happenings. The following shows provide an in-depth view of NASCAR:

➤ *Inside NASCAR.* Shown on TNN

➤ *NASCAR Garage.* Shown on TNN

➤ *RPM2Night.* Shown on ESPN

News and Information Web Sites

➤ **BNSracing.com.** NASCAR Busch North Series

➤ **Fanlinks.com.** NASCAR and ARCA drivers' Web site

➤ **Irace.com.** News from the world of racecar driving

➤ **Jayski.com.** Racing-related links

➤ **Jcmmotorsports.tripod.com/HomePage.html.** Author's page and Busch North Series information

➤ **JCMRacing.com** and **JohnCerbone.com.** Author's Web sites

➤ **members.aol.com/winstongal/.** Free daily NASCAR newsletter, up-to-date information on race results

➤ **Nascaracing.com.** Race information, games, racing simulator, and NASCAR products

➤ **Neracing.com.** New England racing news

➤ **OvalTrack.com.** Links to racing-related sites

➤ **Racecentral.com.** Source for up-to-date racing information

➤ **Raceshops.com.** Listing of NASCAR Winston Cup race shops

➤ **Racingangels.org.** Organization devoted to racing and helping the people in need

➤ **Racin.net.** Racing news and results

➤ **Racingpr.com.** Racing press releases

➤ **Racingtoday.com.** NASCAR racing news and information

➤ **Speedworld.net.** NASCAR news and information

➤ **Thatsracin.com.** NASCAR news coverage

Newspapers, Magazines, and Books

➤ Benay Enterprises, Peter Golenbock, and Greg Fiedlen. *The Stock Car Racing Encyclopedia.* New York: Macmillan, 1997.

➤ *Circle Track Magazine*

➤ Golenbock, Peter. *The Last Lap.* New York: Macmillan, 1998.

➤ *Inside NASCAR* magazine

➤ *Inside Racing Magazine*

➤ *NASCAR Garage* magazine

➤ *Speedway Scene* newspaper

➤ *Stock Car Magazine*

➤ *Winston Cup Scene* newspaper

NASCAR Merchandise Web Sites

➤ Action-Performance.com

➤ Classicollectibles.com

➤ Nascarcollectibles.com

➤ Racingchampions.com

➤ Racingstuff.com

➤ Racingthunder.com

➤ Revel.com

➤ Ticket2race.com

➤ Winnerscircle.com

Winston Cup Drivers' Web Sites

- ➤ John Andretti. Pettyracing.com
- ➤ Johnny Benson. Johnnybenson-fanclub.com
- ➤ Geoffrey Bodine. Geoffbodinefanclub.com
- ➤ Ward Burton. Wardburton.com
- ➤ Wally Dallenbach. Wallydellenbach.net
- ➤ Dale Earnhardt. Rcrracing.com
- ➤ Bill Elliott. Billelliottracing.com
- ➤ Jeff Gordon. Jeffgordon.com
- ➤ Bobby Hamilton. Morgan-Mcclure.com
- ➤ Ernie Irvan. Irvan.com
- ➤ Chad Little. Chadlittle.com
- ➤ Dave Marcis. Marcisracing.com
- ➤ Sterling Marlin. Sterlingmarlin.net
- ➤ Jeremy Mayfield. Jeremymayfieldfan.com
- ➤ Dan Pardus. Danpardus.net
- ➤ Steve Park. Steve-park.com
- ➤ Kyle Petty. Pettyracing.com
- ➤ Ricky Rudd. Rickyrudd.com
- ➤ Kenny Schrader. Schraderracing.com
- ➤ Mike Skinner. Rcrracing.com
- ➤ Jimmy Spencer. Jimmyspencer.net
- ➤ Darrell Waltrip. DW17.com

Winston Cup, Busch, and Busch North Series Tracks' Web Sites

- ➤ Atlanta Motor Speedway. Atlantamotorspeedway.com
- ➤ Beech Ridge Speedway. Beechridge.com
- ➤ Bristol Motor Speedway. Bristolmotorspeedway.com
- ➤ California Speedway. Penskemotorsports.com
- ➤ Darlington Raceway. Darlingtonraceway.com
- ➤ Daytona International Speedway. Daytonausa.com
- ➤ Dover Downs International Speedway. Doverdowns.com/speedway
- ➤ Holland Speedway. Hollandspeedway.com
- ➤ Indianapolis Motor Speedway. Brickyard.com
- ➤ Jennerstown Speedway. Jennerstown.com

- ➤ **Lee USA Speedway.** Leeusaspeedway.com
- ➤ **Lime Rock Park.** Limerock.com
- ➤ **Lowe's Motor Speedway.** Lowesmotorspeedway.com
- ➤ **Martinsville Speedway.** Martinsvillespeedway.com
- ➤ **Michigan Speedway.** Penskemotorsports.com
- ➤ **The Milwaukee Mile.** Themile@milwaukeemile.com
- ➤ **Nazareth Speedway.** Penskemotorsports.com
- ➤ **New Hampshire International Speedway.** Nhis.com
- ➤ **North Carolina Speedway.** Penskemotorsports.com
- ➤ **Phoenix International Raceway.** Daytonausa.com/pir/
- ➤ **Pocono Raceway.** Poconoraceway.com
- ➤ **Richmond International Raceway.** Rir.com
- ➤ **Sears Point Raceway.** Searspoint.com
- ➤ **Stafford Speedway.** Staffordspeedway.com
- ➤ **Star Speedway.** Starspeedway.com
- ➤ **Talladega Superspeedway.** Talladegasuperspeedway.com
- ➤ **Texas Motor Speedway.** Texasmotorspeedway.com
- ➤ **Watkins Glen International.** Theglen.com

Glossary of Stock Car Terms

Ackerman   Turning one wheel more than the other to shorten the radius of the inside wheel.

air bleeds   Holes in a carburetor to adjust the air mixture.

air temperature   The temperature of the inlet air into the engine or the ambient temperature.

apron   The flat portion adjacent to the track, directly connecting the banking to the infield.

anti-sway bar   Device to limit roll in turns.

balancer   A harmonic dampening device installed on the front of engines to eliminate damaging vibrations.

banking   The cambered or angled part of the track.

barometer   An instrument that determines fluctuations in atmospheric pressure.

blocker   A racer who uses all parts of the track to prevent another car from passing.

boiling points   High limits of temperature for liquids, or the tempered limits of an individual's mental state.

brake cooling ducts   Scoops used to deliver air to brakes.

brake fade   Loosing braking capacity due to overheating.

brake pad compounds   The material strength in a brake pad.

break loose   When the rear of a turning car becomes loose.

brute force   Using excessive force.

Busch North Series   A NASCAR series based in the Northeast with backing from Busch Beer.

bump steer   The toeing in or out of tires due to improper suspension angles.

bump   Nosing up to another car and touching it.

burning up the tires   Abusing the tires and causing premature wear.

burnt pistons   Excessive engine heat that causes pistons to melt.

calipers   The part of the brakes used to squeeze pads onto a rotor.

camber   The angle of the top of the wheel compared to a straight vertical line.

carburetor   A device used to atomize fuel and air.

caster   The inclination of the spindle angle as compared to the upper and lower ball joints.

chase it up the track   When a car loses its back end and the driver is forced to drive into it and run off line.

chassis   The basic structure of the car.

chassis roll   The rolling over of the chassis due to weight transfer in a turn.

cockpit   The area for the driver to sit in.

coil springs   Steel wound in a coil shape and used to suspend a car.

compression   Air and fuel ratio of the amount taken in to the amount the air and fuel are compressed and used for making power.

control arm   Front suspension part used for wheel movement.

come in   Reference to tires as they wear.

comfortable pace   A pace that is good for speed, driver comfort, and little abuse to the car.

corner speed   The speed of the car in the corner.

corrected air density   The combination of relative humidity, air temperature, and air pressure to determine how much usable air is available.

crowning   The bubbling of the face of the tire due to overinflation.

cylinder   The cylindrical part of the motor that the piston travels.

detonation   When rapid combustion occurs inside an engine, usually resulting in a banging or knocking sound.

diamond the turns   Entering the corner low, drifting up high in the center, and returning down low before exiting the corner.

double-file running order   Two-by-two, side-by-side order.

down force   Using the pressure of air pushing down on a car to gain traction.

drive shaft   A tubular object connecting the transmission with the rear gear.

dyno   Short for dynamommeter, a machine used for resistance testing of an engine.

edge   The limit of the car.

engine tuning specialist   One who works specifically to tune an engine to the conditions of the day.

entering the corners   The act of driving from the straightaway into the turn.

exiting the corners   The act of driving off the corner onto the straightaway.

feel   When the driver becomes tuned into the car and how it reacts.

friction   Resistance of an object, or to rub up against.

fuel mileage   How many miles a car can go on a gallon of gas.

gray areas   The portions of the track not regularly run on, and usually full of debris.

groove   The portion of the track more frequently used and usually the fastest way around.

handling   The way a car is working for the driver.

heat-treated   A process of heating and then cooling an object to strengthen it.

heavy traffic   When multiple cars run in a pack.

hit the tire   The act of the suspension applying pressure to the tire.

horsepower   How much strength the engine has to use to propel the car forward.

I-beam style truck   I-beam shaped rear suspension part.

ignition timing   The point at which an ignition fires.

infield   The portion of track inside the race surface.

infield care center   A mini-hospital or care center used for treating injured or sick people.

jet   A part with a specific hole drilled in it to regulate fuel, oil, or air.

jockeying for the lead   When two or more drivers change positions or fight to be in first place.

lean out   To remove fuel to create heat and power.

lifting   When air gets under a car or car part and removes traction potential.

light feeling   Feeling of losing control of the car, usually caused by lift or loss of traction.

line   The path around a track that the driver wants to take.

long runs   A period of time during the race with no cautions.

loosen   When the rear of the car loses traction.

loose stuff   Usually found in the gray areas of the track, pieces of cars, rubber, dirt, sand, and so on that limit traction.

master cylinder   The device for applying internal pressure in a braking system.

movement   Suspension travel.

NASCAR   The National Association for Stock Car Auto Racing is the sanctioning body that regulates and controls most stock car racing.

negative camber   Leaning the top of a wheel toward the inside of the car.

nitrogen   Clean air that is free of moisture.

one-groove track   When the track shape or surface make it difficult to run side-by-side in the turns.

on the edge   The limit of a car just before it loses traction.

overinflating   Using too much air, usually in a tire.

panhard bar   The straight bar used to locate the rear of the car and to adjust the rear roll center.

passing   Getting past another car on the track.

patience   Using time to your advantage and waiting for your chance to pass.

pedal feel   The feel drivers have under their feet in terms of how they determine braking or accelerating.

personality   The way a car or driver reacts.

pit road   The place on the edge of the infield used by teams to service their racecars during the race.

pit stop   A quick stop used to service the vehicle.

positive camber   The top of a wheel leaning away from the car.

push   Term used when the driver turns the steering wheel and the car continues going straight or doesn't turn as much as the wheel is turned.

qualifying   Procedure used to determine the fastest cars and establish racing position.

race pace   The speed the cars go during the race.

racey   Something a driver feels mentally. When a driver is confident and will push the issue because he is sure of himself.

rebound   The extension of a shock.

relative humidity   The amount of moisture in the air in relation to how much could be in that particular air.

restrictor plate   Metal plate used under a carburetor to limit its air intake.

rich   Too much fuel for the available air.

ride height   Heights of the chassis in relation to the ground.

roll centers   The intersecting points of the front suspension.

roll over   When the chassis shifts to the side of weight transfer.

rotors   The disc portions of the brakes.

rough riding Using excessive force to pass or ride next to a competitor.

RPMs The speed of the engine as it rotates.

run up the corner When the car enters a turn and can't stay on the bottom, it moves up the track.

seat time The amount of time a driver has spent driving a racecar.

setup The way the car's suspension is adjusted.

shocks A dampening device used with a spring.

shock setup The adjustments or valving of a shock.

sidewall The sides of the tire.

side loads The amount of pressure put on a car's tires in a turn.

solid anti-sway bar Nontubular sway bar.

spindle Part of the car used to mount the hubs and wheels.

spinning out When a car loses traction or control and turns around.

split A term used to determine the difference there is in the spring rate or caster adjustment in the front of the car.

spotter Crew member who watches the entire track and notifies a driver of impending situations.

spring rubber A rubber device used inside the coils of the spring to increase the spring rate of the spring.

spring rate How much pressure per inch a particular spring will apply.

stay under you Keeping the car in control in an uncontrollable situation.

street car Typical, regular car.

suspension An assembly of parts used to control movement on car.

sway bars Also called an anti-sway bar, these are used for limiting suspension travel or rollover in a turn.

taping Applying tape to close a hole in the car, such as the front grills.

the outside The groove of the track against the wall or nearest to the wall as compared with a competitor.

tight The inability to turn a car. Also called *push*.

timing light The instrument used for adjusting the ignition timing.

tire patch The amount of tire touching the track.

tire pressure The amount of air pressure inside the tire.

tire temperature The amount of heat on or inside a tire.

tie rod ends The parts of the front steering used to adjust toe.

tire wear   The amount of tire deterioration.

toe   The adjustment of the front wheels to determine if they are parallel.

torque   The low end of horsepower used to power a vehicle off a corner.

traction   The adhesion of the tires to the track.

track bar   Same as panhard bar, it centers the rear end in the car and controls the rear roll center.

transfer weight   The act of rollover to transfer weight to control a wheel.

trick   Slang word used for a cool or nonregular part made to do a specific part.

truck arms   Rear suspension parts that hold the rear end in the car.

tubular   A part made in a tube form or from another part.

tuning   Testing and making changes to make a particular part perform to its potential.

underinflating   Too little air pressure.

unloading   When the suspension breaks traction.

use the car   When a driver is abusing the car.

valving   This term refers to the adjustments of a shock.

valve stacks   The parts used to adjust the dampening of a shock.

wall thickness   The measurement of the thickness of a tubular object.

weather station   A device used for measuring humidity, air temperature, and air density.

Winston Cup   The supreme series in stock car racing. Winston, RJR Reynolds corporation supports and sponsors this series.

Index

T